HINDI GRAMMAR

D1882707

Owing to the antiquity and rarity of this book, certain pages are regrettably absent, and readability is compromised due to the blurring of the original text. If you possess any insights regarding the availability of these missing sections, kindly inform us. Your assistance is crucial in ensuring the completion of this significant work for the benefit of future generations.

HINDI GRAMMAR

EDWIN GREAVES

GYAN

Published by

Gyan Publishing House
5, Ansari Road
Daryaganj, New Delhi-110002
Phone: 011-47034999, 9811692060
E-mail: books@gyanbooks.com

Distribution Network
gyanbooks.com
India, USA, Canada, UK, Australia

© Publisher

All rights reserved. No part of this work may be reproduced, stored, adapted, or transmitted in any form or by any means, electronic, mechanical, photocopying, micro-filming, recording or otherwise, or translated in any language, without the prior written permission of the copyright owner and the publisher.

ISBN: 978-93-7225-782-3 (PB)

First Published, 1921

2nd Impression 2025

Printed at: Gyan Press, Delhi.

The book is sold subject to the condition that it shall not, by way of trade or otherwise, be lent, resold, hired out, or otherwise circulated without the prior publisher's written consent.

HINDI GRAMMAR
Author: EDWIN GREAVES

HINDI GRAMMAR

BY

EDWIN GREAVES

LONDON MISSIONARY SOCIETY, BENARES

Allahabad

PRINTED AT THE INDIAN PRESS, LTD.

1921

CORRIGENDA.

(All that can be offered in the way of extenuation for this long *Corrigenda* is the fact that the author was in England while the Grammar was passing through the Press in Allahabad, consequently correction of proots was very limited.)

PAGE.	LINE.	FOR	READ.
7	2	बर्ग	बर्ग
16	19	संदर	सुंदर
18	21	o	of
32	14	The second ग्च	is badly printed
34	2	rost	frost
49	1	omit "so"	
52	last	लड़केा	लड़के
58	10	पुँल्लिंग	पुल्लिंग
62	24	छेाटा टापू	छेाटी टापू
75	heading	Faminine	Feminine
80	7	पुस्तक, book under second column	
84	11	Class I	Class II
92	12	Genetive	Genitive
101	heading	Cases	Case
101	last	के	केा
108	10	ज स	जिस

Page	Line	For	Read.
119	3	regard	regarded
120	22	Genetive	Genitive
126	14	more	more more
129	heading	ompound	Compound
133	8	43	143
153	7	prefixes	suffixes
158	5	अपेक्षा,	अपेक्षा.
162	9	alone	alone is
175	17	n essitates	necessitates
175	23	Th	The
185	heading	Çoerelative	Correlative
185	18	konw	know
186	23	Wha	What
188	19	वे आवेंगे.	वे आवेंगे?
197	17	सुल	सूल

(As the later printed sheets did not reach England in time, these corrections could only be carried as far as page 208.—E. G.)

PREFACE.

DR. KELLOGG'S "GRAMMAR OF THE HINDI LANGUAGE" is the standard work on the subject and occupies a position of unquestioned supremacy. The very fulness of the work, however, detracts somewhat from its value for a student commencing the study of Hindi, and thus there is room for a Grammar of less pretentious size and scope.

In 1896, my "Grammar of Modern Hindi" was published by the late Dr. Lazarus at his "Medical Hall Press," Benares. Another edition, revised and slightly enlarged, was published at the same Press in 1908. Finding that the second edition was nearly exhausted, I decided not to revise and republish the old work but to prepare a new Grammar. Over 20 years of further residence and work in India ought, I felt, to enable me to produce a better book. Such an attempt has been made. A comparison of the two Grammars will make manifest the fact that there are great differences in the two books, and it is hoped that these changes are for the better in the way of clearness and simplicity.

Apart from a few notes on the Braj Bhasha, no attempt has been made to treat of dialectical differences, and Urdu has not been included. The language dealt with is modern Hindi in the form that many of its best friends are endeavouring to standardize it, a self-respecting Hindi which is not for ever parading its aristocratic ancestry by filling its pages with Sanskrit words, nor affecting *modernity* by the cultivation of Persian vocabulary and idioms.

The hope is entertained that the present volume may more than fill the place of the book which has done over 20 years of service and may now be allowed to retire

EDWIN GREAVES.

CONTENTS.

CHAPTER III.

CHAPTER IV.

CHAPTER V.

CHAPTER VI.

CHAPTER VII.

CHAPTER VIII.

CHAPTER IX.

CHAPTER X.

CHAPTER XI.

CHAPTER XVII.

CHAPTER XVIII.

CHAPTER I.

THE HINDI LANGUAGE.

1. Hindi, Urdu, Hindustani.

These three names are used very loosely by many writers and speakers, and possibly no definitions are possible which will compel general acceptance.

It might be wise to discard the use of the word Hindustani as applied to literature and confine its application to the language so widely *spoken* throughout India and employed in the ordinary affairs of business and social life. Most of the words included in the vocabulary of this *lingua franca* are common to both Hindi and Urdu.

Hindustani might, with some measure of fitness, be used of one class of literature affected by certain writers who employ a vocabulary which is largely Urdu, but have the works printed in the Nagari character.

Hindi may stand for those forms of the language which are the outcome of the languages which the early Aryan settlers brought with them, combined with, and affected by, the languages of Madhya-desh or Mid-India. It would seem that from the commingling of these came into being various so-called Prakrits (and Sanskrit). From the former of these were evolved what Sir George Grierson terms the Apabranshas (*i.e., fallen* or *corrupted*). Prakrit may be taken to mean "natural" or "colloquial" as contrasted with Sanskrit which is the polished language burnished up for literary purposes. The Apabranshas were later modifications of the Prakrits, and from these came the various forms of Hindi current since, say, about the twelfth century.

Urdu may be appropriately used of the language in which the verbs and many other words are common to both Urdu and Hindi, but are supplemented by a considerable vocabulary of Persian or Arabic origin. Urdu is generally printed in the Persian character, but quite a considerable literature has grown up, largely used by the Christian communities, which is printed in the Roman character.

2. Modern Hindi.

In the beginning of the 18th century two pundits in Calcutta, Lallu Jî Lâl and Sadal Misra, instructed and inspired by the European head of the college in which they were professors, initiated, or to speak more exactly, developed, a movement which is largely responsible for the existence of modern Hindi. The endeavour was made to draw on the Prakrits or Apabranshas and, to some extent, on Sanskrit, for the vocabulary, and to exclude, as far as practicable, Persian and Arabic words not already naturalized. Combined with this was the endeavour to standardise certain verbal and other forms instead of perpetuating dialectical differences.

In recent times Hindi has suffered not a little in the house of those of its friends who are eager to crowd their pages with pure Sanskrit words. A few parade the range of their learning by introducing Persian and Arabic words, thus still further increasing the trials of their readers.

The Prakrits and their descendants differed widely in different parts of India. The aim of modern writers, more or less consistently carried out, is to perfect and make current a language freed from provincialisms and suited to be a literary vehicle for the use of all who speak any of the dialects of Hindi.

The whole question of the rise of Hindi is discussed with great ability, though necessarily not very fully, by Sir George Grierson in his chapter on the "Languages of India," in Vol. I of "The Indian Empire"—one of the four volumes written as introductory to the *Imperial Gazetteer of India*. There is also an interesting little book on the subject in Hindi, "Hindî bhâshâ kî Utapatti" (The Birth of Hindi), by Pundit Mahabir Prasad, published at The Indian Press, Allahabad.

It should be recognized that the Hindi represented in this Grammar is to some extent an artificial language used chiefly in literature. It is the language which writers are endeavouring to make the common literary medium for all the Hindi-speaking peoples. The colloquials which they use in their own homes and in social intercourse may differ widely from this and vary much in different parts of even the same Province. For literary purposes, however, the language dealt with in this Grammar may, be regarded as generally accepted not only in the United Provinces, but also in Bihar, Central India and Rajputana.

By some this language has been called High Hindi, but this term should rather be kept sacred for the productions of those who delight to cram their pages with high-sounding Sanskrit words.

Up to the time of Lallu Jî nearly all, and even since then many, works were written in verse. In these the language is very different from modern prose. The Braj Bhâshâ, Avadhî and other dialects were used. The Sûr Sâgar of Sûr Dâs and the Râmâyan (Râmcharit Mânas) of Tulsî Dâs stand out as two great models of this class of literature.

During recent years the endeavour has been made to popularise poetry written in the standardised modern Hindi, but even to the ear of a foreigner the successes, achieved up to the present, appear doubtful, the verses lack the swing and sweetness of the poetry written in the dialectical forms. However, the "Kharī bolī" poetry has probably come to stay.

The study of the Hindi given in this Grammar is essential for every student of Hindi, as it is increasingly the standard language. Every one, however, who is brought into contact with the people, especially in rural districts, will have to familiarise himself with the dialect of the District in which his lot is cast.

3. Tatsamas and Tadbhavas.

Words closely akin to the Sanskrit forms are called Tatsamas तत्सम (*like that*). The term Tadbhavas तद्भव (*produced from that*) is applied to those words which have been modified from their original forms in their transition through the Prakrits and Apabranshas.

Purism in Hindi is sheer folly. Words of Persian and Arabic origin, and words imported also from English and other languages, have made their home in Hindi, and it is futile to try and oust them from their place. Pedants, who have struggled to exclude all such words and to supply their places by unfamiliar Sanskrit words or manufactured compounds, have done not a little to stay the progress of Hindi. The wise writer or speaker is the man who selects with discrimination his words from the already available material. There is a large vocabulary awaiting his use, furnishing words which will probably well express his meaning and convey it to the ordinary reader or listener.

CHAPTER II.

THE HINDI ALPHABET.

4\. वर्णमाला — Alphabet.

वर्ग — A group of related 5 consonants; gutturals, palatals, etc.

अक्षर or वर्ण — Letter.

आकार — Its form.

उच्चारण — Its pronunciation.

उच्चारण-स्थान — The part of the mouth from which the sound is produced.

स्वर — Vowel.

व्यंजन — Consonant.

अनुस्वार (ं) — Anusvâr or Nasal.

बिन्दु — The name of the sign (ं)

अनुनासिक (ँ) — Anunâsik or Nasalization.

चन्द्रबिन्दु or अर्द्धचन्द्र — The sign (ँ)

विसर्ग (:) — Visarg. The final aspiration.

हल — A consonant with no vowel sound following it. A closed consonant.

हलन्त	A word terminating with a closed consonant.
विराम (्)	The sign under the consonant to indicate that it is "hal."
ह्रस्व	Short vowel.
दीर्घ	Long ,,
प्लुत	Extra long vowel.
मात्रा	A syllable or "instant."
संयोग	The joining of two or more consonants.
संयुक्त अक्षर or संयुक्ताक्षर	Compound consonant thus joined.

5. The Hindi Alphabet differs but slightly from the Sanskrit. Indian grammarians are not unanimous in their views as to the number of the letters. For practical purposes, the number of the letters may be taken as 46, *i.e.*, 11 vowels and 35 consonants. The 3 vowels ऋ, ऌ, ॡ, rí, lri and lrí, are pure Sanskrit and have no place in Hindi. ड़ and ढ़ are added to the consonants, as they are quite distinct in sound from ड and ढ. Anusvâr, Anunâsik and Visarg are not strictly letters, and are therefore not included in the 46.

THE HINDI ALPHABET.

6. The Vowels.

Initial Form.	Medial or Final Form.	Initial.	Medial or Final.
a. अ	(unwritten)	â. आ	ा
i. इ	ि	î. ई	ी
u. उ	ु	û. ऊ	ू
ri. ऋ	ृ		
e. ए	े	ai. ऐ	ै
o. ओ	ो	au. औ	ौ

Nasal (अनुस्वार)

Nasalization (अनुनासिक)

Final aspiration (विसर्ग) :

7. Consonants.

Gutturals	क k	ख kh	ग g	घ gh	ङ ñ	... कवर्ग
Palatals	च ch	छ chh	ज j	झ jh	ञ ṅ	... चवर्ग
Cerebrals	ट ṭ	ठ ṭh	ड ḍ	ढ ḍh	ण ṇ	... टवर्ग
				ड़ ṛ	ढ़ ṛh	
Dentals	त t	थ th	द d	ध dh	न n	... तवर्ग
Labials	प p	फ ph	ब b	भ bh	म m	... पवर्ग
Semi-Vowels	य y	र r	ल l	व w or v		... अन्तस्थ
Sibilants	श sh	ष sh	स s		}	ऊष्म
Aspirate	ह h				}	

By the use of a dot written under a letter, a few other sounds are indicated.

क़ q ख़ kh ग़ gh ज़ z फ़ f

These five stand for sounds found in Urdu words; क़ for ق; ख़ for خ; ग़ for غ; ज़ for ز، ض and ذ; फ़ for ف. The last two are fairly represented by the English *z* and *f*; the first 3 are gutturals having no equivalents in English.

ज्ञ and क्ष or क्ष are sometimes included as letters of the alphabet, but this is incorrect; they are conjunct letters: ज्ञ = ज् + ञ and क्ष = क् + ष.

Modified forms of some of the letters are used in some fonts of type, *e.g.*, अ for अ, भ for भ, फ , for फ etc.

PRONUNCIATION.

8. Pronunciation of Vowels.

In seeking to acquire a correct pronunciation, it may be well to consider three points: 1. The pronunciation must be learned from the lips of an Indian teacher; watching attentively the speaker as well as listening to the sounds, is a matter of much importance; every endeavour should be made to ascertain HOW the sounds are made, where the tongue is placed, etc. 2. The pronunciation of the letters should be learned *as the letters occur in words.* 3. It is still better to group the words in phrases or short sentences, for sounds do not assume their true balance and power until they take their place as parts of words and sentences. What foreigner would learn the pronunciation of "the" until he had learned it as part of a sentence?

The Hindi alphabet is peculiarly scientific, as will be discovered by carefully studying the "classification of letters" chart given later on. Phonetics is no modern discovery in India.

It should be noted that each Hindi letter has its own proper sound, there is not one symbol for several different sounds as in English, *e.g.*, how different is the sound of *a* in such words as *lad, lace, lard, call.*

While insisting on the importance of what has been written above about learning the sounds from the lips of an Indian, a few remarks are offered on some of the sounds as subsidiary helps.

अ represents a sound approximately like the English *a* in the words *arise, avert* or *u* in *suggest.*

आ is much like the *a* in the English *father, mart.*			
इ ...	... *i* ...	... *fit, wrist.*	
ई ...	... *ee* or *ea*	... *feel, seat.*	
उ ...	... *u* or *oo*	... *put, foot.*	
ऊ ...	... *oo* ...	... *pool, fool.*	
ऋ ...	... *ri* ...	... *drink, bring.*	

The vowels ए and ओ require great attention and care. It is sometimes stated that they correspond with the English *a* and *o* in such words as *same* and *so.* This is misleading, as the sounds mentioned in English are much more drawled than the Hindi ए and ओ; they commonly are pronounced in English with what is called the "glide," a prolongation of the vowel sound and a gradual dying away of it. In Hindi, though not *clipped*, these sounds are single and sustained until they suddenly close without any drawl. Possibly the first *a* in the phrase "*Davidic Psalms*," and *o* in the words *opaque* and *oration* are about as near as the English language will furnish.

Let the student ask his pundit to repeat again and again the two phrases ले लो and दे दो. It will at once be evident to the ear how very widely these sounds differ, not only in the consonants of the second, but in the vowels of both, from the English *lay low* and *dado* (room decoration).

ऐ (अ+इ) and औ (आ + उ) somewhat approximate to the *ai* and *ou* in the words *aisle* and *stout*; but in Hindi the amalgamation of the two elements of the diphthong seems to be more complete than in the English sounds, and the अ and आ retain more of their power. The difference may be felt by listening to an

Indian's pronunciation of बैल (*bullock*) and comparing this with the sound in English *aisle* or *pile*, or लौंडा (boy) with the Eng. *pound*.

When final in a word, after a consonant, इ and उ are sometimes very short, *e.g.*, in such words as स्तुति, भूमि, भानु, ऋतु.

The long vowels ए and ओ are also very much shortened at times, especially in verse, *e.g.*, जेहि, मोहि. The shortening is so marked in some instances as to lead to the vowel being reckoned as short instead of long. (compare the sound with *o* in *molest*.)

9. The Visarg can be easily disposed of. It is infrequent in Hindi. It can only be described as an aspiration at the end of a syllable. It is almost like an English *ha* reversed, as though, *e.g.*, *hauoo*, should be pronounced backwards *ool-lah*. The sound must be learned from an Indian speaker.

As illustrations of its use, take प्रातःकाल, *morning*; अन्तःकरण, *mind*.

10. **Annsvar and Anunasik.**

Some would contend that both these are simply nasalizations of different degrees, and that Anusvâr is distinct from the nasal letters. It seems, however, to the writer that this is not so; there are not two nasalizations and the five nasal letters distinct from both but one nasalization (the Anunâsik), and the five nasal letters which may be represented by the Anusvâr at the option of the writer. The nasalization represented by the Anunâsik may vary in intensity; but there is no room between them and the nasal letter sounds for another nasalization. That there are degrees of intensity in the nasalization, will be very evident if attention be given to the pronunciation of the three words, जँहँ, जहाँ and आऊँ; the nasalization increases in the order in which the words are given.

The difficulty in this matter is increased by the fact that much inconsistency exists with reference to the writing and printing of Anusvâr and Anunâsik, Very frequently the former (ं) is found where the sound of the latter (ँ) is correct. The student may be assured that there is little practical difficulty in the matter. After a short time it will be found that the correct pronunciation, nasal or nasalization, will come quite naturally and the reader will scarcely notice whether the Anusvâr or Anunâsik be printed.

The use of Anusvâr as the equivalent of one of the five nasal letters, must be treated in a separate paragraph.

11. The Pronunciation of the Consonants.

The Five N's. Although these do not take the first place among the consonants, it may be well to deal with them at once so as to conclude the consideration of the subject raised in para. 10.

Five nasal letters may be regarded as an unnecessarily large supply; but a little consideration will disclose the fact that English comes little short of this though it is more economical in its symbols to represent them. The English " n " stands for ङ, ञ and न; "m" for म; the Hindi ण has no eqivalent in English.

It will be noticed that there is a nasal for each of the five groups of gutturals, palatals, etc.; and the nasal naturally assumes its proper sound when joined to any of these letters. It is on this ground that in so many cases the special " n " is not printed, but the more simple Anusvâr used instead. This becomes, with the letter following it, a conjunct consonant, and the second letter decides the pronunciation to be given to the Anusvâr.

Some illustrations are appended which should be carefully practised with a pundit.

ङ with one of the gutturals. अंक, *a mark*; अंग, *a member of the body*; ऊँघना, *to doze*. Compare with these the English *ink, longer*. Note that in other words, such as आँख, it is Anunâsik, not Anusvâr; the sound is a nasalization, not a letter.

ञ with a palatal. पंच, *a committee of five*; पंछी, *a bird*; अंजन, *collyrium*; संझा, *evening*. As an illustration of the inconsistencies existing with reference to the use of the Anusvâr and the Anunâsik, the words

पंच and पाँच may be noticed; although, etymologically, very closely allied in पंच, the sound is unmistakeably the full nasal letter; while in पाँच, as pronounced by most speakers, there is only a nasalization.

ण with cerebrals. In some words there is clearly a full nasal letter: *e.g.*, घण्टा, *a gong*; अण्डा, *egg*; उण्डेलना, *to empty out*; but in many cases the sound is only a nasalization: *e.g.*, ऊँट, *camel*; बाँटना, *to distribute*; च्यूँटी, *an ant*; होँठ, *lip*; गाँठ, *knot*. In the word ढूँढना, it will be found that on the lips of some speakers, the sound is a full nasal letter, with others hardly more than a nasalization: very frequently the word becomes ढूँढ़ना, in which case there is only a nasalization.

With the two letters, ड़ and ढ़, the sound is perhaps always only a nasalization, *i.e.*, Anunâsik. साँड़, *a bull*; कोँढ़ा or कोँहरा, *a gourd*.

न with the dentals. In this series there is some variation. In such words as सन्त, *a devotee* or *saint*; पन्थ, *a path*; सुंदर, *beautiful*; अन्धा, *blind*; बन्धक, *a pledge*, there is a full nasal; but in other words, such as दाँत, *tooth*; गाँथना, *to bind*, it is only a nasalization that is heard.

With the labials, the full nasal म is often found, as in चम्पा, *a certain flower*; सम्बन्ध, *connection*;

सम्भालना, *to support.* Compare the English *impossible, impolite, immoderate.* In English, however, the "n" is frequently not changed to "m" before a labial, *e.g., unpolished, unborn, unburnt.*

In Hindi, before the labials, there is often only a nasalization, *e.g.,* **साँप**, *a snake* ; **सौंपना**, *to commit to the care of.*

With reference to the other letters. It will be found from the classification of letters to which group any letter belongs, the Anusvâr before a letter commonly assumes the nasal belonging to that group. No rigid rule, however, can be formulated: sometimes Anusvâr is used, sometimes the Anunâsik. As examples of the use of Anunasik take the following :—**साँस**, *breath* ; **आँसू** *tears* ; **बाँस**, *bamboo* ; **बाँह**, *arm* ; **साँवला**, *brown or dark coloured.* But it is the Anusvâr in the following :—**सन्यासी**, a devotee ; (*cf.* English *onion*) ; **संसार**, *the universe* ; (*cf.* English *unsafe*) ; **अंश**, *a portion* ; (*cf. bunch*); **सिंह**, *a lion* ; (*cf.* English *unholy*). This word **सिंह** is not uncommonly pronounced as though written **सिंघ**.

The exact pronunciation of these nasals must be acquired from an Indian ; as a matter of fact, however, if the pronunciation of the following letter be already acquired, there is no great difficulty as in anticipation of the following sound, the organs of the mouth prepare themselves and the nasal appropriate to it is formed.

When followed by a vowel, the nasals have their fullest sound. The two ङ and ञ are not used in this way; न and म are about equivalent to the English *n* and *m*. Compare the Hindi नाम, *name*, with English *name* or *nasty*, and मारना, *to strike*, with English *mart*. The Hindi ण has no equivalent in English. Practise such words as चरण, *a foot*; गण, *a host*; गुण, *quality*.

12. The aspirated letters ख, घ, छ, झ, etc.

These may be treated of in one section, as, so far as the aspiration of the letters is concerned, the same principles are involved. The combinations in English, *ch*, *ph* *rh*, *sh* yield no help as the *h* is not aspirated. In the English words *church*, *cholera*, *philosophy*, *rhetoric*, *ship* we have somewhat the equivalents of छ, फ, the Urdu फ़, र, and श. The English words *ghost* and *which* do render some assistance, as these words, as pronounced by some speakers, do give a distinct aspiration to the *h*.

Perhaps the nearest equivalents to the Hindi sounds to be found in English are in those cases where one two words ends in one of the consonants referred to and the following word begins with *h*. If the earlier part of the first word be eliminated and only the last letter be pronounced in close conjunction with the second word.

beginning with *h*, we get something suggestive of these aspirated Hindi letters. Take the following as examples:—

(si) ck-hound	pronounce	khound	खौंड
(bi) g-hound	...	ghound	घौंड
(tou) ch-hole	...	chhole	छोल
(spon) ge-house	...	jhause	झौस
(u)p hill	...	phill	फिल
(ca)b-horse	...	bhorse	भ...
(a) bhorrent	...	bhorrent	भ...

Of course, in Hindi the two letters bcome more unified into a single sound than occurs in these illustrations from the English words, but the illustrations may start the student on the right lines for acquiring these Hindi sounds.

13. क and ग.

About equivalent to the English *k* and *g* (hard), in such words as *kill* (किल), *gum* (गम), the Hindi letters are, however, formed further back towards the throat than the English sounds and the tongue is slightly broadened out.

च and ज. These two letters are about the same as the English *ch* and *j* or soft *g* in *cheap* (चीप) and *gin*, (जिन). Probably in the Hindi the tongue touches the palate a little further back than in the production of the English sounds. Even in Hindi, however, there are slight differences in the pronunciation of the letters, *e.g.*, the च in चिल्लाना (to cry out), seems to be somewhat sharper than the same letter in चुप (be silent), probably because of the vowel sound which follows the च in the second word being formed further back in the mouth than the earlier word.

The Cerebral and Dental letters. The pronunciaton of the letters in the ट and त series is found difficult by some. Often this only arises through insufficient care in studying the method of producing these sounds. The part of the palate used by the tongue for producing *t* and *d* in English is about midway between the parts used for the enunciation of ट, ड and त, द. Some teachers of Hindi write of turning the tip of the tongue upwards and backwards against the roof of the mouth to obtain right pronunciation of ट and ड, but it seems to the writer that this is incorrect; the tip of the tongue is rather broadened out and lumped together, pressed against the palate rather far back, and then somewhat sharply brought away as the sound is uttered.

It is worth while calling the attention of the student to the fact that all speakers do not produce sounds in identically the same way.

Indians consider our *t* and *d* nearer to ट and ड than to त and द, as in transliterating English words into the Nagari character the ट and ड are used. Listen to an uneducated Indian using the word टिकट or बोट (*ticket* and *boat*). Or, to take an illustration already used in another connection, listen to the word देदो, and notice the distinction between that and the English *dado*.

It is worth much trouble to acquire the correct pronunciation of these two groups of letters, and with attention and practice there is no serious difficulty.

ड़ and ढ़. These are cerebral *r* and *rh*, and are produced in the same way as that mentioned above for the production of the other Cerebrals.

For the enunciation of the त and द series the tongue is brought forward against the upper teeth, or even between the teeth (some say at the junction of the palate with the upper teeth). These sounds are distinctly softer and more dental than the *t* and *d* in English.

प and ब. These are very similar to English *p* and *b*. Compare English *pull* with Hindi पुल, *a bridge*, and *bin* with बिन, *without*. Possibly in Hindi the lips are not quite so tense as in the production of the English letters.

य is the equivalent to the English *y*. Compare यूँ and *youth*. Possibly in Hindi the tongue is a trifle more forward against the palate. This letter is often pronounced by the less educated as ज and is not infrequently so printed: *e.g.*, जुग for युग, *an age*.

र is crisper and not so dull as the English *r*. Indian grammarians class it as one of the Cerebrals; but the writer is disposed to think that it should be placed among the Palatals. The tongue is placed well forward against the palate just behind where it joins the teeth. Compare English *rip* with रिपु, *an enemy.*

ल is not so thick and muffled as the English *l.* It is produced further forward. It will be noticed that it is classed as a Dental. The English *l* is often pronounced as a Palatal sometimes as a Cerebral. Compare English *loam* with Hindi लोमड़ी, *a fox.*

व is somewhere between the English *v* and *w*, but nearer to *w*. The lips, however, are not so pressed together as in the production of *w*, in fact scarcely touch one another.

It should be noticed that in words brought into Hindi from the Sanskrit, व is largely replaced by ब even in printing, and still more so in pronunciation.

श and ष. The distinction in pronunciation between these two letters is not generally maintained even by Indians. There is, however, a distinction, श being classed as a Palatal, ष as a Cerebral. Some suggestion as to the difference may be found in the pronunciation of the two English words, *sheet* and *shoot.* In the former, the tongue is thrown further forward, in the latter, further back: this is on account of the vowels which follow and affects to some degree the sound of the *sh.*

ष is sometimes pronounced ख and sometimes printed so, *e.g.*, भाखा and मनुख for भाषा and मनुष्य.

स is practically equal to the English *s*, though slightly more dental. Compare सिसकी, a *sob* or *sigh* with *sister*.

ह corresponds with the English *h*. Compare हाँफना, *to pant*, with English *half*.

The following table, shewing the classification of letters according to Indian grammarians, is worth very careful study. It indicates very clearly the highly scientific character of the Alphabet and the attention which has been given to phonetics. The classification given by Indian grammarians has been adhered to; but it seems to the writer that र and ऋ are more strictly Palatals than Cerebrals; the cerebral *r* is ड़, Again, ल is perhaps rather a Palatal than a Labial.

14. Classification of letters.

		HARD. विवृत प्रयत्न or अघोष प्रयत्न			SOFT. घोष प्रयत्न					
		HARD MUTES. अल्पप्राण	HARD MUTES. Aspirated. महाप्राण	Sibilants. These 3 Sibilants and ह are called ऊष्म.	SOFT MUTES. अल्पप्राण	SOFT MUTES. Aspirated. महाप्राण	Nasals अनुनासिक or सानुनासिक	Liquids or Semi-Vowels. अन्तस्थ	Aspirate.	VOWELS.
Gutturals.	कंठ्य	क	ख		ग	घ	ङ		ह	अ आ ः
Palatals.	तालव्य	च	छ	श	ज	झ	ञ	य		इ ई ए ऐ

Cerebrals.	मूर्धन्य	ट	ठ	ष	ड	ढ	ण	र[4]	ऋ[4]			
Dentals.	दन्त्य	त	थ	स	द	ध	न	ल[5]				
Labials.	ओष्ठ्य	प	फ		ब	भ	म	व[3]	उ	ऊ	ओ[2]	औ[2]

ड़ and ढ़ are called द्विस्पृष्ट, and come under Cerebrals.

1. 1. More precisely called Gutturo-palatals, कंठतालव्य
2. 2. ,, ,, ,, Dento-labials, दंतोष्ठ्य
3. ,, ,, ,, Gutturo-labials, कंठोष्ठ्य
4. Rather, perhaps, Palatals.
5. ,, ,, ,,

VARIOUS.

15. The Hindi Syllable.

It is important to understand the divisions of words in Hindi which roughly correspond with our Engish syllables. This matter of syllables or मात्रा is of chief importance in Prosody but is well to briefly notice it here.

The Hindi मात्रा consists of a vowel alone or of a consonant, simple or compound, with its accompanying vowel. To make the distinction between the English and Hindi method as marked as possible, take the following word, *insuppressible.* In English, the division would be in-sup-pres-si-ble, in Hindi i-nsu-ppre-ssi-ble. Apart from its being a closed letter, no syllable ends in a consonant, एक, *one*, is not one syllable, but two ए+क (e-ka); सकरा, *narrow* is not *sak-râ*, but *sa-ka-râ.* We should be tempted to divide इकट्ठा thus—*i-kat-thâ*, it is *i-ka-tthâ.*

16. Closed consonants. Viram.

When a consonant is not followed by a vowel, it is said to be closed, हल, and the fact is indicated by the sign ... ... called विराम, being written under the closed consonant. Thus हल् is not *ha-la*. but *hal.*

The *hal* has another use besides that of being written under a final consonant. It is sometimes written under the first of two consonants which form a conjunct consonant when they are not compounded into one form, thus indicating that there is no vowel sound between the two letters, but that they are to be regarded as a conjunct. कुल्हाड़ी, *axe*, may be printed कुल्हाड़ी or कुल्‌हाड़ी.

17 Use of the Initial and Medial or Final forms of the Vowels.

The fuller forms of the vowels are used when they commence a word or follow a vowel; when following a consonant, the contracted forms are used. Thus 1. आना, *to come*; 2. लाना, *to bring*; 3. जूआ, *a yoke*; 4. ओला, *hail*; 5. लोहा, *iron*; 6. आओगे, *you will come*. 7. सोएंगे, *they will sleep*. In 1. & 6. आ, full form because initial; in 3. because following another vowel; in 1. 2. 4. 5., etc., contracted form because following a consonant. So ओ full form in 4. because initial, and in 6 because following another vowel; short in 5. because following a consonant.

No contracted form for अ exists. The full form is used in the same way as the full form of the other vowels. अ is understood in all cases where a consonant bears no other vowel, where the consonant is not the first member of a conjunct consonant, and where it has not the sign of virâm under it. In all these cases, though unwritten, the अ is understood and sounded. Thus बन = *a forest*, ब + अ + न + अ; स्मशान, *cremation ground*, स + अ + थ + आ + न + अ; समय, *time*, स + अ + म + अ + य + अ.

Where the fuller form of a vowel follows a consonant, this fact indicates that the अ is understood between the consonant and the vowel, otherwise the short form would be used. Thus गई = ग + अ + ई. If the word were simply ग + ई, it would be printed गी.

In many cases, the अ sound is very slight, but, with care, can be distinguished; उनका, *their*, is not sounded exactly like उंका, nor लगता like लग्ता.

It should be noted that an anusvâr and the following consonant constitute a conjunct consonant, therefore अ is not understood between them. अंक = अ + ङ्क + अ, not अ + न + अ + क + अ.

Very occasionally an initial अ following a vowel is indicated by the sign ऽ, *e.g.*, आज्ञाऽनुसार, *according to order*.

18. Note that the contracted form for इ is written *before* its consonant, although read after it. Thus कि = क + इ; इ + क would be printed इक. The forms ा, ी, ो, ौ, are written after the consonant; .. ु ... ू ... ृ are written under, and े ै above.

Where a consonant has anusvâr or the shortened form of र above it, the upper part of ो or ौ is thrown back a little, *e.g.*, लों, पर्वों (प + अ + र्व + ओं + ...).

This also appllies to े...and.....ै, which are written above their consonant.

CONJUNCTS.

19. When two consonants are to be sounded together without the occurrence of any vowel between, they must be joined together, otherwise an inherent अ would be understood after the first. The only two exceptions to this are :—

1. When there be an Anusvâr on the first consonant. That and the consonant following are regarded as a conjunct, although the two letters are not joined together, *e.g.*, संत is the same as though it were printed सन्त, *i.e.*, *sant* not *sanat*. But it should be noted that there is the inherent अ between the स and the Anusvâr.

2. If the Virâm be found under the first consonant. In this case, the consonant marked with Virâm and the following consonant become a conjunct. Thus स्‌तुति would be read as though written स्तुति, (*praise.*)

In being joined with another consonant, the letter र entirely changes its form. If the first member of the compound, it assumes the form...र्... (called then रेफ) and is written over the following letter; if the second member, a small stroke is joined to the letter after which it is sounded. कर्म = क + अ + र् म + अ; but क्रम is = क्‌र + अ + म + अ.

Attention should be directed to the letters क, ग, घ, the forms of which are considerably modified when they appear in conjuncts. The conjunct द्ध appears as though it must stand for ध + द, instead of, as it is, द + ध.

In two other conjunct letters the forms are so changed as not to be recognizable, क्ष = क + ष and ज्ञ = ज + ञ. Some Grammarians print these with the alphabet as separate letters. The conjunct त्र = त + र.

20. A list of the principal conjuncts is appended, arranged in alphabetical order. To save space, illustrative words are not given :

Initial क. क्क kk, क्ख kkh, क्त kt, क्म km, क्य ky,
क्र kr, क्ल kl, क्व kw, क्ष or क्ष *ksh*, क्ष्म or क्ष्म *kshm*, क्ष्य *kshy*.

" ख. ख्य khy, ख्व khw.

" ग. ग्ग gg, ग्ध gdh, ग्न gn, ग्य gy, ग्र gr, ग्ल gl, ग्व gw.

" घ. घ्न ghn, घ्र ghr.

" ङ. ङ्क nk, ङ्ख nkh, ङ्ग ng, ङ्घ ngh (The ङ, however, is generally printed as anusvâr on the previous letter) thus, अंक, अंग, उलंघन.

" च. च्च or च्च chch, च्छ chh., च्य chy.

" ज. ज्ज jj, ज्झ jjh, ज्ञ or ज्ञ (ज + ञ. This conjunct is pronounced like ग्य gy, and is not infrequently so written and printed.) ज्म jm, ज्य jy, ज्र jr, ज्व jw.

„ ञ, ञ्च nch, ञ्छ nchh, ञ्ज nj, ञ्झ njh. The ञ, however, is generally printed as anusvâr on the previous letter; thus, आंच, पंछी, अंजन, झंझट.

„ ट. ट्ट ṭṭ, ट्ठ ṭṭh, ट्य ṭy.

„ ड. ड्ग ḍg, ड्ड ḍḍ.

„ ण. ण्ट ṇṭ, ण्ठ ṇṭh, ण्ड ṇḍ, ण्य ṇy. The ण is often printed as anusvâr over the previous letter.

„ त. त्क tk, त्त tt, त्थ tth, त्न tn, त्प tp, त्म tm, त्य ty, त्र tr, त्व tw, त्स ts.

„ थ. थ्य thy, थ्व thw.

„ द. द्द or द्‌द dd, द्ध ddh, द्भ dbh, द्य dy, द्र dr, द्व dw.

„ ध. ध्य dhy, ध्र dhr, ध्व dhw.

„ न. न्त nt, न्त्य nty, न्त्र ntr, न्थ nth, न्द nd, न्द्र ndr, न्ध ndh, न्ध्य ndhy, न्न nn, न्म nm, न्य ny, न्व nw, न्श nsh, न्स ns. The न is often printed as anusvâr over the previous letter.

„ प. प्त pt, प्न pn, प्प pp, प्य py, प्र pr, प्स ps.

" ब. ब्ज bj, ब्द bd, ब्ध bdh, ब्ब or ब्ब bb, ब्य by, ब्र br.

" भ. भ्य bhy, भ्र bhr.

" म. म्प mp, म्न mn, म्ब mb, म्भ mbh, म्म mm, म्य my, म्र mr, म्ल ml, म्ह mh. The म is occasionally printed as anusvár over the previous letter.

" र. These conjuncts are numerous, but need not be enumerated; they are all written in the way already explained र्क, र्ग, etc.

" ल. ल्क lk, ल्प lp, ल्म lm, ल्य ly, ल्ल or ल्ल ll, ल्ह lh.

" व. व्य wy, व्व or व्व ww.

" श. श्च or श्च shch, श्न shn, श्म shm, श्य shy, श्र shr, श्ल shl, श्व or श्व shw.

" ष. ष्ट sh̲ṭ, ष्ठ sh̲ṭh, ष्ण sh̲n, ष्प sh̲p, ष्फ sh̲ph, ष्म sh̲m, ष्य shy.

" स. स्क sk, स्त st, स्त्य sty, स्त्र str, स्थ sth, स्न sn, स्प sp, स्फ sph, स्म sm, स्य sy, स्र sr, स्व sw, स्स ss.

" ह. ह्म hm, ह्य hy, ह्र hr, ह्ल hl, ह्व hw.

Some of these conjuncts are only necessitated by words derived from the Arabic and Persian. Others are being formed and brought into use as occasion demands.

Thus क्च may be met with to do service in लेक्चर (Lecture).

SANDHI.

21. Sandhi means *junction, combination*, and is used technically to indicate those changes which occur in the last letter of one word and the first of a second when the two words are combined into one. In Sanskrit such euphonic changes occur not only in the formation of compound words, but may more or less apply to all the words in a sentence. Whole lines assume the form of one long compound word, and apart from some knowledge of the rules of Sandhi it is impossible to know where one word terminates and another commences.

These Sandhi changes are found not only in, strictly speaking, compound words, but in cases where a prefix or suffix is added to a simple word.

Most of these changes are effected in the Sanskrit before the words are imported into Hindi, but this is not always the case. This being so, though it may not be necessary for the student of Hindi to enter upon the full consideration of all the elaborate rules of Sandhi found in Sanskrit grammars, yet it is wise to understand the general principles and gain some knowledge of the fundamental rules which operate in effecting the changes. Apart from other considerations, it is a distinct advantage to be able to recognize the constituent elements of a word, to know, *e.g.*, that Himalaya is from हिमः, *frost, ice* and आलय, *abode.*

The changes are mainly of three kinds.

1. A letter may disappear, being merged into another, *e.g.*, परमात्मा, *the supreme spirit*; the inherent अ at the end of परम has been merged in the initial आ of आत्मा.

2. The two letters brought together may be combined into another letter, *e.g.*, in परमेश्वर, *the Supreme God*; the inherent अ in परम and the initial ई of ईश्वर are combined into ए.

3. One letter may be changed so as to euphonize with the other, *e.g.*, जगन्नाथ from जगत्, *world,* and नाथ, *lord.* The त being changed into न, so as to accord with the following न.

A few of the principal Sandhi changes are given below. The full rules and their numerous exceptions are far too elaborate to be included in a small Hindi Grammar.

22. **Changes of vowels.**

Two similar vowels, whether both short, both long, or one short and one long, become the corresponding long vowel, *e.g.*, अ + अ or आ + आ, or अ + आ become आ. Similarly with इ, ई, उ, ऊ, etc. Thus

मुनि + इन्द्र = मुनीन्द्र ; मुनि + ईश = मुनीश.

अ + इ or ई = ए, *e.g.*, जग + ईश्वर = जगेश्वर,
Lord of the world.

आ + उ or ऊ = ओ. पर + उपकार = परोपकार,
Help of another.

अ + ऋ = अर. परम + ऋषि = परमर्षि,
Chief Saint.

अ or आ + ए or ऐ = ऐ ,, हित + एषी = हितैषी,
Well-wisher.

अ or आ + ओ or औ = औ

आ + इ or ई = ऐ

,, ,, उ or ऊ = ओ or औ

,, ,, ऋ = अर or आर, *e.g.*, महा + ऋषि = महर्षि,
Great Saint.

इ or ई followed by a different vowel is changed to य

उ or ऊ ... ... व

ऋ ... ... र

ए ... ... अय

ऐ ... ... आय

ओ .. .. अव

औ ... ... आव

e.g., इति + आदि = इत्यादि, *et cetera*; प्रति + एक = प्रत्येक, *each one*; मनु + अन्तर = मन्वन्तर, *an age of 4,320,000 years.* It will be noticed that, according to the "Classification of Letters" table, य has close affinity with इ, ई, ए, ऐ, and व with उ, ऊ, ओ, औ; र and ऋ are closely related. Thus in the case of many words such as नैन and नयन, *eye*, and औतार and अवतार, *incarnation*, both forms are found.

23. Changes of Consonants.

Nothing beyond a few general principles can be given under this head, as the consonantal changes are very numerous and complicated and belong more properly to Sanskrit Grammar.

a. It is generally the last letter of the first word that is assimilated to the first letter of the second, or moderated in some way, not the reverse, *e.g.*, सत् + जन = सज्जन, *a good person.*

b. A hard consonant may be changed to its corresponding soft letter before a soft consonant, *e.g.*, दिक् + विजय = दिग्विजय, *world-wide conquest*; षट् + दर्शन = षड्दर्शन, *the six systems* (*of philosophy*).

c. Or it may be changed to its corresponding nasal before another nasal, *e.g.*, जगत् + नाथ = जगन्नाथ, *Lord of the world.*

d. In numerous cases the changes are greater than those indicated above, a letter being changed to one of another class. A few examples are appended :

सत् + चित् + आनन्द = सच्चिदानन्द	*Existence, thought, joy.*
निस् + सन्देह = निःसन्देह	*Without doubt.*
निस् + कपट = निष्कपट	*Without hypocrisy.*
निस् + धन = निर्धन	*Without wealth.*
निस् + शंका = निःशंका	*Without doubt.*

The above paragraphs must suffice to indicate the general principles. The English reader may be reminded that such changes are not foreign to the English language, though they are perhaps more commonly found in the addition of prefixes and suffixes than in the formation of compound words. It may be also remarked that the euphonic changes are not so scientifically worked out. We have *unmoved*, but *immaterial*; *impolite*, but *unproved*.

OTHER CHANGES OF LETTERS.

24. Many other changes of letters occur in Hindi, which are neither sanctioned by Grammar nor subject to grammatical rules. These are common in colloquial speech and are also found in literature. ज is often used for य; ब for व; स for श; ख for ष; न for ण. Thus जोग for योग्य, *suitable*; बस for वश, *power*; बिख for विष, *poison*; चरन for चरण, *foot*.

Sometimes र is substituted for ल, *e.g.*, बारना, बालना, *to light*; छ or च्छ for क्ष; अच्छय. अक्षय, *indestructible.* The letters ड़ and र are sometimes interchanged, *e.g.*, खड़ी बोली, खरी बोली, commonly used of the language freed from provincialisms.

Among the illiterate, letters are sometimes reversed in a word, thus आमदी for आदमी, *man.* Other corruptions are very frequent, but have perhaps no right to a place in a Grammar.

ABBREVIATIONS, PUNCTUATION, ETC.

25. Abbreviations.

The sign • indicates that the word is contracted, just as in English *tr.* for *translation*, or *etc.*, for *et cetera*, so in Hindi दो॰ stands for दोहा, Doha; ई॰ for ईस्वी, *the Christian Era* (A. D.); प॰ for पण्डित, Pundit, etc. In a book where any word is repeated again and again, a contraction may be adopted, though it may not be a widely recognized one, *e.g.*, उ॰ for उदाहरण (example).

A figure printed after a word indicates that the word is to be repeated that number of times, *e.g.*, किसी २ का यह मत है...... *i.e.*, किसी किसी का, *the view of this or that one is*......The words श्री ५ signify that the honorific title श्री is to be repeated five times after such a person's name. श्री १०८ is, we believe, the limit in this matter. It is suggestive of so many guns.

26. Punctuation.

Until recently the only marks of punctuation commonly used in Hindi were । and ॥, called एक पाई and दो पाई. The latter is placed at the end of a line of poetry or couplet, the former is less intensive and marks the conclusion of the first half. In prose the double line marks the end of a paragraph, the single that of a sentence.

Of recent years there has been an increasing readiness to adopt many of the English signs for punctuation, etc. The comma aud full-stop (फुल इस्टाप) are very much used, the semi-colon and colon very much less. The note of interrogation is widely used. Perhaps still more popular is the note of exclamation ; a few writers appear to have a perfect passion for ! ! ! ! !s. Inverted commas and parenthetical marks are not uncommonly used, sometimes the latter not very correctly

ACCENT.

27. Accent in Hindi is not so common as in English, but is by no means absent. Very misleading statements have been sometimes made on this point by writers and teachers, and the writer must confess to have been guilty in this matter in his Grammar written years ago. As a matter of fact, accent, both on words in sentences and on syllables in words, is quite common. Possibly no rules can be formulated for the latter, as we recognize that in English no rule can be relied on. In *manly*, *dentistry*, *pungent*, the accent is as clearly on the first syllable as it is on the second in *indent*, *restrict*, *domain*. The general rule about the accent being on the antepenultimate in polysyllabic words, is by no means universal in its application. Under these circumstances, there is no reasonable ground for complaint if the accentuation in Hindi has to be learned by practice, not by rule.

Accent of words in sentences. In Hindi, as in English, this largely depends on the meaning to be conveyed, *e.g.*, यह और किसी का नहीं, उसी का है. *It belongs to no one else, it is his*, the accent naturally falls on उसी का, *his*. Again, कोई नहीं सुनता, *No one hears*, the stress comes on कोई. In the sentence न कोई सुनता न कोई करता, *No one listens no one obeys* (lit. "does"), there is practically no accent on any special word, but in वह सुनता तो है पर करता नहीं, *He hears indeed, but doesn't do* (*it*), the accent is clearly on सुनता, *hears*.

The use of accent or stress on words in sentences varies greatly. Some speakers go evenly on their way and leave their sense to be elucidated by the structure of the sentence; others pursue the exactly opposite course and, so to speak, underline and italicize very many of their words. In some cases tone and emphasis are very necessary, if the exact meaning of the speaker is to be conveyed to the hearer, *e.g.*, in वह करेगा, *He will do (it)*, and वह करेगा ? the meaning depends more on tone; but if the point be as to whether *he* or somebody else will do the work, then stress or accent comes in. वह करेगा may be so pronounced as to indicate very plainly that it is *he who will do it, not another person.* In printing, as underlining is little used, the sentence would probably appear वही करेगा.

28. Accentuated syllables in words.

That accent on syllables exists widely cannot be questioned. In मेरा, तेरा, *mine, thine*, the accent is distinctly on the first syllable; in हमारा, तुम्हारा, *ours, yours*, as distinctly on the second. In करूंगा, मरेगा, *I will do (it), He will die*, however, although these are three-syllabled words, the accent is not on the second, but on the first syllables. The matter of long and short vowels evidently does not decide the matter as to which syllable is to receive the accent. In समाना, *to be contained*, the accent is on मा; but in the word समाचार, it is not on मा, but on the स that the accent falls.

In Verbs the general tendency is for the accent to fall on to the stem rather than on to the termination. Thus in

करूंगा, *I will do*; मरा, *He died*; रोएगा, *He will cry*; गायेंगे, *They will sing*, the accent is on क, म, रो, गा.

In Causal Verbs the accent generally falls on the second syllable of the stem. Compare लगा, *It was affixed*, with लगा (Imperative from लगाना), or लगाता है, *He affixes it*. In the first the accent is on ल, in the second and third on गा. Compare also बैठो, *sit down*, and बैठाओ, *seat* (*another person*). In the first, the accent is on बै, in the second on ठा.

The ear at once distinguishes between the non-accented रे in करेगा and the accented हे in पहेली, *a riddle*. In पति, *husband*, the accent is on प, in पतिव्रता on the ति.

	Accent on.		Accent on.
समाचार, *good news*	स	मसाला, *spices, etc.*	सा
कुशल, *prosperous*	कु	कुचाल, *disorderly walk*	चा
लदा, *laden*	ल	सहारा, *help*	हा
सदा, *always*	स		
दया, *mercy*	द	दयालु, *a merciful one*	या
बोलूंगा, *I will speak*	बो	लूंगा, *I will take*	लू
लौटा, *he returned*	लौ	पौराणिक, *connected with the Purans*	रा

Illustrations need not be multiplied. The student must exercise his ear and imitate. To say आएगा, with a strong accent on ए, is about as indicative of ignorance or carelessness as to say ini-*mic*-al instead of in-*im*-i-cal in English.

The accent in Poetry will arise for consideration in the special chapter on Prosody.

OTHER ALPHABETS.

29. Besides the Nâgarî alphabet, used generally in writing and printing Hindi, modified forms are in use, *e.g.*, the Banioutî used by Baniyas or shop-keepers, the Mahâjanî, adopted by bankers, and the Kaithî, very widely used by patwaris and others, especially in Bihar. The Kaithî is a rough script modified from the ordinary Nâgarî, with the upper line omitted. Like handwriting in English some of the letters may vary. Note, *e.g.*, how differently *g,k,p,s,* etc., are written by different people. For speed and ease of writing Kaithî has distinct advantages. The writer has used it for many years and found it a real saving of labour. It means re-writing for the Press, but a copyist can generally be easily procured.

Several books have been published in Kaithî. Quite well printed books may be obtained from Macmillan & Co., Calcutta, the Kharg Bilas Press, Patna, and other presses. There is quite a good specimen of Kaithî to be obtained at the Bible Society, 23 Chowringhee Road, Calcutta, *viz.*, The Psalms. I—XLI. Price 1 pice. Some books have been published as Kaithî which are not genuine Kaithî ; let the student beware of such.

30. The Kaithi Alphabet.

अ		𑂃		च	𑂒	3	प	𑂣	
आ	ा	𑂄	𑂰	छ	𑂓		फ	𑂤	
इ	ि	𑂅	𑂱	ज	𑂔		ब	𑂥	
ई	ी	𑂆	𑂲	झ	𑂕		भ	𑂦	4
उ	ु	𑂇	𑂳	ञ			म	𑂧	5
ऊ	ू	𑂈	𑂴						
ऋ	ृ		ृ	ट	𑂗		य	𑂨	
ए	े	𑂉	𑂵	ठ	𑂘		र	𑂩	
ऐ	ै	𑂊	𑂶	ड	𑂙		ल	𑂪	𑂪
ओ	ो	𑂋	𑂷	ढ	𑂛		व	𑂫	
औ	ौ	𑂌	𑂸	ण	𑂝				
क		𑂍		त	𑂞		श	𑂬	
ख		𑂎	𑂭 1	थ	𑂟		ष	𑂭	
ग		𑂏		द	𑂠		स	𑂮	
घ		𑂐	2	ध	𑂡				
ङ				न	𑂢		ह	𑂯	

1. It is safer perhaps to use the ordinray Nâgarî ख.

2. .... घ.

3. This too much like घ, 𑆔 is preferable.

4. It is important to begin 𑆨 well to the left and, 𑆩 well to the right 𑆨 भ, 𑆩 म, otherwise 𑆨 and 𑆩 are easily mistaken for one another

CHAPTER III.

DIVISIONS OF HINDI GRAMMAR. PARTS OF SPEECH. SUBSTITUTES FOR THE ARTICLE.

31a. Grammar. **व्याकरण.** Prefix and Suffix.

Part I. Letters. **वर्णविचार.** **उपसर्ग, प्रत्यय.**

„ II. Words. **शब्दविचार.**

„ III. Sentences. **वाक्यविचार.**

Etymology. **व्युत्पत्ति.**

Composition and Syntax. **रचना, वाक्यों की रचना.**

The three divisions of the Parts of Speech:

1. **संज्ञा** ...... Including Nouns, Pronouns and Adjectives.

2. **क्रिया**...... Verb.

3. **अव्यय**...... (Uninflected). Including Adverb, Postposition, Conjunction and Disjunction, Interjection.

Noun. **संज्ञा.**

Pronoun. **सर्वनाम.**

Adjective. **विशेषण.**

Verb. **क्रिया.**

Adverb. **क्रियाविशेषण.**

Postposition. **सम्बन्धबोधक.**

Conjunction & Disjunction. **संयोजक, विभाजक.**

Interjection. **विस्मयादिबोधक.**

31b. As this is a Hindi Grammar for English-speaking students, it would be unwise to attempt to write it from a purely Hindi standpoint; at the same time it is believed that it will prove of considerable assistance to the student to have his attention directed to the divisions of Grammar recognized by Indian Grammarians, to adopt, in some measure, their order in the presentation of the various matters to be considered and to give the technical terms which they use. The knowledge thus gained will be helpful in later reading and study.

We are not disposed to follow their method too closely, nor adopt all their divisions and sub-divisions, which are sometimes traditional, fanciful and conventional and of small practical service. Too much attention has been given by many of the writers of Hindi Grammars to Sanskrit Grammar and too little consideration to the actual principles and rules which prevail in modern Hindi.

32. The 3 main divisions of Hindi Grammar are: 1. **वर्णविचार** — the consideration of the letters. 2. **शब्द विचार** —the consideration of words. 3. **वाक्यविचार**

—the consideration of sentences. Under 2, might come व्युत्पत्ति, Etymology. Under 3, comes रचना, *making*, or वाक्यों की रचना, which may be considered to cover both Composition and Syntax. Prefixes and Suffixes, उपसर्ग and प्रत्यय, may be included under 2. A short chapter will be devoted to this important subject.

For the most part, the Syntax of Hindi will not be dealt with separately, but included in the various sections as the subjects arise with which the different rules of Syntax are connected.

33. The Parts of Speech are divided into 3 classes: 1. संज्ञा, which includes the Noun, Pronoun and Adjective. 2. क्रिया, Verb, and 3. अव्यय, (*i.e.*, unchanging, not liable to inflection), in which are included Adverb, Preposition, (or better, Postposition), Conjunction, (or, as the Hindi Grammarians wisely put it, Conjunction and Disjunction), and Interjection.

1. संज्ञा, Noun. There is a growing tendency among Indian Grammarians to confine the use of this word to mean Noun and not to include Pronouns and Adjectives under the term. It is not difficult to understand how the Pronoun should have been included in the term संज्ञा (that which names or designates), as the Pronoun takes the place of a Noun, but it is not so

so easy to find the ground for the Adjective having been included. Possibly the fact that many Adjectives are used as Nouns may give some clue.

2. **सर्वनाम,** Pronoun. **सर्वनाम,** etymologically, means *all+name*, *i.e.*, a common name applicable to all. Pronominal Adjectives will also be treated under the Pronoun. **प्रतिनिधि** (substitute) is sometimes found for Pronoun.

3. **विशेषण,** Adjective. That which distinguishes. The Hindi **गुणवाचक** is also found to designate the Adjective.

4. **क्रिया,** Verb. (the doing).

5. **क्रियाविशेषण,** Adverb. (that which specializes or discriminates).

6. **सम्बन्धबोधक** (that which indicates connection), corresponds in many respects with the English Preposition, but, as in Hindi it does not precede but follows its Noun or other word, it is more appropriately called Postposition.

7. **संयोजक** and **विभाजक** (that which connects and that which separates). These may well be called Conjunctions and Disjunctions.

8. **विस्मयादिबोधक,** Interjection. (That which indicates dismay, or wonder, etc.)

SUBSTITUTES FOR THE ARTICLE.

34. There is not only no term for the Article in Hindi, but no words which correspond with the English *a* and *the*. Equivalents for them are, however, found.

1. Very frequently the Noun is used without any addition, *e.g.*, *His mother was a widow*, would be simply **उसकी माँ विधवा थी.** A good man never lies, **अच्छा मनुष्य कभी झूठ नहीं बोलता.** What was the cause of it? **उसका क्या कारण था?** He was the greatest of them all, **वह सब में से बड़ा था.** The king began to enquire, **राजा पूछने लगे.**

2. Not infrequently **एक** (one) is used where "*a*" would occur in an English sentence. **एक मनुष्य ने कहा,** *A man said.* **दशरथ ने एक समय प्रसन्न होकर केकयी को दो वर दिये थे,** *Once on a time Dasharath, having been pleased, had given Kekayi two boons.* **एक पुस्तक में यह लिखा है,** *In a book this is written.*

3. Occasionally, **कोई** may be about the equivalent of "*a*," *e.g.*, **कोई स्त्री आकर कहने लगी,** *A woman came and said.* But this might also be rendered, *A certain woman.* **कोई** has generally *something* of the force of, *a certain one*, or *some one*, or *anyone*. **कोई नहीं आया,** *No one came*; lit., *Anyone did not come.*

4. For the Definite Article यह, *this*, or वह, *that, that one*, may sometimes be used, but only in cases where the English *the* carries somewhat of the same force. There are sentences in which the English *the* is quite definite, and yet any equivalent in Hindi might be unnecessary, *e.g.*, *The house is far from here*, might well be rendered घर यहाँ से दूर है ....; the fact that some particular house was being referred to, would be understood from the context. On the other hand, in such a sentence as, *the man is a fool*, meaning some particular man, the Hindi would probably be यह मनुष्य मूर्ख है or वह मनुष्य मूर्ख है. Similarly, वह राजा जिसके पुत्र शास्त्र में ज्ञान नहीं रखते थे, *The king whose sons did not possess a knowledge of the sacred book.* Here the English rendering might equally well be, *that king*. In Hindi, the more usual construction of the sentence would be, जिस राजा के पुत्र शास्त्र में ज्ञान नहीं रखते थे वह..........., *Of which raja the sons...........he...........*Such a phrase as, *The man who went, died*, would be जो गया सो मर गया. In both the English and the Hindi it is not perfectly clear whether the man referred to is some particular man, or whether the statement is a general one.

CHAPTER IV.

DECLENSION OF NOUNS, PRONOUNS AND ADJECTIVES.

THE EIGHT CASES.

35. The Eight Cases. **कारक**

Nominative.

कर्त्ता, (the doer.) — लड़का (boy.) / लड़के ने (Sometimes called the Agentive Case.)

Accusative.

कर्म, (that which is done.) — लड़के को / लड़का

Dative.

सम्प्रदान, (to whom, or for whom given.) — लड़के को

Instrumental.

करण, (producing, causing.) — लड़के से

Ablative.

अपादान, (taking from.) — लड़के से

Genitive.

सम्बन्ध, (bound up with, related.) — लड़के का, की, के

Locative.

अधिकरण, (placing upon.) — लड़के में, पर, etc.

Vocative.

सम्बोधन, (calling to.) — लड़को

36. Much in the way of detail regarding the forms and uses of the Cases, must be left for consideration until the following chapters, but, inasmuch as the broad principles apply equally to Nouns, Pronouns and Adjectives, it seems wise to deal with these broad principles at once.

37. The Cases are indicated by the addition of suffixes. **विभक्ति**, or postpositions, **प्रत्यय.** The original form may or may not undergo change before such addition be made. This Case declension may not be carried out with complete consistency, but is carefully worked out, and presents a striking contrast with the elements of declension to be found in Pronouns and Nouns in English. In Nouns, the "'s" is all that can be brought forward. In Pronouns, we are better off, but far from complete. *My, thy, his, its; our, your, their; me, us, thee, him, them.* It is true that in Hindi we have not a special form for each Case, but there is a complete system, by the use of the **विभक्ति.**

The form with **ने**, given under the Nominative, is sometimes reckoned a separate Case, and called the Agentive. There is some justification for such a course, as the use of the form with **ने** leads to a reconstruction of the sentence in which it occurs; but, in spite of this, it is practically the subject of the sentence and so, in common with Indian grammarians, we include it with the Nominative, regarding it as a special form of that Case.

38. That form of the Accusative which is identical with the simple form of the Nominative will be explained in the chapter on the Noun.

39. The form of the Dative is identical with the form of the Accusative with को. This leads to some confusion at times. In not a few instances a word which is regarded by some as a second Accusative is in reality a Dative.

के लिये (for, for the sake of) is used sometimes with the Dative instead of को.

40. The forms for the Instrumental and Ablative are exactly the same and, in instances not a few, to decide whether the से indicates the Instrumental or Ablative Case is not easy. In राजा ने अपने मनुष्यों से उसको मरवा डाला, *The king slew him by his own men*, it is clearly the Instrumental. In समुद्र से निकाला गया था, *It was taken out of the sea*, there can be no question, it is undoubtedly the Ablative; but in such sentences as स्त्री ने अपने भाई से पूछा, *The woman asked her brother*; यह उससे छोटा है, *This is smaller than that*, it is not so immediately evident under which Case it should come.

41. For the Genitive Case, the Hindi name सम्बन्ध is peculiarly suitable, signifying any relation or connection which may exist between two or more persons or things. उसका बेटा, *His son* ; यह तो एक पैसे की पुस्तक है, *This is a one pice book* ; चान्दी की चूड़ी, *A silver bangle,* are simple illustrations of the use of the Genitive. The relations covered in the use of this Case are exceedingly numerous.

42. The Locative with में, *in*, and पर, *upon*, sweeps a wide area. It has reference to place, time, and logical sequence.

43. The Vocative is the Case used when a person or persons are directly addressed.

44. The following sentence includes all the Cases. हे गुरु मैंने राजा के सेवक को आज्ञा दी कि तुम नगर से घोड़े को लाकर घर में रस्सी से बान्धो, *Oh guru! I gave command to the raja's servant to bring the horse from the city and fasten it up by a rope to the house.*

45. Inflectional changes.

A special form of the word does not exist for each Case. With some Nouns, no change of form occurs at all in the singular, the Case being indicated by the addition of the Case-suffix or विभक्ति. In all Nouns, the Plural has an inflected form differing from the Nom. This may be called the oblique stem, or inflected stem. The same name is appropriate for the stem in the sing. when such a changed stem is used. The inflectional changes are greater with the Pronouns than with Nouns.

46. Case endings.

Some of the Case endings may be regarded as words, such as **में**, *in* ; **पर**, *upon* ; others partake more of the nature of suffixes, having no meaning by themselves. It might, of course, be urged that the postpositions also are incapable of expressing an idea unless joined to other words in a sentence. It will, however, be felt that there is a distinction between **का, की, को** and **में, पर**; even as in English we should not call "'s" in "*dog's*" a word, nor "*...ship*" in "*partnership*," but we do call "*in*," "*upon*" words.

47. Case endings. How written.

The opinion of Hindi scholars as to the correct way of writing the Case endings is not unanimous. Should they be joined to their word or written separately ?

It will be found that generally the following rules are accepted. In the case of Nouns, the Case endings should be printed separately from the words, but should be united with the Pronouns. Thus :—**सरकार ने, पुस्तक का, राजा की, नगर को, धन से, परीक्षा में,**

चेष्टा करने पर; but उसकी, उन्होंने, इसमें, जिसको, उनके, etc.

Details concerning the Cases will be given in the several chapters dealing with Nouns, Pronouns and Adjectives.

CHAPTER V

THE NOUN

48a. Noun संज्ञा

Word शब्द

Word with its Case suffix पद

Case कारक (see for list, previous chapter.)

Case suffix विभक्ति

Affix उपसर्ग, प्रत्यय

Gender लिंग

Masculine पुँल्लिंग

Feminine स्त्रीलिंग

Neuter (not used in Hindi.) नपुंसक लिंग

Number वचन

Singular एकवचन

Plural बहुवचन

Dual (not found in Hindi.) द्विवचन

Compound word समास

48b. The various divisions of words and Nouns adopted by Indian Grammarians is not a matter of supreme importance for the foreign student, nor of great practical moment, but is well worthy of some consideration.

Sounds are said to be of two kinds : 1. **ध्वन्यात्मक,** *i.e.*, mere sounds as made by animals. 2. **वर्णात्मक,** *i.e.*, composed of letters. This definition must be taken for what it is worth ; words exist long before letters are invented to make a record of them possible. This 2nd class of sounds is again divided into : 1. **सार्थक,** *possessing meaning*, and 2. **निरर्थक,** *without meaning.*

Grammar, of course, only deals with this second class, with Words. Words are classed according to their origin or the character of their formation.

1. **रूढ़ि.** A word which is a simple original sound ; an arbitrary sound possessing a definite meaning, as **मनुष्य,** *a man.*

2. **यौगिक.** A word formed from combined roots. Here the word is no longer an arbitrary sound, its meaning rests on its etymology, *e.g.*, **पूजक,** *a worshipper*, from **पूज,** relating to *worship* and **क** contracted from **करना,** *to do.* Thus **पूजक** means, *one who does worship.*

3. **योगरूढ़ि.** These words are **यौगिक** forasmuch as they are derived from roots giving meaning according to etymology, and are **रूढ़ि,** because the meaning of the word when it has been formed is attached arbitrarily to some special object, *e.g.*, **पंकज,** *a lotus*, from **पंक,** *mud*, and **ज,** *born of.* The meaning is plain from the etymology ; but to attach the word to the *lotus* must

be regarded as arbitrary, as there are other mud-born things besides the lotus.

4. **समास,** Compound word, is not always included in these divisions, but appears to belong here. It differs mainly from **यौगिक** words, in that it is formed from two words rather than from two roots. Example, **महाराजा,** *a great king*, from **महा,** *great*, and **राजा,** *a king*.

49. Nouns

A three-fold division of Nouns is generally adopted.

1. **जातिवाचक,** Common Noun. One of a class as **पशु,** *animal* : **पक्षी,** *a bird* : **वृक्ष,** *a tree*.

2. **व्यक्तिवाचक,** Proper Noun. From **व्यक्ति,** *an individual, e.g.,* **विष्णु,** *the god Vishnu* ; **गंगा,** *the river Ganges*.

3. **भाववाचक.** More or less corresponding with the English Abstract Noun, but covering more than can be strictly included in that term. **सुंदरता,** *beauty*, is abstract, but another example given, *viz.*, **मार पीट,** *striking and cudgelling*, must be regarded, by at least the recipient, as not strictly abstract.

There are various other divisions of Nouns adopted by some Indian grammarians such as those indicating rank or office, *e.g.*, **चौधरी,** *a head man* ; those indicating relationship, *e.g.*, **भाई,** *brother* ; measure or weight, **सेर,**

a weight of about 2 lbs.; occupation, बढ़ई, *carpenter*; Collective Nouns, सभा, *an association* or *assembly*.

There are many Verbal Nouns in Hindi, *e.g.*, the Infinitive is a Noun in very frequent use, करना, *to do, the doing*. This is called in Hindi the क्रियार्थक संज्ञा. Another group bears the name of कृदन्त. These include such words as करनेवाला, a doer.

The Infinitive is fully capable of inflection as regards Case, Gender and Number.

50. There are four matters calling for special attention in connection with Nouns. These will now be dealt with: 1. Gender. 2. Number. 3. Cases. 4. Compound Nouns.

GENDER.

51. The Gender of Nouns is, in Hindi, a matter of great importance and of about equal difficulty. Its importance rests on the fact that the gender of the Nominative often affects the form of the Verb; also the gender of the Noun affects the form of the Adjective or Participle. The difficulty arises from this that, as there is no neuter gender in Hindi, every noun is either masculine or feminine, though so many must obviously be quite devoid of any sex distinction. The termination of the Noun may at times afford some help, but no reliable rule can be formulated on that basis. For instance, from the fact that आ

and ई are the characteristic terminations, respectively, of masc. and fem. Adjectives and Participles, and also of many parts of the Verb, one might naturally be led to conclude that Nouns ending in आ and ई would likewise be masc. and fem. Such a conclusion would be very misleading; probably something like 75 per cent. of Nouns ending in आ are not masc. but fem., and a very large number of Nouns ending in ई are masc.

52. After stating that living creatures of the male sex are masc. and of the female fem., the only general principle or tendency that can be laid down is this, that larger things are commonly masc. and smaller things and abstract nouns fem., but this is only a broad principle, not a rule.

Indian writers often set forward this statement as a help to the student,—*Nouns which require the masc. form of the Adjective are masc., those which require the fem. form are fem.* This statement is obviously correct. but, we are at first inclined to conclude, as obviously futile, as it begs the whole question. The statement, however, is quite serviceable for the *Indian* student and yields a suggestion for the foreign student of considerable value. The Indian student will try words by his ear. He will say "**बड़ा टापू**," a large island, "**छोटा टापू**," and will decide that the former is right, the second impossible, in the same way that we repeat a sentence and by the ear conclude what is correct and what incorrect. The suggestion that is forthcoming is this: Let the foreign student, instead of attempting to commit to memory the genders of long lists of words, learn to associate with each Noun an Adjective, or to connect it with other words in a phrase, in which the form of the Verb or some other word will settle the gender of the Noun. In this way, he will not only be fixing the gender of the Noun in his memory but, at the same time, enlarging his vocabulary, *e.g.*, अच्छा फल, *good fruit*; पण्डित का आदर करना, *Shew honour to the man of learning*; ईश्वर के अनुग्रह से, *By God's grace*: लम्बी भुजा, *A long arm*; लड़के की आँखें खुल गयीं, *The eyes of the boy opened*: राजा की दया, *The king's mercy*. This is a far more effective method of learning that फल, आदर and अनुग्रह are masc. and भुजा, आँख and दया fem. than the bald *memoriter* system.

53. Some general rules about genders may prove of some service, but the student must remember that they are only *general*.

MASCULINE.

54. According to ending.

1. Ending in ई. Many of these are somewhat adjectival in their formation and meaning. Not a few of

them can be used as either Adjectives or Nouns, *e.g.*, लोभी, an avaricious man; लोभी गुरु, an avaricious teacher. So again, बंगाली, a Bengali; बंगाली मिठाई, Bengali sweetmeat. This remark applies to many other Nouns as well as those ending in ई.

a. Many Nouns in which ई is added as a suffix to a Noun signifying some quality, and thus means the possessor of that quality, *e.g.*,

पापी	a sinner.	मन्त्री	a counsellor.
प्रेमी	one who loves.	अपराधी	a transgressor.
द्रोही	an enemy.	शास्त्री	a learned man.
लोभी	an avaricious man.		

One exception may be noticed. उदासी is *dejection*. उदास, *a dejected man*. This is similar to the Urdu in which it is the quality which ends in ई; the possessor of the quality has not the ई at the end. Thus:—

ग़रीबी غريبي, *poverty*; ग़रीब, a poor man.
आजिज़ी عاجزي, *helplessness*; आजिज़, a helpless one.

Such Urdu words ending in ई are fem., and retain their Urdu gender when used in Hindi.

b. A Class of Nouns used of members of castes or trades.

It should be borne in mind that membership of a

caste does not necessarily involve that the member should follow the occupation of the caste. Mr. Glover is not in all cases a maker or seller of gloves. To a large extent, however, the members of the caste do follow the occupation, and identification with the caste cannot be evaded.

द्विवेदी, तिवारी two classes of Brahmans.

पुजारी a temple priest.

धोबी a washerman.

तम्बोली a betel-leaf seller.

मोची a shoemaker.

c. Indicating nationality, place of residence of the person, etc.

बंगाली, कश्मीरी, कमाउनी, a native of Bengal, Cashmere or Kamaun.

रघुवंशी, One who belongs to the race of Raghu.

बासी, A resident of, as काशीबासी, a resident of Kashi. As we may say, "He is a Plymouthian," *i.e.*, a resident of Plymouth.

d. A class of Nouns of which the second part is formed from a verbal root and conveys the idea of a possessor of, or doer of, that which is contained in the first part of the word.

बलात्कारी, An oppressor (doer of violence.)

उपकारी, A benefactor (doer of help.)

अपकारी, An injurious person (doer of injury.)

बकवादी, A chatterbox (a garrulous person.)

सत्यवादी, A truthful person (a speaker of the truth.)

सहगामी, A fellow-traveller (a goer with.)

सहकर्मी, A fellow-worker (a worker with.)

दुःखदाई, A troubler (a giver of trouble.)

सुखदाई, One who gives happiness to others.

55. 2. Ending in **आ.**

आ is a very characteristic masc. termination, but of Nouns ending in **आ** probably not less than about 75 per cent. are fem.

a. Verbal Nouns formed by adding **वाला** or **हारा** to the inflected form of the Infinitive. These become fem. by changing **आ** into **ई.**

करनेवाला A doer.

जानेवाला One who goes, or is about to go.

आनेवाला One who comes, or is about to come.

देनेवाला A giver.

The termination **हारा** is little used in modern Hindi.

b. Nouns indicating family relationship.

पिता, *father*; **बेटा,** *son*: **दादा, नाना,** *paternal and maternal grandfather*; **पोता,** *grandson*: **परपोता,**

great grandson; काका, चचा, मामा, फुप्पा, मौसा, various kinds of uncles, according as they are on the father's or mother's side, actual uncle or only the aunt's husband.

As will be pointed out in the section on Number, many of these Nouns are not inflected in the singular.

c. A few ending in इया, indicating occupation.

गवइया, a singer; छवइया, a thatcher;

मुखिया, headman; करवइया or करवैया, a doer.

d. Many others which it would be difficult to classify, *e.g.*,

राजा, a king; उल्था, a translation; खम्भा, a pillar; चोला, a body; छुटकारा, deliverance; डेरा, a tent; मेला, a festive gathering of people; सहारा, help; सोना, gold; लोहा, iron.

56. 3. Ending in क.

This क is connected with करना, and conveys the idea of a doer of. Thus शिक्षक, both *tutor* and *pupil*, one who either imparts or receives शिक्षा, instruction. पालक, one who nourishes or protects. लेखक, a writer; सेवक, a servant.

Not all these Nouns are personal. We have, for instance, रोचक, that which is tasty; बन्धक, a pledge.

57. 4. Ending in **त्व.**

These are Abstract Nouns. **पुरुषत्व,** *manliness, prowess* ; **मनुष्यत्व,** the quality of humanity : **महत्व,** *greatness* ; **दासत्व,** the condition of servitude. A few end in **त्त्व,** *e.g.*, **तत्त्व,** essence, element.

58. 5. Ending in **आव.**

These are of the nature of Verbal Nouns, and have a meaning somewhat similar to that conveyed by the use of the Infinitive as a Verbal Noun. Examples : **झुकाव,** *bending* ; **खिंचाव,** *attraction, tension* ; **पछताव,** *regret* ; **बचाव,** *being saved*; as in such a sentence as **उसका बचाव नहीं बनेगा,** *It will not be possible to save him* ; **हटाव,** *the being thrust back.*

59. 6. Ending in **ऊ.**

Sometimes this ending conveys much the same meaning as the **आव** given above.

उपजाऊ, *productiveness* ; **खाऊ,** *eating ravenously*, or *a glutton* ; **गिराऊ,** *falling* ; **ढलाऊ,** *sloping.*

Words ending in **आव** and **ऊ** masc. and **हट** fem. have much in common.

60. 7. Ending in **पन.**

These also are Abstract Nouns. **भोलापन,** *simplicity* ; **लड़कपन,** *childhood* ; **पागलपन,** *madness* ; **मोटापन,** *thickness* ; **कालापन,** *blackness.*

61. According to meaning.

1. Many natural objects, especially if large, are masc. सूर्य्य, सूरज, *the sun*; चान्द, चन्द्रमा, *the moon*; संसार, *the universe*; जगत, *the world*; तारा, *a star*; आकाश, *the firmament*; स्वर्ग, *heaven*; वायु, *the air*; द्वीप, *a continent*; देश, *a country*; टापू, *an island*; समुद्र, *a sea*; ताल, तालाव, पोखरा, *lake, pond*; नद, *a river*.

But पृथिवी, *the earth*; नदी, *a river*; झील, *a shallow lake*, are fem.

62. 2. Minerals and precious stones, *e.g.*, धातु, *a mineral*; सोना, *gold*; रूपा, *silver*; लोहा, *iron*; ताम्बा, *copper*; पीतल, *brass*; रत्न, *a precious stone*; हीरा, *a diamond*; माणिक, *a ruby*.

But चान्दी, silver, and words for earth, मट्टी, मिट्टी, मृत्तिका, are fem.

63. 3. Parts of the body.

तन, तनु, शरीर, चोला, *body*; धड़, *trunk*; सिर, शिर, *head*; मुँह, मुख, *face*; खोपरा, *skull*; बाल, (generally plural.) *hair*; कान, *ear*; गाल, *cheek*; होंठ, *lip*; दांत, *tooth*; नेत्र, लोचन, *eye*; कन्धा, *shoulder*; हाथ, कर, पाणि, *hand*; पेट, *belly*; पाँव, *leg*; चरण, *foot*; शव, *a corpse*; and many more are masc.

But कटि, करिहाँव, *loins or waist* ; छाती, *breast* ; बाँह, भुजा, *arm* ; ग्रीवा, *neck*. आँख, *eye* ; जीभ, *tongue* : नासिका, *nose*, are fem. : लोथ, *corpse* ; खोपरी or खोपड़ी, skull, also are fem. देह, *body*, is generally fem., but occasionally masc.

64. 4. Divisions of time.

काल, समय, *time* ; युग, *an age* ; बरस, *a year* ; मास, महीना, *a month* ; ऋतु, *a period of two months* ; पक्ष, *half a lunar month* : दिन, दिवस, *a day* ; बिहान, *morning* ; पहर, *a period of three hours*, are all masc.

But रात, रात्रि, *night* : सांझ, *evening* ; घड़ी, *a period of 24 minutes*, are fem.

65 5. Some emotions and mental states.

प्रेम, स्नेह, *love* ; क्रोध, रोष, *anger* ; घमण्ड, अहंकार, अभिमान, गर्व, *pride* ; लालच, *avarice* ; आनन्द, हर्ष, सुख, *joy, pleasure* ; दुःख, *pain* ; शोक, *grief*.

But many such qualities, especially those representing the more tender feelings, are fem.

FEMININE.

66. I. Ending in ई. The termination ई is characteristic of the fem., even as आ is of the masc. ; but Nouns ending in ई are by no means exclusively fem. Probably quite as many are masc.

A. The fems. of corresponding Nouns in masc., ending in आ.

a. Indicating relations. दादी, नानी, *paternal* and *maternal grandmother.* बेटी, *daughter*; पोती, *grand-daughter* (son's *daughter*).; काकी, चची, *aunt* (father's brother's wife.); मामी, *aunt* (mother's brother's wife.); फूफी, *aunt* (father's sister.); मौसी, *aunt* (mother's sister.)

It is interesting to note that, while a son's daughter is पोती, a daughter's daughter is not (generally) नाती but नातिन. The word नाता is reserved for the meaning of a relative of any kind, a kinsman. The form नाती is appropriated for daughter's son, and the fem. of this is नातिन.

b. Nouns of Agency.

करनेवाली, a doer.

सुननेवाली, a hearer.

c. Other Nouns.

लड़की, *a girl*; छोकरी, *a lass*: चेली, *a disciple*: कुत्ती (or कुतिया), *a bitch*; बकरी, *a she-goat*; घोड़ी, *a mare.*

These Nouns are not very numerous, nor are they

consistently worked out. भैंसा is *a buffalo*, but the fem. is not भैंसी, but भैंस. हाथी is not a female elephant but a male. The fem. is हथनी . दासी is a female slave, but there is no masc. दासा, it is दास.

So the masc. of पुत्री, *daughter*, is पुत्र, son.
" " भेड़ी, *female sheep*, is भेड़.
" " हरिणी, *female deer*, is हरिण.

A few Nouns for inanimate things are found with a masc. in आ and a corresponding fem. in ई. These latter are generally diminutives, or regarded as inferior in some way.

रस्सी, *rope*; masc. रस्सा.
कुल्हाड़ी, *hatchet*; " कुल्हाड़ा.
जूती, *shoe*; " जूता.
नाली, *a drain*; " नाला.

Often a masc. in आ is not found, *e.g.*, नदी, *river*, corresponds with नद, *a very large river*. We have खिड़की for *a small window* or *door*, but no such word as खिड़का is in use.

67. B. A certain number of words ending in आई, having, in many cases, an abstract meaning.

सच्चाई, *truthfulness*; भलाई, *prosperity*: बड़ाई, *greatness*; बुराई, *depravity*; लम्बाई, *length*; चौड़ाई, *breadth*.

Such forms as सुन्दरताई, *beauty*; पवित्रताई, *holiness*, should be avoided; the ई is quite redundant, the ता already fully conveying the abstract idea.

68. C. A number of words indicating cost of labour of various kinds, and sometimes the work itself.

धुलाई, price of washing, washing.
ढुलाई, price of carrying, porterage.
कटाई, price of reaping, cutting.
सिलाई, price of sewing, sewing.
कमाई, earnings.
पकाई, cooking.
जुताई, tillage.

Also बिनाई, बनवाई, पिसाई, cost of weaving, making, grinding, and many other similar words.

69. II. Ending in इ.

Of words ending in इ very many are fem. Of these many are distinctly abstract in meaning.

भक्ति, *religious fervour*: पुष्टि, *bodily fitness*; शक्ति, *power*: उन्नति, *advancement*: अवनति, *decline*; बुद्धि, *wisdom*; सृष्टि, *creating*; दृष्टि, *vision*; शान्ति, *tranquillity*; स्तुति, *praise*; रीति, भांति, *method*; भूमि, *the ground*.

A few mascs. in इ are found. ऋषि, मुनि, *saint*; कपि, monkey; राशि, *a heap*, etc.

70. III. Ending in **आ.**

A. Some of these are the names of moral qualities. A few are Collective Nouns; a considerable number must be classed miscellaneous.

a. **करुणा,** *compassion*: **दया,** *mercy*: **कृपा,** *favour*; **घृणा,** *contempt*; **आशा,** *expectation*; **अभिलाषा, कांक्षा,** *desire*; **लज्जा,** *shame*; **ईर्षा,** *envy*: **शंका,** *doubt.*

b. **सभा,** *an association* or *assembly*: **प्रजा,** *subjects of a king. cf.* the English "this people." **सेना,** *an army.*

c. **विद्या,** *learning*; **प्रशंसा,** *praise*: **निन्दा,** *abuse, insult*: **महिमा,** *glory*; **दिशा,** *direction.*

आज्ञा, *command*; **भाषा,** *language* or *dialect*; **सेवा,** *service*; **मूर्च्छा,** *a swoon*; **रक्षा,** *protection*; **चिन्ता,** *thought, anxiety*; **धारा,** *flow (of a stream)*; **बाधा,** *hindrance*; **टीका,** *a commentary*: **मदिरा,** *intoxicating drink.*

बालिका, *a girl*; **महिला, कमला, अबला,** *woman*; **कथा,** *a story*; **पीड़ा,** *pain*; **चेष्टा,** *effort*; **प्रथा,** *custom*; **प्रतिज्ञा,** *promise*; **संख्या,** *number.*

71. B. There is a very large class of Abstract Nouns ending in **ता.** Indian writers tack this **ता** on to well nigh innumerable words. The suffix has much the force of "ness" in English, as in *sweetness*, *goodness*, *freshness*. A few examples are given :—

अज्ञानता, *ignorance.*	**एकता**, *oneness.*
अधिकता, *excess.*	**कोमलता**, *softness.*
अमूल्यता, *pricelessness.*	**चतुरता**, *ability.*
आवश्यकता, *indispensableness.*	**नम्रता**, *softness.*
उत्तमता, *excellence.*	**प्रसन्नता**, *pleasure.*
उदारता, *liberality.*	**योग्यता**, *fitness.*

72. C. A considerable number of fem. Nouns ending in **ना**, including a few in **णा**. These Nouns have generally somewhat of a verbal force, *the doing of*. Examples :—

प्रार्थना, *prayer, supplication.*	**रचना**, *make, workmanship.*
आराधना, *worship.*	**कल्पना**, *thought, imagining.*
उपासना, *worship.*	**सम्भावना**, *possibility.*
कामना, *desire.*	**सूचना**, *information.*
घटना, *occurrence.*	**स्थापना**, *placing.*
ताड़ना, *chastisement.*	**प्रेरणा**, *instigation.*

विवेचना, *discrimination.*

73. IV. Ending in **इन**, **आइन**, **नी** or **आनी**.

These are mostly formed from masculines. Very many of them are caste designations.

A. *a*. From mascs. ending in ई.

धोबिन	fem. of	धोबी, washerman.
मालिन	„	माली, gardener.
तम्बोलिन	„	तम्बोली, betel-leaf seller.

b. From mascs. ending in आ.

Sometimes the आ is retained before the addition of इन; sometimes dropped.

बनियाइन	fem. of	बनिया, shopkeeper.
धुनियाइन	„ ...	धुनिया, wool-carder.
ठठेरिन	„ ...	ठठेरा, brass-worker.
कसेरिन	„ ...	कसेरा, copper-worker.

c. From mascs. ending in a consonant.

सेानारिन	fem. of	सेानार, goldsmith.
चमारिन	„ ...	चमार, leather-worker.
लोहारिन	„ ...	लोहार, blacksmith.

This इन may be अन in some instances: *e.g.*, चितेरन for fem. of चितेरा (*painter*), लोहारन for लोहारिन fem. of लोहार (*blacksmith*).

d. In some cases, there is an alternate feminine, *e.g.*, चमाइन for चमारिन, and a few more.

74. B. Ending in आइन. These are from mascs. of various endings.

गुरुआइन or गुरुआनी fem. of गुरु, a religious teacher.

पण्डिताइन...... „ पण्डित, a learned man.

ठाकुराइन......... „

also ठाकुरानी, ठकुरानी ठाकुर, a landowner, etc.

75. C. Ending in नी, इनी and आनी.

It should be noticed that a long vowel in one of the syllables of the masc. is sometimes shortened in the formation of the fem.

These Nouns are not only the names of castes, but for other classes of words, relatives, animals, etc.

a. Many are from mascs. ending in ई, the ई being changed into इनी.

भिखारिनी fem. of भिखारी, a beggar.

अपराधिनी...... „ अपराधी, a transgressor.

पापिनी „ पापी, a sinner.

गजगामिनी, or गजगमिनी, a woman whose stately walk is compared with the gait of an elephant.

b. From mascs. ending in a consonant, etc.

कल्वारिनी fem. of कल्वार, a distiller.

शुक्लानी „ शुक्ल, a certain class of Brahmans.

सिठानी „ सेठ, a banker.

जुलाहिन „ जुलाहा, a weaver.

जेठानी, wife of a woman's husband's elder brother (जेठ)

देवरानी... „ ....younger.... „ ......(देवर)

नागिनी	fem. of	नाग, a snake.
ऊँटनी......	„ ...	ऊँट, a camel.
सिंघनी......	„ ...	सिंघ or सिंह, a lion.
हथनी......	„ ...	हाथी, an elephant.

76. D. Ending in ट.

These have often somewhat of an abstract meaning, *e.g.*, उसकी सजावट देखने योग्य है, *Its make up* (*or ornamental get up*) *is worth looking at.*

घबराहट,	perturbation.
सड़ाहट,	rottenness.
बनावट,	make.
थकावट,	weariness.
चिकनाहट,	smoothness.
आहट,	sound of a footstep.

77. The above general rules and illustrations must suffice. . As is natural, where no neuter gender exists, uncertainty attaches to the whole question of gender. Any rules framed can only be of a general character, having many exceptions. Indian writers differ as to the gender of various words. This is partly due to local usage, *e.g.*, देह, *body*, is generally fem.; but in some

parts masc. The word पुस्तक, *book*, used to be masc. It is now invariably fem., probably owing to the fact that the Urdu word for book, *kitâb*, is fem. Again, the word आत्मा, *spirit*, though still generally masc., is used as fem. by some writers. This, likewise, is probably due to the influence of Urdu, the word "*rûh*," *spirit*, being fem. in Urdu.

One word, खोज, is both masc. and fem., and the meaning differs as the masc. or fem. is used. As masc., it means "*trace*," as fem. "*search*." उसकी खोज करो, *Search for it.* खोज नहीं मिला, *no trace of it was found.* The word ओर, *direction*, is used both as masc. and fem.; a note on this will be found later in the Grammar.

Careful observation and frequent recourse to the Dictionary is the only course. In accordance with the suggestion already made, let the student train his ear by associating other words with Nouns and thus accustom himself to *feel* what gender a Noun is.

78. A few words are given below as worthy of special note :

Masculine.	*Feminine.*
आसरा, hope.	(but आशा of somewhat similar meaning.)
पानी, water.	रोटी, bread.
प्रश्न, question.	माला, rosary, garland.

Masc.	Fem.
उत्तर, answer.	महिमा, glory.
जी, life.	पीड़ा, pain.
विश्वास, faith.	मृत्यु, death.
आत्मा, spirit.	आग, fire.
मोती, pearl.	जड़, root.

पुस्तक, book.

चिड़िया, bird, and बिल्ली, cat, are both fem.; but are commonly used for birds and cats, regardless of sex. The same might be said about certain other words.

79. Gender indicated by different words.

In some cases, a feminine Noun, pairing off with a corresponding masculine, is not a modified form of the latter, but a distinct word, *e.g.*,

father, पिता	mother, माता
brother, भाई	sister, बहिन
man, पुरुष	woman, स्त्री

Another word for man, मनुष्य, is often used with a generic force as including woman, in the way that *man* is used in such a phrase as "man is mortal."

king, राजा	queen, रानी or राणी

A masc. राना or राणा is used for king in some parts of India.

bullock, बैल	cow, गाय

लाल and मुनिया, male and female of a certain small bird.

80. Gender of Compound Nouns.

The last word in a Compound Noun decides its gender, the earlier word simply qualifying the latter. Thus प्रजापति, *king, etc.*; सभापति, *president of an assembly*; अग्निकुण्ड, *a fire-pit*, are masc., although प्रजा, सभा and अग्नि are fem.

In the same way, राजधानी, *capital*; जलयात्रा, *a voyage*, are fem., although राजा and जल are masc.

81. Urdu words do not come under the general rules given above; they retain their own genders when brought into Hindi. Very many Urdu words ending in आ and ह are masc. many ending in ई, त and इश are fem.

NUMBER.

82. There are two Numbers in Hindi, Singular and Plural. A Dual Number exists in Sanskrit but has not been brought into Hindi.

Only the Nominative Case will be referred to in this section; the forms of Oblique Cases will be dealt with in the section on the Cases.

The majority of masculine Nouns do not possess a different form for the Nominative Plural; consequently, it is only by the forms of other words in the same sentence, or by the context, that it can be decided whether a Noun be sing. or plural. In not a few instances it is the context alone that can make the matter clear. In the sentence, राजा आये हैं, it is impossible to tell whether the translation should be "*the king has come*" or "*the kings have come.*" The verb is in the plural, but this would be quite appropriate if only one king were referred to, the plural verb being honorific.

83. The Four Declensions of Nouns.

In dealing with Number and Cases of Nouns, we may place the Nouns in 4 classes:

I. Some mascs. ending in आ.

II. All other mascs. Some ending in आ must be included in this class, those ending in any other vowel, and those ending in a consonant.

III. Fems. ending in इ, ई, उ, ऊ.

IV. Fems. ending in any other letter.

84. For deciding whether a masc. Noun ending in आ, should be included in the 1st or 2nd class, the rule has been given that Tadbhavas in आ belong to Class I, Tatsamas to Class II. It is evident, however, that such a rule is worthless to any but an advanced scholar. The best course to take is to try and fix the mascs. ending in आ that belong to II (and they are quite limited in number), the rest may then be regarded as belonging to Class I.

85. I. Mascs. ending in आ belonging to Class II.

a. A few indicating relationship:

पिता, father;

दादा, paternal grandfather;

नाना, maternal grandfather;

पुरुखा or पुरखा, ancestor;

चचा or चाचा, uncle;

काका, „

मामा, „

पोता, grandson;

and a few others.

b. Other Nouns not easily classified as regards meaning:

राजा, a king.
राना or राणा, a king.
विधाता, creator or disposer.
कर्त्ता, doer, Creator.
देवता, a god.
आत्मा, spirit.
परमात्मा, great spirit.
भर्ता, protector.
बाबा, a term of respect to the aged.
ज्ञाता, a learned man.
दाता, a giver.
वक्ता, a speaker.
श्रोता, a hearer.
रचयिता, an author.
योधा, a warrior.
सखा, a companion.
युवा, a young man.
नेता, a leader.
अगुआ, a guide or forerunner.

86. II. Mascs. ending in other vowels come under this Class II. (See sections 54 and 59.)

Under this come such Nouns as **पापी, धोबी, बंगाली, बकवादी, मुनि, डाकू,** *a robber*: **गुरु,** *a teacher*; **अतिथि,** *a guest*.

87. III. Mascs. ending in consonants. Such as :—

नाम, name : **कुल,** race ; **पत्थर,** stone ; **स्थान,** place ; **शोक,** sorrow : **रोग,** disease : **तीर,** arrow ; **पाँव,** leg ; **पाप,** sin : **कुण्ड,** pool ; **कोट,** fort : **नेत्र,** eye ; **उपाय,** arrangementor device.

With all these Nouns in Class I, the Nom. Pl. is the same as the Nom. Sing., and the form does not undergo any change in the oblique cases in the singular.

88. Class I. Mascs. ending in **आ.**

This Class is so miscellaneous as regards meaning that no classification is attempted :

बेटा, a son ;
लड़का, boy ;
कुत्ता, dog ;
पता, trace, clue ;
धोखा, deception ;
नेवता, invitation ;
टोना, spell ;

and the numerous words ending in **वाला,** such as **देनेवाला,** *a giver* ; **करनेवाला,** *a doer*.

These Nouns make their plural Nom. by changing आ into ए, *i.e.*, बेटे, लड़के, कुत्ते, etc. The same inflection is made before adding the Case endings in the oblique forms of the singular.

88b. Class III.

This class includes feminine Nouns ending in ई and इ. They form their Nom. pl. by changing both ई and इ to इय and adding आँ.

स्त्री, woman.	स्त्रियाँ, women.
लड़की, girl.	लड़कियाँ, girls
नदी, river.	नदियाँ, rivers.
रीति, method.	रीतियाँ, methods.
सखी, companion.	सखियाँ, companions.

Occasionally, the termination एं, is found. Thus सखियें, companions; स्त्रियें, women; कहानियें, stories.

Nouns ending in इया generally form their Nom. pl. by the simple addition of anunasik. Thus बिटिया, little daughter. pl. बिटियाँ. For चिड़िया, *bird*, both plurals are used चिड़ियाँ and चिड़ियाएँ.

89. Class IV. All other feminines must be included in this class.

The oblique cases of the singular are uninflected; the Nom. pl. is formed by adding एँ to the sing. Nom.:

पुस्तक,	book,	plural	पुस्तकें
बात,	word,	„	बातें
तरंग,	wave,	„	तरंगें
जड़,	root,	„	जड़ें
सेना,	army,	„	सेनाएँ
यात्रा,	journey,	„	यात्राएँ
वस्तु,	thing,	„	वस्तुएँ

89b. Irregularities.

There are many inconsistencies to be met with in the formation of plurals. The form राजे, Nom. pl., instead of राजा, is to be found in the works of thoroughly good Hindi writers. वस्तें for वस्तुएँ is occasionally met with, and for the stem of the oblique cases in the plural वस्तुन instead of वस्तुओं. It has been noticed in the last paragraph that the forms स्त्रियें, कहानियें (and so with, other similar Nouns), are used by some writers.

A measure of uncertainty exists with reference to some mascs. ending in आ as to whether they should be included in Class I or Class II, *e.g.*, पोता, *a grandson*; बीघा, *a land measure.*

All Nouns are inflected for the oblique stem of the cases of the plural. The forms will be found in the next section, that on the Cases.

90. Special uses of Singular and Plural.

Singular form with Plural meaning. In Hindi, it is not uncommon to find the sing. form used where the meaning is evidently plural. This principally occurs with the Nominative Case, but not exclusively so. **सब स्त्री चकित हो गयीं,** *All the women became greatly bewildered.* **कुछ घड़ी यौंहीं बीतीं,** *Some hours passed in this way.* **सोलह २ मात्रा होती हैं,** *There are sixteen instants (in each line).* **बहुत सी बस्तु ऐसी हैं,** *There are many things like this.*

उस ने अनेक भाषा सीखीं, *He learned several languages.* **चार फल के दाता,** *The giver of the four fruits.* **बहुत सा रुपया चाहिये,** *Many rupees are needed.* **थोड़े दिन में,** *In a few days.* **छही महीने पीछे,** *After exactly six months.* **उसका हाथ पाँव बान्धकर,** *Having bound his hands and feet.*

Occasionally, the Verb remains in the sing. where the Nom. is evidently to be understood as pl., *e.g.*, **आँसू बह रहा था,** *Tears were flowing.* **जिन २ राजाओं का नाम आया है,** *Whatever kings' names are mentioned.* **कई लाख रुपया उसमें ख़र्च हो गया,** *Several lakhs of rupees were spent in that.*

91. Plural used where sing. would be used in English.

In some of the instances given as illustrations it will be noted that in English the plural is intended, though the singular form of the Noun is retained.

With articles of food where the names of grain are referred to :

चाँवलों को धोकर, *Having washed the rice.* **धानों के खेत,** *Fields of rice.* The plural is used also with the word **खीलें,** *parched grain.* **उन चनों को भुँजवा कर,** *Having had the gram roasted.* With this compare the English, "*Having had the chick-peas roasted.*"

प्राण, *life,* is generally used in the plural, possibly with the idea of vital functions, centres of life. **उसके प्राण बच गये,** *His life was saved.* **राजा को प्राण छोड़ने पड़े,** *It fell to the king to give up his life.* **न जानें मेरे प्राण कैसे हैं,** *What sort of a life mine is, is not to be understood.* **मैंने तेरे प्राण बचाये,** *I saved your life.*

Similarly, with **साँस,** *breath.* **उसकी साँसें चल रही थीं,** *He was panting for breath.* The word **रुधिर,** *blood,* is also found used in the same way. **रुधिर बह रहे थे,** *Blood flowed.*

बाल, *hair,* is generally used in the plural. **उसने बाल बढ़ा रखे हैं,** *He has let his hair grow long.*

दाम, *price,* is often in the plural. **बड़े २ दामों पर बेच डाली,** *He sold (the wood) for a high price.*

दर्शन, *sight.* **हमको श्री रामचन्द्रजी के दर्शन होंगे,** *We shall get a sight of Ram Chandra ji.* This word is generally used with this sense in the plural, but not invariably so. Probably the variation in use depends upon the idea as to whether there is to be one peep or a more prolonged "look" or "looks."

समाचार, *intelligence.* This is not in any way an equivalent to the use of the English word "news;" that is only plural in appearance. **समाचार** is used both in the sing. and plural, though more often in the latter **उसने राजा भोज को सब शुभ समाचार कह सुनाए,** *He caused Raja Bhoj to hear all the good news.* Later, in the same story, we have the sing. "**का समाचार**" (Cf. the Eng. *tidings.*) **भोजन,** *food,* is sometimes used in the plural, **तूने भोजन नहीं किये,** *You have not taken food.*

भूख, *hunger.* **वे भूखों मरते हैं,** *They are dying of hunger.* As though repeated fastings (unwilling fastings) were referred to.

भाग, *fortune.* This is occasionally used in the pl. **अपने भागों को दोष लगाने लगा,** *He began to throw blame on his fortune.*

92. The formation of plurals by the use of **गण** and **लोग.**

The words **गण,** *multitude,* and **लोग,** *people,* are sometimes added to Nouns as suffixes, giving them a plural meaning, with something of a collective force. **जन,** *person,* is occasionally found similarly used.

पाठकगण, *readers.* पाठक-पाठिकागण, *readers, men and women.* महिलागण, *women.* सुग्रीव ने सीता खोजने को कपिगण भेजे, *Sugriva sent the monkeys to search for Sita.* बड़े बड़े देवगण ऋषिगण और मुनिगण निमंत्रित किये गये, *Great gods and saints and holy men were invited.* दो चार लोगों ने उसको पहुँचाया, *Two or three caused him to reach his destination.*

A fem. of लोग, *viz.*, लुगाई, is occasionally used. लोग लुगाई सब उनकी निन्दा कर, *All the people, men and women, having abused them.* पापीजन, *sinners.* स्त्रीजन, *women.* बन्धुजन, *kinsfolk.*

Notice that these are not true Collective Nouns; they generally take a plural verb.

THE CASES.

93. The classification already made for Nouns under Gender holds for the Cases also.

The names of the eight Cases have been already given in Ch. IV. Under Gender, the Nom. plural has been considered. We have now to note the inflectional changes made for the Oblique Cases, and the use of these Cases. The Vocative Case will be referred to under its own head, as regards the inflection as well as its idiomatic use. The following particulars apply to the remaining six Cases.

In Classes II, III and IV there is no inflectional change in the sing. In Class I the आ is changed to ए—लड़का, लड़के.

In the plural, the termination ओं is common to all the 4 Classes: some slight modification in the stem may occur.

In Class I, आ is changed to ओं—लड़का, लड़कों.
" II, generally no modification. काम, पिता —कामों, पिताओं;
but ई is changed to इयों—पापी, पापियों.
इ ... " ... इयों—मुनि, मुनियों.
ऊ " ुओं—डाकू, डाकुओं.
उ ... " ... ुओं—गुरु, गुरुओं.

III. The ई and इ are changed in the same way as indicated under Class II.

IV. In words ending in a consonant, and in आ, the ओं only is added; the ending ऊ is changed to ुओं, *e.g.*, बहू, *daughter-in-law*, बहुओं.

This classification probably covers nearly all the ground. Possibly a few words do not conform to the foregoing remarks, and inconsistencies occur among writers and speakers.

It will be seen by the table of Cases here given that there are two forms of the Accusative, and a second form of the Nominative for some Verbs, in some of their Tenses.

94. **Declension of Nouns.**

		Class I. (Masc.)	Class II. (Masc.)	Class III. (Fem.)	Class IV. (Fem.)
Singular.		लड़का, a boy.	पिता, a father.	स्त्री, a woman.	बात, a word.
Nominative.	कर्ता.	लड़का	पिता	स्त्री	बात
,,	Agentive form.	लड़के ने	,, ने	,, ने	,, ने
Accusative.	कर्म.	लड़के को	,, को	,, को	,, को
,,	Nom. form.	लड़का	,,	,,	,,
Dative.	सम्प्रदान.	लड़के को	,, को	,, को	,, को
Instrumental.	करण.	,, से	,, से	,, से	,, से
Ablative.	अपादान.	,, से	,, से	,, से	,, से
Genetive	सम्बन्ध.	,, का, की, के.	,, का, की, के.	,, का, की, के.	,, का, की, के.
Locative.	अधिकरण.	,, में, पर, etc.	,, में, पर, etc.	,, में, पर, etc.	,, में, पर, etc.
Vocative.	सम्बोधन.	लड़के or लड़का	,,	,,	,,

Plural.	Class I.	Class II.	Class III.	Class IV.
Nominative.	लड़के	पिता	स्त्रियाँ	बातें
„ Agentive form.	लड़कों ने	पिताओं ने	स्त्रियों ने	बातों ने
Accusative.	„ को	„ को	„ को	„ को
„ Nom. form.	लड़के	पिता	स्त्रियाँ	बातें
Dative.	लड़कों को	पिताओं को	स्त्रियों को	बातों को
Instrumental.	„ से	„ से	„ से	„ से
Ablative.	„ से	„ से	„ से	„ से
Genitive.	„ का, की, के.	„ का, की, के.	„ का, की, के.	„ का, की, के.
Locative.	„ में, पर, etc.	„ में, पर, etc.	„ में, पर, etc.	„ में, पर, etc.
Vocative.	लड़को	पिताओ	स्त्रियो	बातो

THE NOMINATIVE.

95. There are two forms of the Nominative Case. The second with **ने** is often called the Agentive Case; but for all practical purposes it is a second Nominative. It is not, like the second form for the Accusative, an alternative form which may be used or not at the discretion of the speaker or writer; with certain Tenses of certain Verbs it *must* be used. With all the Tenses formed from the Perfect Participle of Transitive Verbs, its use is compulsory. Further particulars concerning this very important matter will be found in its appropriate place in the chapter on the Verb. By some writers on Grammar this form is regarded as a Case quite distinct from the Nom., its Verb being used with an impersonal or passive force. Thus **मन्त्री ने राजा को देखा,** would mean, *By the minister there was a seeing of the raja;* but it is far simpler to look upon **मन्त्री ने** as a Nom. Case. Thus we have for the Present Tense **मन्त्री राजा को देखता है,** and for the Past **मन्त्री ने राजा को देखा,** *The minister sees the king; The minister saw the king.* The minister is the subject and the Nom. in both cases.

This form of the Nom. is used with the following Tenses:—

Indefinite Perfect.	**उसने अपने भाई को देखा,**	He saw his brother.

Present Perfect.	उसने अपने भाई को देखा है.	He has seen his brother.
Past Perfect.	" " " देखा था.	He had seen his brother.
Contingent Perfect.	" " " देखा हो.	Should he have seen his brother.
Presumptive Perfect.	" " " देखा होगा.	He must have seen his brother.
Past Contingent Perfect.	" " " देखा होता.	If he had seen his brother.

96. The Nominative Case is much used, but little explanation concerning its use is necessary, as, apart from the Nom. with ने, its use is exceedingly simple.

1. As the Subject of the Verb. दोनों भाई चलने के श्रम से थक गये थे, *Both brothers had become tired through the toil of travelling.* उन्हों ने ऐसा किया, *They did so.* राजा कल जाएँगे, *The king will go to-morrow.* पण्डित की बुद्धि मारी गयी है, *The pundit's wisdom has been smitten*, i. e., *He has lost his senses.*

2. Predicatively. Either with the Verb "to be," with a Passive Verb, also with some other Verbs. मैं पापी हूँ, *I am a sinner.* रामसिंह अपराधी गिना जाता है, *Ram Sinha is reckoned a transgressor.* कुछ दिन पीछे एक दूसरा मनुष्य मन्त्री ठहराया

गया, *After a time another man was appointed prime minister.* तीनों दास चोर निकले, *The three servants turned out to be thieves.* लड़ते २ वे वीर बन गये, *Fighting on they became warriors.*

The question of agreement between Subject and Verb, as regards Number and Gender, will be considered in the chapter on the Verb.

THE ACCUSATIVE CASE.

97. The Accusative Case may take the form of the Nom., or the form to which को is attached. To form a rule, or rules, by which it can be decided which form should be used in each individual instance is impossible. No rule exists on the subject, and not in all cases can it be said that the matter is regulated by idiomatic usage, for sentences could be, given which in other respects thoroughly correspond, yet को is used in one, but not in the other. It is, in not a few sentences, a matter of taste, one writer affecting a larger and another a smaller use of this or that form.

Having made such a statement, it must be carefully guarded and restricted in its application. It should be fully recognized that in many cases idiom *does* decide that not only is one form distinctly better than the other, but that one is right, the other practically impossible.

There are certain broad principles which may be helpful.

a. With Pronouns, the form with **को** is very generally used.

मैंने उसको देखा, *I saw him*, is right ; **मैंने वह देखा,** it would be difficult to find in, perhaps, any writer.

b. The form with **को** is very widely used with proper names. **रामदत्त को बुलाओ,** *Call Ram Datta.*

c. The form without **को** is found more often with lifeless things and with animals than with persons, *e.g.*, **राजा ने पैर पूजे,** *The king worshipped his feet.* **मैंने घोड़े चलाये थे,** *I had driven on the horses.* On the other hand, we find **दुःख को, प्रार्थना को, वंश को.**

d. Where a Dative is used in the same sentence, and no other equivalent takes the place of **को** with the Dative, the Accusative is generally used in the Nom. form, thus avoiding the occurrence of two **को**'s in the same sentence.

e. Where the connection between the verb and the Noun is very close, the **को** is often omitted. **स्त्री ने यह बात सुनी,** *The woman heard this word.* Many words joined closely up with **मारना** have the Accus., without the **को** and the Noun indicating the person struck, with the **को**. This is probably a Dative, though many prefer to call it a second Accusative.

घोड़े ने लड़के को लात मारी, *The horse kicked the boy.* According to Hindi, it is the "kick" that the horse strikes, not the "boy." The boy is the recipient of the kick and, therefore, in the Dative. Compare the English phrases, "*He struck a bargain with the man*" and "*He struck the boy a blow.*"

f. While the omission of को may suggest closeness of connection between the Verb and Noun, the use of को has a tendency to indicate stress and emphasis.

98. Double Accusatives. Double Accusatives do occur; but in many sentences which might be brought forward as illustrations, careful consideration will possibly lead to the conclusion that one of the so-called Accusatives is more strictly speaking a Dative.

Take the following as illustrations of the genuine Double Accusative : राजा ने अयोध्या को अपनी राजधानी बनाई, *The king made Ayodhya his capital.* उसने कुतुबुद्दीन ऐबकको अपना प्रधान नियत कर. *Having appointed Kutub-ud-din Aibak his chief man.* In such sentences, the principal Acc. bears the को. In the two sentences printed above, it is *Ayodhya* and *Kutub-ud-din* which are the principal Accusatives ; "*his capital*" and "*his chief man*" are, in a sense, predicated of these.

In sentences like the following, the word with को is more strictly a Dative than a second Accusative: अपने २ लड़के लड़कियों को उत्तमोत्तम वस्त्र और आभूषण पहिना कर, *Having had his sons and daughters clothed with the very choicest clothes and jewels.* What the king had put on was the clothes and jewels—on *to* his children. सेवक ने लड़के को जूते पहिना दिये, *The servant put shoes on to the boy's feet.* Here the दिये shews that लड़के को is a true Dative. उसने चौरासी राजाओं को नेवता भेजा, *He sent an invitation to 84 kings.* "To the kings" is clearly Dative. So, again, in राजा ने राज अपने भतीजे को सौंपा, *He entrusted the kingdom to his nephew.*

It is similar with the two Nouns after such words as खिलाना, पिलाना, बतलाना, etc. What is caused to be eaten, or drunk, or explained, is the food, the drink, the matter, these are the Accusatives, the people who do the eating and drinking and have the matter explained to them are the recipients, they are in the Dative Case.

99. Where there are two Accusatives, one complementing the other, the Case sign, the को, is used only after the second; the first is generally written in the Nom. form. अपने चारों पुत्र और पतोहुओं को साथ ले, *Taking his four sons and daughters-in-law with him.*

Notice that पुत्र is not only in the Nom. form, but in the singular, although the meaning is plural.

100. Accusative of place.

The Accusative is often used of the place to which motion is directed or the place which is reached. उन्हें उसने युद्ध में मार यमपुर को भेज दिया, *Having slain them in battle, he sent them to the realm of Death.* एक ओर को ले गया, *(He) took him off in a certain direction.*

Sometimes the Case sign is omitted, *e.g.*, सब अपने अपने घर चले गये,. *They all went off, each to his own house.*

101. Accusative of time.

The Accusative is similarly used with reference to time. लोगों को आगे को दुःख पहुँचने का डर है, *There is the fear of trouble coming to the people hereafter.* आज रात को तू छिप कर बैठ जा, *Sit carefully concealed for the night.*

With time also as with place, the को is sometimes omitted. इस समय कोई नहीं है, *At this time there is no one (here).*

THE DATIVE CASE.

102. The usual sign of the Dative, as of the Accusative Case, is को. The Dative, however, may be indicated in other ways, *e.g.*, by के लिये, के निमित्त, के अर्थ.

There is one use of the Infinitive with a Dative of the Noun in which the **को** may be omitted, although the construct. stem is retained, *e. g.*, **वह देखने गया,** *He went to see.* This might also be expressed—**वह देखने को**—or **देखने के लिये—गया.**

Another form for the Dative of Pronouns exists, but the consideration of that will come in the chapter on Pronouns.

The Dative has various uses, but they may probably be fairly comprised under three headings.

103. The Dative of the recipient

राजा ने दोनों भाइयों को बहुत ग्राम दिये, *The king gave many villages to both the brothers.* **उसने पाँच रुपया एक लड़के को और दस रुपया उसके बड़े भाई को दिये,** *He gave five rupees to one boy and ten to his elder brother.*

104. The Dative of Possession or Acquisition.

This covers not merely material possessions, but also mental and moral qualities and responsibilities. Many of these uses are met in English by the word "has" or "had." We can say that a man *has* a *cat,* or a *cold* or a *conscience,* a *garden* or a *bad temper*, a *great joy*, a *sense of responsibility*, a *suspicion.*

The following illustrations will suggest the wide use of which the Dative is capable: **पहले पहाड़ों के पंख**

होते थे, *In the days of old the mountains had wings.* किसी को काम मिल जाय, *If any one get work.* उन रानियों में से किसी को भी बालक न हुआ, *No child had been born to any of the queens.* लोगों को बड़ी सहायता मिलती है, *People are greatly helped.* प्राचीन भारत के विद्वानों को इतिहास से विशेष प्रेम न था, *The learned men of ancient India had no special love for history.* लोगों को उनके कहने पर सहज ही विश्वास न आवे, *On their testimony people will not readily believe (it).* हम लोगों को ऐसा मालूम होता है, *It seems so to us.* उन को मन ही मन परमानन्द हुआ, *A great joy filled his soul.* (Lit. *to him, in his heart of hearts great joy became.*)

105. The Dative of purpose, Duty, Responsibility. etc.

For this, the Infinitive is very largely used. This will be more fully treated of when the Infinitive is brought to our notice. Two or three illustrations are given here :

बस हम लोगों को इतना ही निवेदन करना है, *Let this suffice, we have merely to state this.* बड़े भाई को पालन करना पड़ता है, *It falls to the elder brother to support (her).* तुम्हारी बहिन को हानि उठानी पड़ेगी, *Harm will befall your sister.* (Lit. *To your sister it will befall that she must take up injury*). इस काम के लिये उन्होंने एक ब्रह्मचारी को चुना, *They chose a student for this work.* देखने को गये हैं, *They have gone to see.*

If an Accusative with को occur in the same sentence, के लिये may be used for the Dative. लड़के उसको देखने के लिये गये हैं, *The boys have gone to see it.* Or the Dative sign may be dropped altogether, thus, रत्न किसी को ढूँढ़ने नहीं जाता है, *A jewel does not go in search of anyone.*

Very occasionally, two Datives with को may be found in the same sentence, *e.g.*, उनको खाने को चारा भी नहीं मिलता था, *They could not even get any fodder to eat.* Many writers would avoid the two को's by writing the sentence thus—उन्हें खाने को, etc.

THE INSTRUMENTAL CASE.

106. The particle से is used with both the Instrumental and Ablative cases. It is probably this fact and the difficulty of deciding in many instances under which case a word should be classified that has led to the two cases being united under the name "Ablative" by some. There appears, however, no sufficient justification for adopting this course. Undoubtedly, it is not easy to decide in all instances under what case a certain word with से should be placed, but it is perfectly clear that the two cases are not identical. There are many instances where a word is Instrumental (करण), and it could not be classed as Ablative without great violence.

Under the Instrumental may be included such sentences as the following :—

a. By means of a person. ऐसे मूर्ख से बहुत हानि होगी, *Much harm will come through such a fool.* लड़के से तो कोई अपराध नहीं बन पड़ा, *No fault was committed by the boy.* लड़की से नहीं किया जाएगा, *It can't be done by a girl.*

b. By means of other than a person. उन्होंने बड़े परिश्रम से किया, *They accomplished it with great labour.* उस पर ध्यान देने से, *Through carefully considering this.* धन-विज्ञान आदि नामों से कह सकते हैं, *We can speak of this by such names as "Science of Wealth."* खोज से यह बात भ्रममूलक सिद्ध हुई है, *Through investigation it is proved that this is founded on a delusion.* उसने अपने हाथ से किया, *He did it with his own hand.*

c. Various ; answering to English "with," etc. धनी पुरुष बड़े कष्ट से धन इकट्ठा करते हैं, *The rich amass wealth with great difficulty.* वे उसे तुच्छ दृष्टि से देखते थे, *They looked at him with a contemptuous glance.* युधिष्ठिर ने बहुत ही प्रेम के साथ भीमसेन

को गले से लगा लिया, *Yudhishthir with great affection clasped Bhimsen to his neck* (lit. *by the throat.*)

The following is a very good illustration of the use of the Instrumental : धनी पुरुष को, राजा से, चोरों से, शत्रुओं से, स्वजनों से, पशुपक्षियों से, भिखारियों से, मृत्यु से और अपने से भी नित्य भय बना रहता है, *A rich man is always living in fear either of the king or of thieves or enemies or his own people, of birds and beasts or of beggars, of death or of himself.*

Instances where it is doubtful whether they should be assigned to the Instrumental or Ablative Case, will be noticed under the Ablative.

Sometimes the से is omitted. आप क्या अपनी आँखों नहीं देख रहे थे, *What, were you not observing (it) with your own eyes?* इस कारण वे भाग गये, *On this account they fled.* अपना काम अपने हाथों ही करते थे, *He did his work with his own hands.*

THE ABLATIVE CASE.

107. Under this Case must be included not a few sentences in which the idea of "ablation" can only be reached in a very roundabout way, and yet seem to be more connected with the Ablative than with the Instrumental Case. As a matter of fact, the से alone seldom represents the true and full sense of the Ablative ; it only corresponds with the English "from" or "than." The full "Ablative," *i.e.*, "out of" is generally expressed in Hindi by the combination of the Case endings for both the Locative and Ablative, *i.e.*, by **में से,** as will be seen under division "*a*" following.

a. The true Ablative. **सेाना खानों में से निकलता है,** *Gold comes out of mines.* **जिस तरह कीचड़ में से कमल की उत्पत्ति होती है,** *In the same way that the lotus springs up out of the mud.* **इन तीनों में से किसी के विषय में उसे पक्षपात नहीं,** *He has no partisanship for any one of the three.* **उसने जेब में से मेातियेां की माला निकाली,** *He took a pearl necklace out of his pocket.*

Sometimes **से** alone is used to convey this full ablative meaning, *e.g.*, **चाँदी भी सेाने की तरह खान से निकलती है,** Silver also comes out of a mine as does gold.

In the following sentence both idioms are used: **यह धरती में से निकलता है परन्तु हमारे देश में कोई ऐसी जगह नहीं जहाँ से यह निकलता हेा,** *This comes out of the earth, but there is no place in our country whence it can be obtained.*

b. "From," with reference to place, etc.

कहाँ से तुम आये हेा? *Where have you come from?*

वह सदा उससे दूर ही रहती है, *She always dwells far from him.* वहाँ से कुछ दूर, *Some distance from there.* मुझसे आज चारपाई से उठा नहीं जाता, *I can't get up from my bed to-day.*

c. Applied to time. "Since." बहुत दिनों से, *ince many days.* तब से आज तक, *From then until to-day.* आज से पहले, *Before to-day.*

d "From" as received from a person. जिस गुरु से हमने क्या शिक्षा ली है—यह सुनिये, *What teaching I have received from which teacher,—Listen to this.* किसी को किसी से कुछ माँगना नहीं पड़ता था, *No one had to ask anything from anyone.*

e. With Verbs of asking, etc. ईश्वर से मेरी यही प्रार्थना है, *This is my prayer from God.* उसने अपने सेवक से पूछा, *He asked his servant.* कंगाल किससे कुछ माँगे ? *From whom can the poor fellow ask anything ?*

f. For marriage with. सीताजी से विवाह किया, *He married Sitaji.*

g. Separation from. दो चार सिपाही सेना से अलग हो गये, *Two or three soldiers became separated from the army.*

h. से *is regularly used with the Verb* कहना,

to speak, though the ablative idea is not at all obvious. गुरु ने अपने चेलों से कहा, *The teacher said to his pupils.*

i. Of manner, used Adverbially. क्रम से, *In order.* आनन्द से स्वीकार किया, *(He) accepted it joyfully.*

j. Indicating the logical ground. इसी से मैं कहता हूँ, *Therefore, I say.*

k. Various. काम क्रोधादि से रहित होकर, *Having become free from passion, anger and the rest.* सभी राजा से डरते हैं, *All fear the king.* जिस से आगे बढ़ने से काम के बिगड़ने का डर है, *In going beyond which there is danger of the work going wrong.* उन्होंने भगवान दत्त से प्रतिज्ञा की, *They promised Bhagwan Datta.* यह किसी से छिपा नहीं है, *This is not hidden from any one.*

l. For comparison. जंगली जानवरों का संग नीच की संगत से अच्छा है, *Association with wild animals is better than fellowship with the despicable.* नामी से भी नामी कवि की कीर्त्ति, *The fame of even the most renowned poet.* उत्तम से उत्तम, *The best of all.* (lit. *best than the best.*)

The uses of this and the Instrumental Case are very numerous and various. The foregoing illustrations will indicate the general lines of those uses.

THE GENITIVE CASE.

108. There are three forms for this case, *viz.*, **का**,**की**, **के**. The form assumed depends on the word which follows, not on that which precedes. In **स्त्री का घर**, *The woman's house* (lit., *of the woman, the house*), the form of the Gen. affix depends on the gender of *house*; the matter is not affected by the gender of the possessor of the house.

का is used when the following Noun is Masculine, Sing., and Nominative.

की is used when the following Noun is Feminine, Sing. or Pl. of any Case.

के is used when the following Noun is Mas. Pl. of any Case, and also when a Sing. Masc. Noun in an Oblique Case follows.

Thus :—

देनेवाले or **देनेवाली का बेटा**, The giver's (mas. or fem.) son.
,, or ,, **की बेटी**, The giver's daughter.
,, or ,, **की बेटियाँ**, The giver's daughters.
,, or ,, **की बेटी से**, From the giver's daughter.
,, or ,, **की बेटियों से**, From the giver's daughters.
,, or ,, **के बेटे**, The giver's sons.
,, or ,, **के बेटों को**, To the giver's sons.

देनेवाले or देनेवाली के बेटे की, पुस्तक. The giver's son's book.

The देनेवाला or देनेवाली being in the Genitive Case, the वाला is changed to the construct. stem before adding the Case sign. In the case of वाली. there is no change of stem. as in fems. the stem is the same throughout in all the Cases in the sing. The form of the Case sign का, की, के, is regulated by the Gender and Number of the following word.

Perhaps the clearest way to regard the matter is to treat the first related word with its affix as an Adjective, and such it is in some respects. As we say, काला घोड़ा, *a black horse*, काली घोड़ी, *a black mare*, काले घोड़े, *black horses* ; so we say, राजा का घोड़ा or मेरा घोड़ा, *the king's horse* or *my horse* ; राजा की घोड़ी or मेरी घोड़ी, *the king's mare or my mare* ; राजा के घोड़े or मेरे घोड़े, *the king's horses* or *my horses*. The का, की, के depend on the sex and number of the horses, not in any way on that of the possessors.

109. An exception to the rule about changing the का to के before a Noun (or Infinitive used as a Noun) should here be noted.

It not infrequently happens that the form का remains unchanged, where a change to the construct. form might be anticipated. Take some instances. चन्द्रमा का न देखे जाने का कारण, *The cause of the non-appearance of the moon* ; but उसके चले जाने पर, *Upon his going.* Again, नियम का पालन करने में, *In observing the rule.* धर्म का ठीक २ पालन करने में, *In the exact observance of duty* (or *righteousness*). पराक्रम का त्याग करने पर शत्रु अवश्य ही हमें जीत लेंगे, *Upon our giving up our prowess the enemies will of a surety conquer us.* ऊँचे कुल और ऊँची जाति का होने से बड़ाई नहीं आती, *Greatness does not come through being of a high race and high caste.* On the other hand, we find उसके घड़ियाल के मुख में पड़ने की बात ठीक जँच गई, *The idea of her falling into the mouth of crocodile was judged to be correct.*

Both idioms are used by writers of good standing.

It would appear that where the का is not changed, the whole phrase is regarded as one piece and only the last case sign is changed, the other words in the phrase being not interfered with. In such a sentence as the second one quoted above, we can quite see that, as the पर throws the preceding चला जाना into the construct. form, that again throws the उसका into the construct. उसके. This is the only explanation we can offer for the alternative idioms.

110. When it is remembered that this Case is called in Hindi **सम्बन्ध कारक**, *i.e.*, the Case of relation or connection, and not merely Possessive or Genitive, as in English, it will be seen at once that it must necessarily cover a very wide ground.

To attempt to classify all the relations for which the Case can be used, is practically impossible. All that we can attempt is to point out some of the principal classes, to give a few illustrations of others which may suggest the variety of relations which may be covered by this Case, and to note some special idiomatic uses of the Case.

111. The Genitive of Possession.

a. This may be the possession of material things. **राजा के धन वैभव की सीमा नहीं**, *There is no limit to the king's wealth and grandeur.* **लड़की की पुस्तक वहाँ पड़ी है**, *The girl's book is lying there.* **बनिये के घर में नहीं मिलेगा**, *It will not be found in the baniya's house.*

b. It may refer to parts of the body. **उस के हाथ में एक पुस्तक है**, *There is a book in his hand.* **राजा ने उस लड़की के मुँह की ओर ध्यान से देखा**, *The raja looked thoughtfully towards the girl's face.* **स्त्री की आँखें खुल गयीं**, *The woman's eyes opened.*

c. Or, to mental qualities, good or bad. उसका यह डर अकारण भी नहीं, *His fear is also not without cause.* राजा के उदार और स्तुत्य गुणों का प्रभाव ऐसा है कि, *The power of the king's generosity and praiseworthy qualties is such that......* उसका क्या अपराध है? *What is his fault?* रामलाल का यह दोष स्वाभाविक है, *This fault of Ram Lal is natural to him.*

112. The Genitive of Relationship (Kinship.) तीनों लड़के एक कंगाल के पुत्र हैं, *The three boys are sons of a poor man.* जिन की माता हैं वे धन्य हैं, *Blessed are they who have mothers.* वह उसकी कौन है? *What relation is she to him?* लड़के का भाई भाग गया था. *The boy's brother had fled.* रजनी की सास उसको समझाने लगी, *Rajani's mother-in-law began to scold her.*

113. Genitive of Office, etc. रामपुर का कोटवाल, *The head police officer of Rampur.* राजा के दोनों मन्त्री आकर कहने लगे, *The king's two ministers came and said.* मैं तुम्हारा सेवक हूँ, *I am your servant.* राजा की प्रजा वहाँ आनन्दपूर्वक रहने लगी, *The king's subjects lived there with great joy.*

114. Genitive of Price and Quantity. दो पैसे की

पुस्तक है, *It is a two-pice book.* चार बीघे की बखरी, *It is a piece of land of four bighas.* बड़े २ मोल के वस्त्र, *Very expensive clothes.* एक एक बक्स दो २ अढ़ाई २ मन का होता है, *Each box weighs 2 or 2½ maunds.* उसकी कितनी लम्बाई चौड़ाई है? *What is its length and breadth?* वह दस बारह रुपया का होगा, *That must be worth ten or twelve rupees.*

115. Of Material of which made, or maker. वह पियाला सोने का था, *It was a gold cup.* पान के पत्तों के दोनों में, *In baskets made of leaves of betel.* मन्दिर का घाट पत्थर का बना है, *The steps of the temple are made of stone.* फूलों की माला, *A garland of flowers.* तुलसीदास की रामायण, *The Ramayan written by Tulsi Das.* यह किस का बनाया है? *By whom was this made?* लोहे की कील, *An iron nail.*

116. The Genitive of Time. वह दस बरस की लड़की थी, *She was a girl of ten years of age.* यह दो बरस की बात है, *This happened two years ago.* कई बरस के परिश्रम का फल, *The fruit of the toil of several years.* कालिदास का समय, *The time of Kali Das, i.e., In his days.* यहाँ के आजकल के लोग, *The people of here and now.*

117. Of Residence. देश २ के लोग इकट्ठे हुए, The people of various countries assembled. काशी के जितने पुजारी होते, *As many officiating priests as there are in Benares.* वह किसी गाँव का कुनबी है, *He is a Kunbi from some village.*

118. Various. उसको लाने की आज्ञा दी गयी, *The order was given to bring him.* प्रजा का उपकार करना उनका मुख्य काम था, *To help his subjects was his chief work.* उसकी बहुत हानि हुई, *He was much injured, or suffered much loss,* वे अपने देश और धर्म का सुधार कर सकते हैं, *They are able to reform their country and religion.* इतने प्यार का क्या कारण है, *What is the reason of so much love?* उपदेश देने की योग्यता, *Fitness for imparting instruction.* उन्हीं में कालिदास की गिनती थी, *Among them was reckoned Kali Das.* राजा की उदारता का वर्णन, *An account of the king's liberality.* पिता जी का वह प्यार का हाथ कहाँ है? *Where is that loving hand of my father?* यह बड़े दुःख की बात है, *This is a matter causing great trouble.* सरजू नाम की एक नदी है, *There is a river called the Sarju.* ऐसों के आने से क्या लाभ होगा, *What good will result from the coming of such?* उसके करने को चेष्टा की, *He endeavoured to do it.*

119. Intensive. To give the idea of completeness or

thoroughness, a word is followed by का (or की or के, and then repeated. सब के सब, *all.* खुले के खुले, *wholly exposed.* दूध का दूध और पानी का पानी, *The milk pure milk, the water pure water.* बात की बात में, *In a moment.* झुण्ड की झुण्ड, Swarms of (flies or any Fem. Noun). With a masc. Noun का or के must be used. झुण्ड का झुण्ड would rather mean, *the whole* swarm. झुण्ड के झुण्ड, *Many swarms.*

120. Separation of related words. Not infrequently, one related word may be separated from the other. पूरा डर उस भेद के खुल जाने का है, *There is great fear of the secret getting out.* ये सब आप ही के हैं दूसरे के नहीं, *These are yours, not another's.* भूमिका में चन्द का तथा उसके ग्रंथ का संक्षेप में वर्णन रहे, *In the Introduction there will be a short account of Chand and of his book.* मुझे उनकी अवस्था का लग भग अस्सी वर्ष की होने का पक्का प्रमाण मिला है, *I have obtained a clear proof of his having been about 80 years of age.*

121. Omission of the related word. Sometimes the related word is not given after का, but is understood. लड़के किसी की नहीं मानते हैं, *The boys won't obey any one,* (*i. e., the word of any one*). राजा ने उसकी नहीं सुनी, *The king did not hear him* (*i.e., his word*). न मालूम हमने उस कम्बख़्त का क्या बिगाड़ा है,

I do not know what affair of that luckless wretch I upset. We must understand काम after कम्बख़्त ——, or some such word. यह कुछ काम का नहीं, *This is of no use.*

122. The use of के where की or का might be expected. Probably, closely connected with the above is an idiom which may present some difficulty to the beginner. Not infrequently, के is found where का or की is looked for. राजा के चार राणियाँ थीं, *The king had four queens.* The explanation generally offered is undoubtedly the correct one. Some word, understood, must be regarded as omitted. In the foregoing sentence, probably घर में, *i.e., In the house of the king were four queens.* So उसके एक स्त्री थी, *He had one wife.* कोई पुत्र उसके नहीं है, *He has no son.* दोनों में से एक के बेटा है और दूसरे के बेटी, *Of the two, one has a son, the other a daughter.* उस बिचारे के कोई भी नहीं, *The poor creature has no one belonging to him.* उसके कोई कन्या नहीं है, *He has no daughter.* जिसके इतना धन था, *He who had so much wealth.* उनके कोई सन्तान न थी, *He had no offspring.* जैसे चक्रवर्त्ती शर्मिष्ठ के हुआ तैसा ही तेरे होगा, *You shall have a world conquering son as Sharmishtha had.*

123. Infinitive as Noun. One of the related words is frequently an Infinitive used as a Noun. दास के आने

पर, *Upon the arrival of the servant.* **उसके करने का यह कारण था,** *The reason of his doing so was this.* **मन्त्री के ऐसा करने का अभिप्राय यह होगा,** *The purpose of the minister so doing must be this.*

124. Alternative of Genitive or Accusative. In some sentences, an alternative construction presents itself, the Genitive may take the place of an Accusative. The two following sentences are taken from one book, from the same page. **उन्होंने प्रतिहारी को पक्षी के लाने की आज्ञा दी,** *He ordered the chamberlain to bring the bird.* **मानो गगनमण्डल को नापने के लिये हाथ फैलाये हो,** *As though he had stretched out his hands to measure the heavens.* In the first sentence, we might have **को** instead of **के,** and in the second, **मण्डल के नापने,** would be quite idiomatic. There are instances where the meaning might be dubious, *e.g.,* **उसके बुलाने से क्या काम,** might be translated, "*What is the good of calling him?*" or, "*What is the good of his calling?*" *i.e.,* calling someone else. If the former be the meaning intended and this be not perfectly clear from the context, the Accusative construction should be adopted.

One or two additional illustrations are given:

उसके जगाने के लिये पिता ने सेवक को भेजा, *The father sent a servant to wake him.*

आपने जो पिता की इस आज्ञा का भंग करना अधर्म समझा, *The breaking of this command of your father which you regard as wrong.* इस लड़के के बचाने के लिये, *To save this boy.* धैर्य्य के छोड़ देने से, *Through giving up steadfastness.* उधार लेना और उस के चुकाने के लिये यत्न न करना, *To borrow and not strive to pay it off.*

The following sentence illustrates the fact that in such sentences the के and को are not always alternative: राजा के बहुत देर तक समझाने बुझाने पर केकयी ने कहा, *Upon the king scolding and explaining for a long time, Kekayi said.* The Hindi *might* mean, *after Kekayi had explained to the King, etc.*, but does not. Had that been the meaning, को would have been the safer idiom ; because को could only have yielded one meaning, के could not have replaced it.

125. Where the question of agreement of the Case ending with two or more words is involved, the general rule, perhaps, is for it to agree in gender with the nearest, but it may be in the plural and masc., so as to cover all the words involved. Thus उसका न भाई है न बहिन, *He has neither brother nor sister.* This might equally well be written, or better, उसके न......... (in accordance with the idiom mentioned in Sect. 122.) उनके मातापिता सम्बन्धी अत्यन्त भय में रहते थे,

Their father and mother and relatives lived in great fear.

In the following two sentences, the हानिलाभ and मातापिता are probably regarded by the writer as Compound Nouns and therefore have the gender of the latter. दूसरों का कोई हानिलाभ नहीं है, *There is no injury or advantage to others.* जिसके मातापिता ने ऐसा किया, *He whose father and mother did so.*

126. A strong negative. The following idiom to express a strong negative is worth noting: ये मनुष्य जाने के नहीं, *These men won't go.* वह देने का नहीं, लेने का है, *He is not a man to give, he is for getting.* उसकी हठ छुटने की नहीं, *His obstinacy will never be given up.*

127. The Genitive with Postpositions.

The inflected form के is much used with Postpositions. The chapter on Postpositions will give fuller particulars about this point.

128. Much more might be written about the Genetive Case, but the above must suffice. To be able to use freely, but discriminately, the various idioms connected with the Genetive is a good test of a student's grasp of Hindi.

THE LOCATIVE CASE.

129. The word Locative very inadequately defines the functions of this Case. The Hindi term, अधिकरण, also falls short. अधि means "over" or "upon." The case with its two Case signs में, *in*, and पर, *on, upon*, has to do not only with place but with time, with mental qualities and with logical relations and conditions.

Other Postpositions are said to put their accompanying Nouns into the Locative Case. These must be left for consideration until the chapter on the Postpositions. Some of the Postpositions certainly appear to be as closely connected with the relations covered by this Case as do the Case signs में and पर, *e.g.*, ऊपर, *above*. नीचे, तले, *beneath*. निकट, *near*. पास. *very near*. तक, लों, *up to*, etc.

A rough classification of the uses of the Locative with में and पर must be attempted, and illustrations given.

130. A. With में.

1. *Of place.* "*in*." इस देश में लोग ऐसी बात नहीं मानते हैं, *In this country people do not accept such a thing as this.* राजा दशरथ पुरी में आये, *King Dasharath arrived in the city.* घर में कोई नहीं है, *There is no one in the house.*

2. *Of mental states.* अर्जुन में भी कैसी दया है, *In Arjun also what mercy there is.* वह क्रोध में ऐसा पागल हो गया, *He became so mad in his anger.* पराक्रम में धीरता में वह सुमेरु पर्वत के तुल्य था,

In valour, in steadfastness, he was like Mount Sumeru. **यह बात सहज ही समझ में आ जाती है,** *This is easily understood.* **विद्या में उनके समान कोई न था,** *In learning none was his equal.*

3. *Of time.* **एक ही बरस में चार पाँच सौ आदमी मर चुके,** *In a single year, four or five hundred people died.* **इतने ही में कई एक बलवान आये,** *Meanwhile several sturdy fellows came.* **सूर्य्य डूबने में थोड़ी ही देर थी,** *It was only a short time to sunset.*

4. *Various.* **नाटक में ऐसा लिखा है,** *It is so written in a play.* **उस उपन्यास में सुखिनी नामक एक स्त्री की कथा है,** *In this novel there is a story of a woman named Sukhini.* **ऐसा करने में यह हानि होती है,** *In so doing there comes about this harm.* **यह जब हमारे और सूर्य्य के बीच में आ जाता है,** *When this comes between us and the sun.* **इसकी ईश्वर में सच्ची प्रीति थी,** *He had a true love for God.* **चारों भाइयों में परस्पर बड़ा ही स्नेह था,** *There was great mutual love between the four brothers.* **इनमें सब से बड़ा पुत्र दुर्योधन हुआ,** *Among them the eldest son of all was Duryodhan.* **सरल हिन्दी में लिखा है,** *It is written in simple Hindi.* **जिसके हाथ में अधिकार है,** *In whose hand there is authority.* **वह पैरों में खड़ाऊँ पहिने थी,** *She wore sandals on her feet.* **पत्तों के दोनों में नारियल का मद्य पिया,**

(They) drank toddy from vessels made of leaves.

5. *Adverbial.* **गुप्त में,** *secretly.* **प्रगट में,** *openly.* **संक्षेप में,** *briefly.*

6. Sometimes **में** and **से** occur together, with the meaning, *from among.* Thus, **उनमें से यह उत्तम है,** *This is the best of them.*

131. Omission of में

Sometimes the **में** is not expressed, though understood.

एक विधवा है जो भाई के घर रहती है, *There is a widow who lives in her brother's house.* **इन दिनों,** *In these days.* **यह इच्छा पूरी करनी पाठकों के हाथ है,** *The accomplishment of this desire is in the hands of the readers.* **उस क्षण दे दी,** *Gave it on the very instant.* **धोबी के घर हुआ,** *This took place at the dhobi's house.*

132. B. With पर.

1. *Of place.* **चबूतरे पर दो मनुष्य खड़े होकर बातचीत कर रहे हैं,** *Standing on the platform two men are carrying on a conversation.* **नाव पर कोई नहीं मिला,** *No one was found on the boat.* **दोनों भाई नदी के तट पर रहने लगे,** *The two brothers took up their abode by the bank of the river.* **घोड़े पर सवार होकर,** *Having mounted a horse.* **उस पर दृष्टि करके,**

Having looked at him. **क्या मैं भूमि पर हूं या स्वर्ग में.** *Am I on earth or in heaven.*

2. *Of mental states, etc.* **इस बात पर विचार करना चाहिये,** *It is necessary to consider this matter.* **राणी उस पर पूरा भरोसा रखती थी,** *The queen placed full reliance on him.* **प्रजा जन अपने राजा पर अनुरक्त नहीं, उसकी सेना भी उससे बहुत प्रसन्न है,** *Not only are his subjects devoted to their king, his army also is pleased with him.*

3. *Various, including temporal sequence.* **इस पर वह कहने लगा,** *Whereupon he began to say.* **दिन पर दिन,** *Day after day.* **उसके चले जाने पर वे कमरे में आये,** *On his going away they came into the room.* **रस्सी खींचने पर टूट जाती है,** *A rope on being pulled breaks.* **टूटने पर नहीं जुड़ता,** *On being broken cannot be joined.* **दस पैसे पर मिल सकता है,** *It can be obtained for ten pice.* **वह आने पर होगा,** *He must be on the point of arriving.* **उसके जाने पर यह हुआ,** *As he was about to go this happened.* (Or, it might be "*just after he had left.*")

4. Sometimes **से** follows **पर,** as is the case with **में.** **मेज पर से उठाकर ले आओ,** *Take (it) from the table and bring (it) along.*

5. *Omission of* **पर.**

Occasionally, we must conclude that पर or some similar word has been omitted from a sentence (being understood). मेरे माथे बड़ा अपवाद लगे गा, *Great blame will rest on my head.* तेरे निकट आकर घड़ियों वार्त्ता करता हूं, *I come near you and talk for hours together.* शरीर तो थोड़े ही दिन रहते हैं, *Our bodies last but for a few days.*

THE VOCATIVE CASE.

133. हे or some other Interjection *may* be used to indicate the Vocative Case, but this is not essential ; very frequently the Vocative is used without any Interjection.

When the Noun belongs to Class I, the आ may be changed to ए for the Vocative, but this is frequently not done. In the other three Classes of Nouns, no oblique form exists in the singular. Thus in a great majority of instances, in the singular, the Locative is the same as the Nominative.

In the plural, however, the Vocative form is in common use. The form is the same as the oblique stem for the other Cases, with the exception that the anusvàr is dropped. Thus we have लड़को, *Oh boys.* राजाओ, Oh kings. लड़कियो, *Girls* ! बहिनो, *Sisters* !

COMPOUND NOUNS. समास

134. The first point to consider is,—What Nouns should be included under this heading ? Some would include all Nouns which are in any way compounded, that is to say, which are made up of any addition or additions to the basis modifying in any degree the meaning of the original word. According to this, such a word as अज्ञानता would be considered a Compound Noun, forasmuch as the privitive अ changes the meaning of ज्ञानता. Similarly, ज्ञानता itself might be regarded as a Compound, because the suffix ता has given an abstract meaning to the original.

Undoubtedly all such words are Compounds but, on the whole, it seems better to leave words compounded in such a way for consideration in the chapter on Prefixes and Suffixes and to confine our attention here to those Compounds which are made up of two or more or less complete words, as, *e.g.*, राजभवन, *king's house, palace.* सास-ससुर-पद-पूजा, *The worship of the feet of the mother-in-law and father-in-law.*

There still remains the difficulty of deciding whether words placed in juxtaposition, but not modified in any way as regards form and meaning, should find a place under the heading of Compound Nouns; such pairs of words, for instance, as रात दिन, *night, day.* सोच विचार, *thought, consideration.* The fact that the Conjunction has been dropped between such pairs of words, does constitute some small ground of justification for their inclusion, and we therefore give them a place.

Mention may be made also of some other words which have a feebler claim to be called Compound Nouns, but for the consideration of which no more suitable place may be found.

The Compounds which are to be considered may consist of two, or more, Nouns, or of a Noun, compounded with an Adjective, an Adverb, a Verbal Noun, or some other Part of Speech.

Some of the words so compounded, are strictly speaking Adjectives, but are also used as Nouns.

135. I. Compounded of two Nouns.

गौशाला, *cow-house.* **मुक्ताहार,** *pearl-necklace.* **भव-सागर,** *the ocean of existence.*

The words which make up these Compounds may be variously related.

a.—The first word may be of the nature of a Genetive in relation to the second word, as **रामकहानी,** *A story of Ram* (commonly applied to any long "yarn.") **क्षत्री-कुल-द्रोही,** *Enemy of the tribe of the Kshatris.* **भूमण्डल,** *The globe of the earth.*

b.—The first word may stand in an Accusative relation to the second. **अन्नदाता,** *He who gives grain, i.e.,* God as the giver of our daily food. **जगत्राता,** *He who delivers the world.* **अग्निपूजक,** *A fire-worshipper.* **मुक्तिखोजक,** *A seeker of salvation.* **मक्खीचूस,**

A miser. A man willing to suck a fly which has fallen into the milk or similar substance, so as not to lose anything.

c. The first word may stand in a Dative relation to the second, as **दीनदयानिधि**, *The treasury of mercy for the distressed.*

d. These and various other relations are found between the two words. **ब्रजवासी**, *A dweller in Braj.* **गुणदायक**, *A giver of good qualities.* **कर्णमुकुट**, *An ear-ring.* **नरककुण्ड**, *The abyss of hell.* **जलचर**, **थलचर**, *Fish. animals, i.e., Goer in the water or on the earth.* **घुड़चढ़**, *Horseman.*

e. Perhaps under this head should be mentioned pairs of words which, owing to the omission of the Conjunction between them, may be regarded as loosely compounded.

(1). Some of these pairs of words are practically identical in meaning. **झगड़ा रगड़ा**, *Quarrelling and wrangling.* **कीट पतंग**, *Insects and flies.* **सोचविचार**, *Thought, consideration.*

(2). Others are pairs of Nouns closely related in meaning, the second conveying something of the idea. "and such like."

मातापिता, *Mother and father.* भाईबन्धु, *Brothers and kinsmen.* अन्नजल, *Food and drink,* lit., *grain and water.*

(3). Some are contrasted words, carrying somewhat of the idea of inclusiveness. दिनरात and रातदिन, *Day and night; continually.* सांझ बिहान, *Evening and morning.* चराचर, *Moving and unmoving, i.e., the entire creation, things which have life and movement and those which do not move.*

136. II. Compounded of a Noun and Adjective, or Participle, or a second Noun used with Adjetctival force. In some words, the Adjective comes first, in others last.

दुष्ट जन्तु, *Evil creature.* कपटवेष, *Disguise,* lit., *deceptive dress.* राजर्षि, *King of sages.* भूतग्रस्त, *Demon-seized, possessed.* मनरंजन, *Captivating the mind.* श्रीयुत, *One possessing great glory.* श्रीहत, *One whose glory has been smitten.*

137. III. Compounded of a Noun and one of the अव्यय, *i.e.,* the undeclinable Parts of Speech. These should be, perhaps, included under Compounds formed by adding Prefixes and Suffixes, but may be mentioned here.

धर्महीन, *A man devoid of righteousness.* यथाकाल, *The suitable time.* अतिशक्ति, *Great strength.*

138. IV. Compounds whose meaning derived from

the words has been appropriated to some special person or thing. **अतिरोग**, *Consumption*, lit., *severe disease.* **मृगतृषा**, *Mirage*, lit., *deer-thirst.* **दशानन**, *Râvan*, *i.e.*, *the ten-faced one.*

139. V. Compounded of a Noun and some numeral. **चतुर्युग**, *The four ages.* **चतुर्मुख**, *Brahma, the four-faced.* **द्विवेदी**, *A caste of Brahmans; one who knows two of the Vedas.* **त्रिलोक**, *The three worlds.*

140. VI. Jingling words thrown together, because of similar sound or meaning. **मारपीट**, *Striking and thumping.* **लड़भिड़**, *Fighting.* **पासपरोस**, *Neighbour.* **नामधाम**, *Name and residence.*

In some of these words, the second has practically no meaning: it is simply added to jingle with the first. There are a great number of such words current in Hindi. Not infrequently, the second is a repetition of the first word, with **ओ** or **व** substituted for the first letter. **खण्डनमण्डन**, *Breaking.* **भीड़भाड़**, *A crowd.* **दौड़धूप**, Exertion. **खोजखाज**, *Seeking.* **टोपीओपी**, *A hat, or hats.* **मेजवेज**, *tables and such things.* **कपड़ावपड़ा**, *Clothes.* I have heard the word **गर्दावर्दा**, for the English "*girder*," *iron beam.*

This classification is neither exhaustive nor detailed, but may serve to indicate the line upon which the Compound Nouns are constructed and the place they take in Hindi. They are greatly used both in literature and in current speech. Indians have a peculiar relish for assonance and alliteration.

CHAPTER VI.

SYNTAX. वाक्यों की रचना.

AGREEMENT. ORDER OF WORDS. ORATIO DIRECTA. REPETITION.

AGREEMENT OF NOUN, ETC., WITH VERB.

141. To treat of the Syntax having reference to the Cases of Nouns alone is quite impracticable, as it is only when Nouns are brought into relation with Verbs and other Parts of Speech that any question of Syntax arises. Accordingly, in this chapter, some points will be brought forward which are as closely connected with the Verb and with other Parts of Speech as with Nouns. Furthermore, some matters may be touched on which do not properly belong to Syntax.

142. I. Agreement of Nominative and Verb.

a. Where there are two or more Nominatives, the Verb may agree with the nearest in Gender and Number.

हर्ष और आश्चर्य हुआ, *Joy and astonishment arose.* सब देवता और प्रजा अत्यन्त प्रसन्न हुई, *All the gods and the subjects of the kingdom became greatly pleased.* चार लड़के और तीन लड़कियाँ हुई, *Four sons and three daughters were born.* क्षमा

ओर अनन्त जीवन और मुक्ति प्राप्त हो गयी, *Forgiveness and eternal life and salvation were secured.* **सौ पुत्र और एक कन्या होगी,** *A hundred sons and a daughter will be born.* **सभ्यता की उन्नति और मस्तिष्क की उन्नति साथ ही साथ होती है,** *The progress of civilization and the development of the brain go together.*

143. *b.* Or, the Verb may be in the plural, agreeing in Gender with the nearest Nominative, or being made masculine.

मेरे माता पिता भी रहते थे, *I had a mother and father, i.e., My parents were living.* **हवा और पानी भी वहाँ बिकते हैं,** *There even air and water are sold.* **सुन्दर** (a man's name) **और हीरा मालिन आते हैं,** *Sundar (m.) and Hira, the woman gardener, are coming along.* **एक बेटा और दो बेटी उत्पन्न हुए,** *One son and two daughters were born.* **एक पुरुष और एक स्त्री रचे गये,** *One man and one woman were created.*

In the following sentence, although the two Nominatives are gathered together under the **सब**, yet the Verb is made to agree with the nearest Nominative in Gender: **जितने मुनि और उनकी जितनी स्त्रियाँ थीं सब उन्हें बहुत चाहती थीं,** *As many saints and their wives as there were, they all loved them much.*

c. In modern Hindi, the most usual course to take,

where there are two or more Nominatives, is to gather hem up into a दोनों, तीनों, सब, or some such word, and then use the masculine plural Verb.

मेरे मन में एक बेर भय और विस्मय दोनों उत्पन्न हुए, *Immediately fear and astonishment both sprang up in my mind.* उनकी कौशिल्या, सुमित्रा और कैकेयी ये तीन रानियाँ थीं, *He had three queens. Kaushilya, Sumitra and Kaikeyi.* मुनि मनुष्य देवता और दैत्य सब तुम्हारी सेवा करते हैं, *Sages, men, gods and demons, all serve thee.* ऐसे अच्छे लड़के पाकर राजा और रानियाँ सब बहुत ख़ुश हुए, *Having obtained such good sons, the king and the queens were all very glad.* धनी दरिद्र ऊँच नीच सभों ने ऐसा किया, *Rich and poor, high and low, all did so.*

d. Where there are two Nominatives, the second of which is more or less predicative of the first. the Verb agrees with the first in Gender.

धूल में मिल जाना एक सहज बात था, *To mingle with the dust was an easy matter.* वह (f.) भीष्म की मृत्यु का कारण हुई, *She became the cause of the death of Bhîshma.* यह बात द्रोण के असन्तोष का कारण हुई, *This became a cause of discontent to Dron.* उसी समय से आगरा नगर

मुग़ल सम्राटों की राजधानी गिनाजाने लगा, *From that time Agra began to be regarded as the capital of the Moghal Empire.*

e. Sometimes, at the conclusion of a sentence, where the Verb requires a Nominative with ने, this Nominative remains unexpressed, being understood from a Nominative without ने in an earlier part of the sentence.

कुछ लोग इकट्ठे हुए और विचार कर यह ठहराया, *Some people came together and, having thought over the matter resolved, that......i.e.,* लोगों ने ठहराया. In the following sentence, the last Verb requires ने, but the वह of the earlier part of the sentence has to suffice. वह बहुत रोई बहुत सिर धुना बहुत विलाप किया, *She wept much, beat her head violently and gave way to lamentation.*

144. II. Accusative and Verb.

In most instances, no difficulty arises, as the Number and Gender of the Verb is regulated by the Nominative, not the Accusative; but with Transitive Verbs, in those Tenses which require the Nominative with ने, difficulties may arise.

(1) *a.* If there be only one Accusative, and that be used in the form without को, the Verb agrees with it

in Number and Gender. स्त्री ने अपना घर छोड़ा, *The woman left her house.* उसने एक पुस्तक मोल ली, *He bought a book.* मैं ने तीन घोड़े भेज दिये, *I sent three horses.*

b. If there be two Accusatives, the verb is generally made to agree with the nearest in Number and Gender.

उसने बड़ा पराक्रम और वीरता दिखाई, *He manifested great prowess and valour.* आप के साथ कुटिलता और कपट करना उसने अब तक नहीं छोड़ा, *He has not yet left off his crookedness and deceitful dealing with you.*

(2) Where the Accusative form with को is used, the Verb is always in the singular Nominative form. किसी ने लड़के को or एक स्त्री को or लड़कों को or स्त्रियों को- देखा, *Some one saw a boy*, or *a woman*, or *boys*, or *women*.

If there be more than one Accusative, the Verb is not in any way affected, but the form of the Accusatives may be. Generally, only the last is changed to the construct. form of the stem, the earlier Accusative remaining in the Nominative form. उसने अपने लड़के लड़कियों को छोड़ दिया, *He forsook his boys and girls.*

(3) With the Accusative, as with the Nominative,

it is usual, when there are more than one, to gather them up into an inculsive सब, or other appropriate word. This may assume the form with को, or remain without it.

In such construction, the Accusatives included are in the Nominative form, not the inflected. उसने काम क्रोध लोभ मोह मद और मत्सर इन छहों शत्रुओं को जीत लिया है, *These six enemies, lust, wrath, covetousness, infatuation, mad passion, envy, he has conquered* इन्होंने राम के लिये माता पिता भाई स्त्री राज सुख आदि सभी कुछ छोड़ दिया, *For the sake of Ram, they have forsaken everything, mother and father, brothers, wife, the pleasures of the royal court, and the rest.* जीवन और नयन दोनों को कृतार्थ करूँगा, I will satisfy both my life and my eyes.

(4). Where a second Accusative is predicative of the first, *it* does not affect the form of the Verb, *that* is regulated by the principal Accusative. गोस्वामी जी ने सब बातों में भरत को राम की परछाहीं माना है, *The Goswami has made Bharat to be the very reflection of Ram in all particulars.* उन्होंने पाटलीपुत्र को अपना विशाल साम्राज्य की राजधानी बनाया, *He made Pataliputra, the capital of his wide empire.*

145. III. The gender of Predicative Adjective or Participle after Accusative.

When an Adjective or a Participle is used predicatively of Nouns in the Accusative, with को, it is generally made singular and masculine, irrespective of the Number and Gender of the Nouns, *but not invariably so.* Thus :— जिन बातों को मैं पहले अच्छा समझता था अब मुझे बुरी मालूम होती हैं, *The things which I at first regarded as good now appear to me as bad.* हम लोग इन तारों को आकाश में चमकता हुआ देखते हैं, *We see these stars shining in the heavens.* बाहुओं को तना हुआ रखकर, *Having placed both the arms in an outstretched position.*

But :—इस विषय की घटी को पूरी करने के लिये, *To fill up the deficiency of this thing* हम अपनी आवश्यकताओं को पूरी कर लेंगे, *We shall satisfy our needs.* राजसिंह ने कुल की लाल पताका को कार्यक्षेत्र में खड़ी किया, *Rajsinha again erected the red standard of his race in the field of active work.* उसने उन तीनों को अपने सेवक बनाया, *He made the three of them his servants.*

When the Accusative form without को is used, the Adjective is generally made to agree with it in Gender and Number. उसने लोहे की मूर्त्ति उन के सामने खड़ी करदी, *He set up the iron image in front of them.* राजा ने सब सामग्री इकट्ठी कर ली, *The king collected all the materials.* उसकी मा ने उसको पूरी

पक्की बना दिया है, *Her mother has made her thoroughly well prepared.*

146. IV. Nouns in the Oblique Cases and their Case signs.

a. When two or more co-ordinate Nouns, in Cases requiring the oblique form, occur, one Case sign generally suffices, and the earlier Nouns are kept in the Nominative form.

सब छोटे और बड़ों के जी में, *In the minds of both great and small.* **हाथी घोड़े पालकी रथ गाजा बाजा झंडे झंडियों का तो कुछ ठिकाना ही न था,** *There's no reckoning the elephants and horses, the palkis and chariots and bands of music and banners (large and small).* **स्वधर्मी परधर्मियों से समान बर्ताव करना,** *To treat alike the followers of one's own and other religions.*

b. Very often the Nouns are gathered up into a **सब** or other appropriate word.

चित्त और ज्ञान दोनों का नाश हो जाता है, *The destruction of both mind and knowledge takes place.* **ज्ञान तो उसने भली और बुरी दोनों प्रकार की नीतियों का प्राप्त कर लिया,** *He acquired a knowledge of both kinds of policy,—good and bad.* **लिखना पढ़ना कुश्ती लड़ना तीर**

चलाना घोड़े की सवारी शिकार खेलना सभी बातें उन्होंने बहुत जल्द सीख डालीं, *They quickly learnt to write and read, to wrestle and shoot arrows, and to ride and hunt.* (Here the Accusatives are in the Nominative form throughout.) आँगन हज़ारों राजाओं के रथों घोड़ों और हाथियों आदि से सदा ही परिपूर्ण रहता है, *The courtyard is always crowded with thousands of royal chariots and horses and elephants and other* ....Note that के and से both serve for several Nouns.

c. Not infrequently, however, the Case sign is repeated to give distributive force.

(Ram and Sugriva are entering into a covenant; Ram is to establish Sugriva as king; Sugriva is to go in search of Sita.) फिर राम ने बाली को मार सुग्रीव को राजा बनाने और उसने सीता की खोज लगाने की परस्पर प्रतिज्ञा की, *Then they mutually promised, Ram to slay Bali and make Sugriva king, Sugriva to institute a search for Sita.* जो किसी को दुःख से नहीं छुड़ाता, उसको उपदेश नहीं देता, वह उसका गुरु नहीं, वह उसका सगा नहीं, वह उसका पिता नहीं, वह उसकी माता नहीं, वह उसका देवता नहीं, वह उसका पति नहीं, वे सब उसके शत्रु हैं. (A literal translation of this passage would not give the real meaning, a free translation is given to make the meaning clear). *Those who do not deliver others from trouble and give them sound advice are their foes. The one who so acts is neither a true teacher nor a good kinsman, is not a good father or mother or god-like friend or husband.* **उसने सीताहरण की और रावण से अपने युद्ध की कथा कह सुनाई,** *He related the story of Sita's abduction and of his own fight with Ravan.*

THE ORDER OF WORDS IN SENTENCES.

147. 1. The Nominative comes first, the Verb follows it. Generally speaking, the Verb is the last in a sentence. **लड़का भाग गया,** *The boy fled.*

2. The Accusative comes between the Nominative and the Verb. **लड़का पुस्तक पढ़ रहा है,** *The boy is reading a book.* So with an Accusative of place. **लड़का घर गया,** *The boy has gone home.*

3. Where there is a secondary Accusative, this follows the principal Accusative. **राजा ने बलराम को सेनापति ठहराया,** *The king appointed Balram general.*

4. A Dative generally comes before the accusative. **गुरु ने लड़के को पुस्तक दी,** *The teacher gave the boy a book.*

5. A second Noun, used predicatively, follows the first and comes before the Verb. **रजवन्ती उसकी पत्नी है,** *Rajwanti is his wife.* **उसकी पत्नी रजवन्ती**

है, *His wife is Rajwanti.* There is, of course, a very great distinction between these two sentences. In the first, Rajwanti is referred to, what her status is ; in the second, the subject considered is, Who did the man marry ?

6. The Instrumental Case ordinarily comes immediately before the Accusative. **राज पक्के मसाले से चौखट लगाता है,** *The mason is fixing the door-frame with mortar.*

7. The Ablative holds a similar place in the sentence. **वह अपने घर से यहाँ आया है,** *He has come from his house here.*

8. The position of the Locative Case cannot be defined. The tendency is, perhaps, for the Locative with **में** to come early in the sentence, for that with **पर** to come late. It is only a *tendency*, the position will depend on the relation of the Nouns in the Locative Case to other Nouns in the sentence. **उसमें कुछ नहीं है,** *There is nothing in this.* **यह पुस्तक भूमि पर पड़ी रही,** *This book was lying on the ground.*

9. As in English, an attributive Adjective is commonly placed before its Noun, when used predicatively, after it. **दो लाल घोड़े बिक गये,** *Two roan horses were sold.* **श्यामलाल का घोड़ा लाल है,** *Shyam Lal's horse is roan.*

10. Relative and correlative. In English, the correlative often comes before the relative; in Hindi it is exactly the reverse. Eng. "The man will be punished who steals." The Hindi for this would be **जो चोरी करेगा सो दण्ड पावेगा,** *i.e., Who steals that man will be punished.* This matter cannot be enlarged on here, but it is one that should have the very careful attention of the student. It is one of those matters where it is very easy for a learner to get into the way of writing English-Hindi and not realising that it is so. Unfortunately, many a teacher would not point out a matter of this kind, for there is no absolute rule on the subject. In thoroughly good Hindi, the correlative does *sometimes* come before the relative.

Let us take one more sentence. "The man whose house is near mine is my brother." The Hindi of this is not **वह मनुष्य जिसका,** etc., but **जिसका घर मेरे घर के पास है वह मेरा भाई है.**

11. This must suffice for the present in the way of rules about the order of words in a sentence. It must be clearly understood that the order indicated is only a "general instruction." There is no absolutely fixed order.

12. In some interrogatory sentences and under circumstances in which special stress is to be laid upon a word, the order of words in a sentence may be completely changed, even to the extent of placing a Verb before

its Nominative, *e.g.*, कौन करेगा, is "Who will do it?" In करेगा कौन, the idea conveyed is that there are plenty of people ready to promise to do it, but who is the man who will not only promise, but actually do the business.

Two or three illustrative sentences may be useful. वे गये थे छः महीने रहने, *He went with the idea of staying for six months.* The idea conveyed is that he went off long before, or long after, he had intended: he intended to stay for six months, but only stayed for perhaps a few days. उनकी वही दशा होगी जो दशा साँप के सिर से उसकी मणि छीनने वाले की होती है, *His condition will be that of the man who goes to take the jewel from a snake's head.* करने योग्य तुम्हारे पक्ष में है कौन, *Who on your side is fit todo it?* The order of words suggests the answer, "No one." मेरे बराबर आज तक कोई राजा हुआ ही नहीं, *Up to the present time there has been no king my equal.* यदि आप को क्रोध न आवेगा तो फिर आवेगा कब, *(Under such circumstances) if you don't get angry, then when will you?*

Very frequent changes from the ordinary order of words occur, and often they are very forcible as regards their meaning. A considerable familiarity with Hindi, however, must be acquired before bold ventures are made in this direction. Some changes of order may prove disastrous.

DIRECT AND INDIRECT NARRATION.

148. A matter of no little importance in the construction of Hindi sentences is the use of the *Oratio directa.* This is far more used in Hindi than in English. Where we should say, "He said he would come," the Hindi would be **उसने कहा कि मैं आऊँगा,** *He said that I will come,* or, as we should print it, He said, "I will come." The **कि** takes the place of the inverted commas, the English quotation marks.

Take two Hindi sentences as illustrations: **उसने उससे पूछा कि क्या बात है,** *He asked him, "What is the matter?"* In English, we should generally say, "He asked what the matter was." Again, **उसने अपने भाई से कह दिया कि भाई क्रोध का समय नहीं है,** *He said to his brother, "Brother, this is not a time for anger."*

In reporting conversations or sending messages, it is necessary to exercise considerable care if misunderstanding is to be avoided. In reporting that we sent a servant yesterday to tell someone to come to-day, we might be tempted to say in Hindi, **मैंने कल सेवक को भेज दिया किसी से कहने के लिये कि आज आवे.** This is English-Hindi, not Hindi. The sentence should run something like this, कल मैं ने सेवक से कहा कि जाकर किसी से यह कह देना कि कल आओ.

At the present time, some modern Hindi writers have been so influenced by their English education that they are more inclined to use the *oratio obliqua* than was the case in days gone by. Again, some use the quotation marks instead of the कि; some use both. A few writers have adopted the use of —. The following are from Hindi books :—

हनुमान जी कहने लगे—
मातु मोहिं दीजै कछु चीन्हा

Hanuman said, "O mother, give me some token."

राजा ने कहा—"देखो दीवान," *The king said, "Look here, Diwan."*

The use of कि is not confined to quotation ; it is used also in narrative. मैं ने प्रतिज्ञा की कि मैं जाऊँगा, *I promised to go.* वे चाहते थे कि हम जो कुछ अनुमान कर रहे हैं मन्त्री भी वही अनुमान करे, (*The king*) *desired that the minister might reach the same conclusion that he himself accepted.* Lit., *He desired that what inference I am deducing the minister also may deduce that inference.*

THE REPETITION OF WORDS.

149. This subject is connected with Idiom rather than with Syntax, but may be allowed a corner in this chapter.

The repetition of a word—Noun, Adjective, Pronoun, Adverb, Participle or Verb—plays quite an important part in Hindi composition. The repetition of the Verb may be left for the present and reference only made in this section to other Parts of Speech.

It should be remembered that the matter now treated of is quite distinct from the doubling of words referred to in the section on Compound Nouns. Here we are speaking of the repetition of exactly the same word. This repetition has a force of considerable power. The force differs with different words, and in different sentences. The following rough classification and illustrations will perhaps sufficiently indicate the main principles of this idiomatic repetition of words.

150. I. **Giving Distributive Force.**

यदि प्रत्येक पीढ़ी के लिये पच्चीस पच्चीस वर्ष का समय रक्खा जाय, *If 25 years be allowed for each generation.* **ध्रुवजी ने एक एक यक्ष के शरीर में तीन तीन बाण मारे,** *Dhruva pierced the body of each Yaksh with three arrows.* **सौ २ दो २ सौ एक साथ होकर चली जातीं,** *They go off together a hundred and two hundred at a time.* **जो जो जाएगा सो सो पावेगा,** *Whoever goes will obtain.* **जहाँ २ कोई जाए वहाँ २ यह देखा जाएगा,** *Wherever any one may go, this will everywhere be seen.*

घर २ में दस दस बारह बारह जन बीमार हो कर पड़े हैं, *In every house, ten or twelve people are lying ill.* बन २ मारे फिरे, *They wandered about in forest after forest.*

The following also belong to this group, but are limited in their scope owing to the words used :—

इस देश के किसी २ प्रान्त में	*In one or another province of this country.*
कहीं कहीं	*Here and there. In some places.*
कुछ कुछ	*To a small extent. A little.*
कोई कोई	*One here and there.*

151. II. Giving Intensive Force.

This includes exactitude, magnitude, multiplicity and the reverse of these. हरे २ पत्तों के योग से वह भी हरा मालूम होता है, *From the proximity of the very green leaves that also appears to be green.* बड़े २ नगरों में, *In very big cities.* थोड़ा २ चाहिये, *Just a very little is needed.* छोटे २ बच्चे यह कर सकते हैं, *Little mites of children can do this.* साथ २ चले जाते थे, *They were going along sticking close together.* पूरा पूरा बँट गया, *It was all distributed.* बाटिका के बीच २ में, *In the very middle of the garden.* इस बात का ज्ञान ठीक २ नहीं होता, *What is known concerning this matter is not exact knowledge.* **पास २**, *Very close.* **लँगड़ाते हुए वह धीरे २ चलने लगा,** *He went limping along very slowly.*

152. III. Sometimes the sign of the Genitive, **का,** is inserted between the first and second writing of the word ; sometimes **ही** is so written (or spoken.) These belong to Class II rather than to I.

सारे का सारा, सारा का सारा, *The whole, the entire lot.* **कुछ का कुछ,** *Somewhat.* **समूह के समूह,** *Great quantities, e.g.,* **पौधों के समूह के समूह देख कर,** *Having seen the great numbers of newly planted out trees.* **झुण्ड के झुण्ड,** *Whole herds.* **तोतों की पाँति की पाँति,** *Whole lines of parrots.* **घोड़ों की पाँतियाँ ही पाँतियाँ,** *Whole lines of horses.* **दुःख ही दुःख,** *Intense pain.* **धूल ही धूल,** *Dust, dust ; completely reduced to dust.* **मन ही मन में,** *In his heart of hearts, i.e., his real thought or feeling.* **मांस या लहू का नाम ही नाम था।** *(Over her bones) there was just the bare name of flesh and blood.*

CHAPTER VII.

THE ADJECTIVE.

153. For Adjective, the Hindi is **विशेषण. गुणवाचक** is also sometimes used; this word, however, is applicable to other Parts of Speech, besides the Adjective, meaning simply any word that predicates quality.

Many Adjectives have the masculine and feminine terminations **आ** and **ई**, and are then inflected in accordance with the Nouns they agree with in Gender, Number and Case, *with some modifications.* Other Adjectives are not subject to any inflection, *e.g.*, **चतुर**, *clever*.

154. Class I. Adjectives subject to inflection.

These end in **आ** for the masculine, **ई** for the feminine, and are inflected in the same way as Nouns masc. of Class I and Nouns fem. of Class III, with this exception that 1. the Case sign is attached to the Noun only, not to the Adjective, and 2. the **ई** of the fem. remains unchanged throughout; thus we have **अच्छी लड़कियों की पुस्तक**, *the book belonging to the good girls,* not **अच्छियों**.

The changes by inflection may be thus tabulated.—

Masc. Nom. Sing.	अच्छा लड़का,	a good boy.
,, Oblique Cases Sing.	अच्छे लड़के को, में, से,	to a good boy, etc., etc.
,, Nom. Pl.	अच्छे लड़के,	good boys.
,, Oblique Cases Pl.	अच्छे लड़कों, को, में, से,	to good boys, etc., etc.
Fem. Nom. Sing.	अच्छी लड़की	a good girl.
,, Oblique Cases Sing.	अच्छी लड़की, को, में, से,	to a good girl, etc., etc.
,, Nom. Pl.	अच्छी लड़कियाँ	good girls.
,, Oblique Cases P.	अच्छी लड़कियों को, में, से,	to good girls, etc., etc.

Participles and the Nouns of Agency, formed from the inflected Infinitive by the addition of वाला and हारा, are, for all practical purposes, Adjectives, and are inflected in the same way as indicated above.

When these are used as Nouns, they are fully inflected. Thus चलनेवाले मनुष्यों के लिये, but चलनेवालों के लिये ; so also with an Adjective used as a Noun. *e.g.*, बड़ों की समझ में यह क्या है, What is this in the estimation of the great?

Some Adjectives, ending in a consonant, possess a form for the fem., ending in आ, or ई, *e.g.*—

दुष्ट,	*evil.*	fem.	दुष्टा
प्रियतम,	*beloved*	,,	प्रियतमा
सुन्दर,	*beautiful*	,,	सुन्दरी
सुशील,	*of a gracious disposition.*	,,	सुशीला

Such fem. forms are affected by some writers, but more generally the masc. form is used as a common gender and made to do service for both genders. Not infrequently, the form in the fem. ending in ई is used as a fem. Noun.

155. Class II. Uninflected Adjectives. All other Adjectives may be regarded as not subject to inflection; such are —

उत्तम,	*excellent.*	मासिक,	*monthly.*
श्रेष्ठ,	*supremely excellent.*	दैनिक,	*daily.*
कठिन,	*difficult.*	बलवान,	*strong.*
दृढ़,	*firm.*	बलवन्त,	*strong.*

There are a few endings in vowels; in ईय, as अद्वितीय, *matchless, without a second*; विश्वासनीय, *worthy of trust*: in ऊ, as दयालू, *merciful*; कृपालू, *gracious*: in ई, as शोकी, *mournful.* Those ending in ई and ऊ are often used as Nouns. In such cases the masc.

ई becomes इणी for fem., *e.g.*, अधिकारी, *ruler* ; fem. अधिकारिणी ; उपकारी, *helper* ; fem. उपकारिणी.

156. Adjectival use of सा (सी, से), सरीखा and नामक.

These cannot strictly be called suffixes, forasmuch as they are usually not joined to the words which precede them, yet they have very much in common with prefixes. They convert the words with which they are used with into Adjectives.

157. सा, सी, से. This सा with its fem. सी and plural से (this form being used also for the oblique Cases of the masc. sing.), is declined in the same way as Adjectives of two terminations, agreeing with the Noun which follows it, and which it qualifies, *e.g.*, चित्र सी स्त्री, *a picture-like woman, i.e.*, what we should call "*like a statue*," devoid of movement or other indications of life. The सी agrees in gender with the fem. स्त्री which follows it, not with the masc. चित्र, to which it is added. If the word qualified were मनुष्य, it would become चित्र सा मनुष्य, or pl. चित्र से मनुष्य.

A few illustrations are appended :

तुम सा मनुष्य इस काम के योग्य नहीं है, lit., *A you-like man is not fit for this work, i.e., a man like you.* उसने ग्रपने भाई को ग्रधमरा सा पड़ा पाया, *He found his brother lying as it were half-dead.* धुग्राँ सा कुछ दिखाई देता है, *Something like smoke appears.* तस्वीरें मिट सी गयी थीं, *The pictures became as though blotted out.* खिस सी होकर, *(She) becoming angry-like, i.e., pretending to be angry.* हँसती हुई सी, *(She) as it were laughing.* ग्राप से पवित्र, *Holy as you.* देखने में तेा ये क्षत्रिय से मालूम पड़ते हैं, *In appearance they are like Kshatriyas.* कुम्भकरण सा भाई, इन्द्रजीत सा पुत्र, *A brother like Kumbhakaran, a son like Indrajit.* The idiomatic use of the सा is slightly different in the following sentence: उसकी सी झझक कर उठ बैठी ग्रैार बौड़ही या भूत लगी सी ग्राँखें फाड़, *Having started up like one suddenly aroused, she sat up and having opened her eyes wide like one mad or bewitched.*

158. There is another use of सा which must be referred to. Dr. Kellog considers this to be derived from another root. In use it certainly differs somewhat from that already given, but there are also great similarities. It is to a large extent pleonastic, adding little or nothing to the meaning of the word to which it is added. Take two illustrations: थोड़ी सी भूमि, *A little land.* वे ग्रपने साथ बहुत सी चीज़ें ले चले, *They passed along,* *taking many things with them.* If by the use of **सी** any force be added to the words **थोड़ी** and **बहुत**, it is of the nature of intensive force.

Occasionally, this **सा** has the meaning of "... ish" in English, *e.g.*, **काला सा**, *blackish*.

159. **सरीखा (ई, ए)**. The form and force of this is practically the same as that of **सा**.

The following sentence illustrates the use of **सरीखा** and of the second use of **सा** : **तुम सरीखे हमने बहुत से देख लिये हैं**, *We have seen many such like as you.* **इन अमृत सरीखे वचन**, *These nectar-like words.* **इनके लिये हम सरीखे लोग तनिक भी चिन्ता नहीं करते**, *Such people as we take no concern whatever about these things.* **मुझ सरीखा दीनों को बैठाना**, *Seat such humble people as I am.*

In the following two sentences the use differs slightly, approximating more to the Postposition : **के समान** or **की नाईं**. **सब लोग कमल सरीखे खिल उठे**, *All the people blossomed out like lotuses.* **वह तेरे ही सरीखे मरेगा**, *He will die like you.*

160. **नामक** The use of this is quite simple. Instead of such a phrase as, *A city named Shripur*, the form, *A Shripur-named city*, **श्रीपुर नामक नगर**, is used. So we have, **निमि के मिथि और मिथि के जनक**

नामक पुत्र हुए, *A son named Mithi was born to Nimi, and to Mithi a son named Janak.* बम्बई के पास बसई नामक गाँव, *In a village called Basai near to Bombay.*

Occasionally, the form नामी is found, with two different forms for the fem. नाम्नी and नामा.

When नाम is used instead of नामक, it is generally in the Genitive Case, भीमसेन नाम का एक राजा, *A king of the name of Bhimsen.* सुन्दर नाम की एक कन्या, A damsel of the name of Sundar. ताड़का नाम की राक्षसी, *A female demon named Taraka.*

161. रूपी, The special use of this word suggests a doubt as to whether it should be noticed under Adjectives. As रूप means "form" or "shape," one might naturally expect that रूपी would be an Adjective, meaning, *form-possessing*, and that क्रोधरूपी अग्नि would mean, *Fire possessing the form of, being like to, wrath, i.e.,* अग्नि being the Noun and क्रोधरूपी its qualifying Adjective, meaning "possessing the form of anger." It, however, works out the other way, meaning "Anger which is like fire." Thus विद्यारूपी द्रव्य, *Learning which is like riches.* प्रजारूपी पुत्रों का पालन करो, *Care for your subjects who are as sons.* मन शरीररूपी नगर का राजा है, *Mind is the king of the body which is like a city.*

Occasionally, a writer may be found using the words in the reverse way, *e.g.*, **अमृतरूपी उपदेश,** where, apparently, the author's meaning is not, *Nectar which is like good teaching*, but, *Good teaching which is like nectar*, and should, therefore, according to the generally accepted idiom, be **उपदेशरूपी अमृत.**

In a recent book, by a very good writer, is the following: **ज्ञान पुरुषरूपी है और भक्ति स्त्रीरूपी,** *Knowledge is manlike and devotion womanlike.*

162. Comparison of Adjectives.

No system of the Comparison of Adjectives exists in Hindi corresponding with that in use in English, but there are idioms by which the results of a comparison can be readily expressed.

A few Sanskrit Comparatives and Superlatives are imported ready-made into Hindi, *e.g.*, **कठिनतर,** *more difficult*; **धनिष्ठ,** *most wealthy*; **प्रियतम,** *most beloved*; but these are stray words, and do not indicate any such system in Hindi.

The most general way of expressing the Comparative is by throwing the person or thing with which the comparison is made into the Ablative Case, with **से,** and using the simple Adjective. Thus **पुरुष स्त्री से बलवान है,** *A man is stronger than a woman.* **यह घर उस से ऊँचा है,** *This house is higher than that.*

Other idioms also are current, *e.g.*, by the use of **बढ़कर**, the Conjunctive Participle of **बढ़ना**, *to go beyond*. **इस नगर में उस से बढ़कर कोई ज्ञानी नहीं है**, *There is no more learned man in the city than he*. By the use of **अपेक्षा**, **उसकी अपेक्षा यह बड़ा है**, *This is greater than that*, or, lit., *In comparison with that this is great*.

Perhaps the most common way of expressing the Superlative is by adding **सब** to the Noun with which the comparison is made and converting it into the plural form, retaining the Ablative **से**, as with the Comparative. Thus Comparative. **यह राजा उस राजा से बड़ा है**, *This king is greater than that*. Superlative: **यह राजा सब राजाओं से बड़ा है**, *This king is greater than all kings*. This is not peculiarly satisfactory, as it is inexact; for it involves logically that he is no longer a king or that he is greater than himself. A more correct idiom is also employed: **में** is used instead of **से**, thus, **सब राजाओं में यह राजा बड़ा है**, *This king is among all kings the great one*, i.e., *the greatest*. For fulness and exactness, the following is perhaps the best idiom of all: **सब राजाओं में, उस राजा से कोई बड़ा नहीं है**, *Among all kings there is none greater than he*; or **सब राजाओं में इस राजा के बराबर कोई नहीं**, *Among all kings there is none his equal*.

There are other ways of expressing something equivalent to the Superlative, *e.g.*, by the use of such words as—

अच्छे से अच्छा, Good than the good, *i.e.*, best of all
उत्तम से उत्तम, do......................do.
कठिन से भी कठिन, Hardest of all.
अधिकाधिक, Most exceedingly.
बड़े से बड़े, Very great (pl.)
छोटे से छोटे, Very small (pl.)

Or, by the addition of an adverb before the, adjective, *e.g.*, अति, अत्यन्त, बहुत, *e.g.*, अति ऊँचा *Very high.* अत्यन्त ऊँचा, *Exceedingly high.* बहुत बड़ा, *Very large.*

CHAPTER VIII.

163. THE PRONOUNS

Pronoun.	सर्वनाम
Personal Pronoun	पुरुषवाचक सर्वनाम
1st person ("I")	उत्तम पुरुष
2nd ,, ("Thou")	मध्यम पुरुष
3rd ,, (He, she, it.) Remote (Demonstrative Pronoun.)	(वह) अन्य पुरुष or प्रथम पुरुष
Near Demonstrative Pronoun	निश्चयवाचक सर्वनाम or संकेतवाचक सर्वनाम
Indefinite Pronoun (कोई)	अनिश्चयवाचक सर्वनाम
Interrogative Pronoun (कौन)	प्रश्नवाचक सर्वनाम
Relative Pronoun (जो)	संबन्धवाचक सर्वनाम
Honorific Pronoun (आप)	आदरप्रदर्शक सर्वनाम
Reflexive Pronoun (आप)	निजवाचक सर्वनाम

164. Hindi has an advantage over English in possessing an Interrogative Pronoun, **कौन,** and a Relative, **जो,** whereas in English "*who,*" has to answer for both. On the other hand, Hindi possesses no Personal Pronoun for the 3rd person. **वह** is simply "that (one)" and has to do duty for *he, she, it.* In the same way, **यह,** the Proximate Demonstrative Pronoun, corresponds with *this man*, *this woman*, *this thing*.

FIRST AND SECOND PERSONAL PRONOUNS.

165. **मैं**, I, and **तू,** Thou, are thus declined:

Singular.

Nominative.	I.	**मैं, मैंने**	Thou.	**तू, तूने**
Constructive Base.		**मुझ**		**तुझ**
Accusative.	Me.	**मुझे, मुझको**	Thee.	**तुझे, तुझको**
Dative.	To me.	,, ,,	To thee.	,, ,,
Instrumental.	By me.	**मुझ से**	By thee.	**तुझ से**
Ablative.	From me.	,, ,,	From thee.	,, ,,
Genitive.	My, mine.	**मेरा, मेरी, मेरे**	Thy, thine.	**तेरा, तेरी, तेरे**
Locative.	In me, on me, etc.	**मुझ में, पर,** etc.	In thee, on thee, etc.	**तुझ में, पर,** etc.

Plural.

Nom.	**हम, हमने**	**तुम, तुमने**
Constr. Base.	**हम**	**तुम**
Acc.	**हमें, हमको**	**तुम्हें, तुमको**
Dat.	,, ,,	,, ,,
Instr.	**हमसे**	**तुमसे**
Abl.	,,	,,
Gen.	**हमारा, री, रे**	**तुम्हारा, री, रे**
Loc.	**हम में, पर,** etc.	**तुम में, पर,** etc.

166. In the plural, there are some additional forms which are little used:

Nom. हमोंने, तुम्होंने Acc. and Dat. हम्हों को, तुम्हों को

Instr. and Abl. हमों से, तुम्हों से Locative हम्हों में, तुम्हों में

167. *The Constructive Base*—When the Pronoun is in apposition with another word or loosely compounded with it, the Constructive base alone is used, the Case sign being appended to the second word.

मुझ कंगाल से क्या हो सकता है? *What can a poor wretch like me do?* मुझ अपने पुत्र को निकालेंगे? '*Will you turn me, your son, out?* हम तीनों भाइयों को उसने बुलाया, *He called us three brothers.*

Instances occur where the Genitive, instead of the Constructive base, is used in this way, निश्चय कोई हमारा सा दुखिया है, *Verily there is some one as great a sufferer as I.* हमारे ऐसे मन्दभाग्यों को, *To those as ill-fated as we are.* Even such forms as मेरे को, मेरे से, हमारे को are occasionally met with; but such forms should not be imitated,

Scholars differ as to which is the better form for the Nom. with ने when compounded with another word, *e.g.*, मैं राजा ने यह आज्ञा दी, or मुझ राजा ने यह

आज्ञा दी, *I, the king, gave this order.* Opinion appears to be about equally divided.

Sometimes ई is joined to this Constructive base. This is equivalent to the addition of ही, giving stress to the Pronoun, but not quite as strong as the full ही. Thus हमी लोगों को भागना पड़ा, *It came about that even we had to take flight.* तुम्ही लोगों पर दोष लगेगा, *On you people the blame will fall.* हमी को नहीं सभों को, *Not only to us, to all ....*

168. *The Accusative and Dative.*—The forms for the Accusative and Dative are identical. Whether there be any difference in the uses of the two forms, and what the difference be, if any exist, it is not easy to understand. The forms without को *are* used for the Accusative, but probably it will be found that there is a tendency to use these forms more for the Dative, and the forms with को for the Accusative. राजा ने तुम्हें ठहरने के लिये घर दिया, *The king gave a house for you to stay in.* वह तुम्हें पारितोषिक देगा, *He will give you a reward.* मुझे अनेक मित्रों से सहायता मिली, I *have received help from many friends.* हमें दुःख भोगना पड़ेगा, *We shall have to endure trouble.* In the following, this form is used for the Acc. तुम्हें भी साथ लेते जाएंगे, *They will go, taking you along with them.*

169. *The Genitive.*—It will be noticed that for the Genitive, the Constructive base is somewhat changed; in the sing., it becomes मे, ते, in the plural हमा, तुम्हा, and to these bases are added रा, री, रे. Thus formed, the Genitives are inflected exactly the same as Adjectives of two terminations. They are, in fact, to all intents, Adjectives. It must be remembered that this termination as regards gender is regulated by the gender of the person or thing possessed, not by that of the possessor. मेरा घोड़ा, *My horse.* मेरी पुस्तक, *My book.* The gender of *horse* and *book* determine the gender form of मेरा and तेरी, not the gender of the owner of these things.

The other cases require no special notice.

170. *The use of the Singular and Plural Personal Pronouns.* A matter of special importance is the right use of the Pronouns in addressing persons, or in speaking and writing about them. It will be well to anticipate slightly and to consider here not only the use of the 1st and 2nd Personal Pronouns, but also the Demonstrative, so far as it has to do for the 3rd Personal Pronoun, and the Honorific Pronoun, आप.

As regards the 1st Person, the Plural may be, and is, to no small extent, used for the singular. Thus, हमारी समझ में, *In my judgment*; हम जाएंगे, *I will go*; हम को चाहिये, *I need it.* There is an increasing tendency, however, among the more cultured and educated classes, to use the singular form in speaking about oneself, and it may be taken as an utterly safe rule to always use the singular in referring to oneself. Let it be recognized, at the same time, that the use of the forms हम and हमारा is not at all equivalent to the "we" in English used as the "plural of majesty," or the "editorial we." In past days, the plural forms were far more used for the singular than they are at present; and this accounts for the fact that in many places लोग is added to हम, to indicate the plural, where the context might not clearly shew whether the singular "I" or plural "we" were meant.

For the 2nd person, there are three Pronouns available, तू, तुम, आप. आप is really a 3rd person, necessitating the Verb in the 3rd plural, but is nevertheless greatly used in direct address for the 2nd person. In English, we have a similar idiom, but such uses are generally reserved for those persons who possess special dignity, "Your Majesty," "Your honour," "Your reverence;" whereas the आप is used in Hindi for very ordinary people.

तू is very little used, and, when it is used, has often in it something bordering on contempt for the person so addressed. It may be wisely excluded from the foreigner's working vocabulary. There is a use for the word far removed from that indicated above. A man may use it to his wife or child with as much kindliness and affection as a Quaker would use "thou." In Hindi, however, the use of the word is confined to those who are younger or in a more "protected" position than the speaker. It may sometimes be used to a servant, indicating a certain familiar relationship of the patriarchal type rather than contempt. A teacher may also use the word to his disciples, indicating something of the nature of paternal affection and care.

तुम and आप are the alternative words, in the discriminating use of which the foreigner may experience some difficulty. To adopt तुम, where आप is the appropriate word, is to be guilty of a great breach of etiquette; to use आप where तुम would be the right word, may be taken for sarcasm, even as, "Will you be graciously pleased to . . . " might be so taken, if addressed to your butcher or baker.

तुम may be used to servants and to children and young people who would be addressed by their Christian names in English. It may also be used in speaking to workmen and petty shopkeepers. Among Indians of equal standing it may be used in familiar intercourse, in somewhat the same way that the "Mr." is dropped among Englishmen where there is considerable familiarity. The foreigner will, however, need great care in venturing on the use of the तुम in this way. आप may be regarded as the general Pronoun to use towards equals, towards those in a superior position and also to subordinates, with whose names we should retain the "Mr." in English. If in doubt, use आप.

171. Pronouns to be used in addressing God. What Pronoun should be used in addressing God, or in referring to Him? Should it be आप and वे with the Verb in the 3rd plural, or तू and वह with the 2nd and 3rd singular? Hindi is only discussed here. तू in Urdu is perfectly correct and needs no discussion.

In this paragraph, the writer uses "I," as he is fully aware that, on this important question, a considerable majority of missionaries differ from him. As regards the translation of the Bible, I regard it as perfectly sound to retain the singular. The attempt to discriminate between the adoption of तू and तुम and आप would continually be involving the translator in the responsibilities which belong to the commentator. A simple translation of the Pronouns for God and for all persons is the easy and safe course. When, however, the question arises of how to address God in prayer and worship, and how to write or speak concerning

God, it seems as appropriate to use आप in direct address and वे in writing or speaking, in Hindi, as it does to spell "Him" with a capital "H" in English. In my reading for many years, I have given particular attention to the matter; and the conclusion which I reached a long time since has been fully confirmed. The matter stands thus. Most missionaries, and, following them, the majority of Indian Christians, use तू. Some, however, of the well-read Indian Christians do not approve of this, and a few missionaries do not. By *some* Hindus, probably through education in Mission Schools, तू has been adopted, but speaking generally of Hindus, the view is clearly that तू is very inappropriate, तुम is slipshod and lacking in reverence, आप and वे are the correct Pronouns to use. I have accepted and adopted this for many years, and to me तू and वह sound as grating as does "you" when used to God in prayer in English.

I could easily produce very many quotations to back up the statement made. I will satisfy myself with giving just some few. भगवान आज क्या करनेवाले हैं! *What is God about to do to-day*! हे परम दयालु परमेश्वर! आप मेरी शुभ इच्छाओं को पूर्ण कीजिये, *O most merciful God, fulfil my desires that are right.*

हे परमेश्वर ! आप प्रकाश रूप हैं, *O God, Thou art the image of light.* And on the same page, कीजिये and दीजिये in address to God. हे प्रभु ! ऐसी कृपा कीजिये, *O Lord! Grant such grace.* ईश्वर क्या करेंगे, *What will God do?* ईश्वर से मैं प्रार्थना करता हूँ कि वे सब को तुम्हारे ही सदृश बेटा दें, *I pray God that He may give to all a son like you.* I note in one book: हे ईश्वर ! तुम अपने नाम को कलङ्कित न करो, *O God, do not bring any stigma upon your name*; but on the same page, उसकी रक्षा भगवान करते हैं, *God protects him.* And a few pages away, अन्तर्यामी भगवान आप के पवित्र हृदय का भाव नहीं समझते हैं, *Does not the heart-knowing God understand the disposition of your holy heart?* ईश्वर तो सब का विचार करते ही हैं, *Verily God thinks of all.*

In one book, in which the plural is elsewhere used, we meet in one place with the singular, ईश्वर उसका रक्षक है, *God is his protector.*

I give one more quotation from a writer on Hindi composition. Having stated that आप is for great respect, तुम to indicate equality or relationship and familiarity, तू to indicate disrespect, he proceeds: कहीं तू को भी बराबरवाले और छोटे लोगों के लिये

बोलते हैं, कहीं कहीं भक्तलोग ईश्वर के लिये भी तू कहते हैं, जैसे :—

हे ईश्वर! आप हमारी रक्षा करो; हे नीच! तू क्या करता है, चन्द, तुम कहाँ जाओगे.

Here and there people use "tu" for equals also and for the little folk; here and there devotees use "tu" for God also, e.g.—

"Oh God! protect us." "What are you up to, you scoundrel?". "Chanda, where will you go?"

Whether it is a misprint, or whether a slip on the part of the writer, is not clear, but आप should certainly have कीजिये, not. करो. Occasionally, such loose writing is met with; but one would not expect it in a book on Composition.

172. *Omission of Pronoun.*

The Pronoun is sometimes unexpressed. In Hindi, this is in many cases quite safe, as the form of the Verb in many of the Tenses indicates the Gender and Number of the subject. Take the following examples: दो तीन मील चलकर एक झील के किनारे पहुँचे, *Having gone two or three miles, (we) arrived at a piece of water.* इस पहाड़ी को पारकर जब दूसरी ओर पहुँचे, *Having reached the other side of this hill, when (we) reached the other side.* कहो जिस काम को गये थे

उस का क्या किया, *Say, what did (you) do about the work (you) went (to do)?* अच्छा, तब राजसिंह को ही मन्त्री बनाऊँगा, *Very well then (I) will make Rajsinha minister.* कहो तो मैं जाऊँगा, *If (you) will speak the word, I will go.*

DEMONSTRATIVE PRONOUNS AND 3RD PERSONAL PRONOUN.

173. In Hindi, there is no Personal Pronoun for the 3rd person, but the two Demonstrative Pronouns, near and remote, quite efficiently supply the place. That these Demonstrative Pronouns (यह and वह, *this, that*) do not indicate the gender, is a defect which they share in common with the real Personal Pronouns for the 1st and 2nd persons. In English also, the 1st and 2nd persons (*I* and *you*) do not indicate gender, but the 3rd does, *he, she, it.*

These two Demonstrative Pronouns not only render service as Personal Pronouns, but also as Correlatives.

	Proximate.	*Remote.*
Singular.		
Nominative.	यह (यिह, यही, यिही)	वह (वुह, वही)
...	इसने	उसने

	Proximate.	*Remote.*
Constr. base.	इस (इसी)	उस (उसी)*
Accus.	इसको, इसे, यह	उसको, उसे, वह
Dat.	इस को, इसे	उसको, उसे
Instr. & Abl.	इससे	उससे
Gen.	इसका, की, के	उसका, की, के
Loc.	इसमें, पर	उसमें, पर
Plural.		
Nominative.	ये, इन्होंने	वे, उन्होंने
Constr. base.	इन, इन्हों	उन, उन्हों
Acc. & Dat.	इन्हों को, इन्हें इनको	उन्हों को, उन्हें उनको
Instr. & Abl.	इन्हों से, इनसे	उन्हों से, उनसे
Gen.	इन्हों का, की, के इन का, की, के	उन्हों का, की, के उनका, की, के
Loc.	इन्हों में, पर, or इन में, पर	उन्हों में, पर, or उन में, पर

* This addition of ई may be added to all the Cases in the sing., except the इसे, उसे forms of Acc. and Dat. It corresponds with the हों in the plural. It *may* indicate a measure of emphasis, but not necessarily so. The additional हों in the plural is more commonly used in some of the Cases than in others, *e.g.*, it is

much preferred in the Nom. with ने The form उनने is practically not used.

Such forms as इन्हीं, इन्हीं लोगों ने, are also met with ; these must be regarded as the addition of the emphatic ही to इन।

When these Pronouns are used with Adjectival force before another word, in a Case requiring the oblique form, the Constr. base is used, but not the Case ending, that is added to the later word, *e.g.*, उस मनुष्य ने कहा, *That man said.* इस पुस्तक का दाम, *The price of this book.* उन मनुष्यों ने कहा, *Those men said.* इन पुस्तकों का दाम, *The price of these books.*

174. Use of Singular and Plural. When used as Personal Pronouns, ये and वे may be substituted for यह and वह as honorific, and the Verb will then be in the Plural, *e.g.*, of a king, ये अब आये हैं, He has now come ; of a rishi, वे कल जाएंगे, *He will go to-morrow.*

On the other hand, in the Nominative, the singular forms यह and वह are sometimes found with a plural meaning, this being indicated by the plural form of the Verb being used. This is due to the influence of Urdu, in which this idiomatic (and sometimes catchy) use of यह and वह greatly prevails. In Hindi, this idiom is of quite recent times, and is by no means generally accepted. It is just a trick of fashion and serves no useful purpose.

175. Idiomatic uses of **यह** and **वह.**

यह and **वह,** as *this* and *that,* are used in reference to a very wide range of subjects, **यह** referring to the present, or historic present, **वह** to the past. They may refer not only to a person or thing, but to an incident, a whole group of circumstances or a logical argument, also to time, *e.g.,* **उसके अनन्तर,** *After that.* **इसके बाद,** *After this.* **इससे यह मालूम होगा,** *From this it will be evident.*

In reporting conversations and incidents, **यह** and **वह** are conveniently used for two persons or things, as "*one,*" "*another,*" or "*the other,*" in English. When so used, the terms "proximate" and "remote" largely lose their significance. It is by no means uncommon to find that a person referred to early in a paragraph as **यह** is referred to later on as **वह,** *e.g.,* in a biography, we have the father's name given, then **इनके ये तीन पुत्र थे,** *This man had these three sons.* A little later, one of these is referred to as **वे भगवद्भक्त थे,** *He was a great devotee.* Then, **उनके एक कन्या और एक पुत्र , दो सन्तान हुए ,** *Two children were born to him, a daughter and a son.*

It has already been mentioned that these Pronouns are much used in the Const. base form, before other words with Adjectival force. **यह मनुष्य, वह मनुष्य,** *this man, that man.* **इन दिनों, उन दिनों,** *In these days, in those days.*

176. Honorific and Reflexive Pronouns.

These two must be very carefully distinguished. Exactly the same in form, one is a Pronoun of respect used in speaking to, or of, a person ; the other is merely a reflexive, applicable to all three persons, corresponding to the English "*self*" or "own." **मैं आप,** *I myself.* **तुम आप जानते हो,** *You yourself know.* **अपनी पुस्तक लेते आओ,** *Come, bringing your own book.*

177. *The Honorific* **आप.** This has already been referred to in Sect. 170. In construction, it is 3rd person, and necessitates the Verb in the plural, but is used for a single individual person, being either addressed to him, or referring to him. It corresponds, in use, with "*your honour*" in English, as regards grammatical form, but not in meaning, as it is far more generally used.

The word is subject to no inflectional changes. The plural is expressed by the addition of **लोग** ; *e.g.,* **आप लोगों ने सुना होगा,** *You people will have heard.*

Though we often find the word translated in English by "*your honour*," in a majority of instances, "you" would better represent the meaning of the word. आप कब जाएंगे, When will.........go? might be used to a member of the nobility, to your uncle or aunt, to an ordinary acquaintance, to a clerk in your office, to any business man of some education and position.

It is used in all the Cases, the word itself remaining unchanged, but taking the Case signs. आप का कहना ठीक है, *What you say is correct.* आप को मिलेगा, *You will get it.* आप लोगों के बीच, *Among you.*

The principal use of आप is in direct address, but it is used, in referring to the same person, *to* a third person (present) or to another person not present. Thus, while at all times, in form and construction, it is a 3rd person, it is used for both 2nd and 3rd persons. आप का कहना, would more commonly mean, *What you say*, but it also may mean, *What he says.* एक बार महाराजा ने आप को बुलवा भेजा, may either mean, *The Maharaja on one occasion sent to call you*, or, *to call him.* In the following, आप is used for the 3rd person, आप का जन्म सं० १७०६ में हुआ था, *He was born in* 1706 (*i.e.*, A. D. 1763). लोग आप का विशेष आदर करते हैं, *People render special honour to him.*

As already stated, the principal use of आप is in direct address, but this second use, for the 3rd person, must not be overlooked. In modern Hindi, this second use is more general than it was.

आप, in direct address, is occasionally found with the second person of the Verb. आप करो, *Please do* (*this*), This is careless writing and not grammaticially defensible.

178. The Reflexive आप.

The consideration of this Pronoun raises some difficulties, both as regards its forms and its uses.

Nom.	आप, अपने आप.
„	आपने, or आप alone after the subject, with ने.
Acc. and Dat.	अपने को, अपने तईं, अपने आप को.
Instr. and Abl.	अपने से, अपने आप से.
Gen.	अपना, अपनी, अपने, occasionally अपने आप का.
Loc.	अपने में, पर; अपने आप में, पर.

In both forms of the Nom., that with, and that without, ने, it generally follows the true subject of the sentence, much the same as in English we have, "He himself went." Thus, राजा आप दूतों से पूँछने

लगे, *The king began to question the messengers himself*; or, राजा ने आप देखा, *The king himself saw.*

The form, अपने आप, is not much used in the Nom. In the following sentence, अपने आप has probably more affinity with the Iustrumental or Ablative Case than with the Nominative: संसार की अद्भुत रचना अपने आप स्वयं हो गई है, *The marvellous order (*lit. *make) of the universe has come about of itself.*

Both अपने आप and अपने, with the Case signs, are used in the Oblique Cases. We have अपने आप को भूलना, *To forget oneself.* राजपूत वीर अपने आप को भूल गये *The Rajput warriors forgot themselves, i.e.,* were so engrossed in fighting as to lose all concern about their own safety. उसे अपने आप से बाहर कर रखा था, *He had driven him crazy.* Lit., *Had placed him outside of himself.* वह उन्हें अपने में खैंच लेता है, *It draws them into itself.* दोनों राजकुमार अपने से बड़े लोगों का आदर करते थे, *The two princes rendered honour to those who were greater than themselves.*

आप से आप means "spontaneously." अपने आप may be similarly used. Thus, यह बाजा अपने आप बज रहा है, *This instrument is playing of itself.*

Connected with this Pronoun is the word **आपस**, *mutual.* **आपस की फूट देख कर,** *Having seen that they were quarrelling among themselves.* **वे आपस में बहुत प्रेम रखते थे**, *They loved each other very much.* **आपस की सन्धि उन्हों ने तोड़ डाली,** *They broke the treaty that had existed between them.*

179. *The Genitive* **अपना.** This **अपना** may, in all respects, be treated as an Adjective of two terminations, agreeing in Gender and Number with the Noun which it qualifies. It must be remembered that it has no connection whatever with the Gender and Number of the subject. **लड़की अपने भाइयों को बुला रही है,** *The girl is calling her brothers.* **लड़का अपनी बहिनों को बुला रहा है,** *The boy is calling his sisters.*

अपना is used with all three persons, and generally refers to the subject of the main Verb in the sentence, **उन्होंने अपने नौकरों को भेज दिया**, *They sent their own servants.* This sentence remains the same, whether **उन्होंने** refers to a masc. or fem. "they," and the latter part of the sentence would remain the same if "he," "she" or "it" took the place of "they." If the servants belonging to some other person be intended, then some other Pronoun, or Noun, must replace the **अपना,** *e.g.*, if A sent the servants of B, then the sentence must run, उस (*i.e.*, A) ने उस (*i.e*, B) के नौकरों को भेज दिया, *A sent B's servants*, or उसने मेरे नौकरों को भेज दिया, *He sent my servants.*

अपना does not *always* refer to the main Verb. It may belong to a secondary Verb. उसने उनको अपने लड़कों को साथ लेकर आते हुए देखा, *He saw them coming along bringing their children with them.* Here the अपने refers not to the main Verb of the sentence, but to the subject of the participial form of लेते आना. In the following sentence, although as regards construction, the अपनी might refer to कामिनी मोहन, it does *not* but to the subject of the main Verb. The man was not staring at himself, but at the Pundit. पण्डित ने कामिनी मोहन को अपनी ओर निरासा भरी डीठ से बार बार ताकते देख कर कहा, *Having seen Kamini Mohan looking towards him again and again with a look full of despair, the Pundit said.*

Note also such sentences as the following: जब मज़दूरों को अपना वेतन कम मालूम होता है *When their wages appear to the workmen to be too little* इसे अपनी भी सुध नहीं है, *He takes no thought of himself.* हार जीत अपने हाथ में नहीं है, *Defeat an victory are not in one's own power* (lit. *hand.*) जब रात को राजा महलों में आये तब रानी को अपनी जगह

न पाया, *When the king, at night, came into the chambers, he did not find the queen in her own place.* Here the अपनी has no Verb to the subject to which it refers, but the meaning is quite evident. So, in the following, हम राजा को अपनी करनी का फल चखावेंगे, *We will make the king taste the fruit of his own doings.* These instances, and many more of a similar character, do not, however, diminish the general value of the rule given about the अपना referring to the subject of the main Verb.

180. निज. Occasionally, निज is added to अपना to strengthen it, giving to it something like the force of the English "*one's very own.*" अपने निज देश में पहुँचते ही उसे बहुत आनन्द हुआ, *On arriving in his own country he experienced great joy.*

Sometimes निज is used without अपना, *e.g.*, वह मेरी निज की है, *She* is my very own. वे आप के निज के लोग हैं, *They are your very own people.*

181. पराया. This word is an Adjective, not a Pronoun; but its right to mention in this chapter is quite as strong as that of अपना, and its consideration here is quite as appropriate. As अपना means *one's own*, so पराया stands for *another's.* It is declined as an Adjective of two terminations. पराई पीड़ा से जिसका कलेजा

नहीं कसकता, *He whose heart does not suffer at the pain of another.* एक न एक दिन तो पराये घर जाना ही है, *One of these days she will have to go to the house of another.* पराये हाथ से, *By the hand of another.* (If it were "*another hand,*" the Hindi would be दूसरे हाथ से). किसी को अपना पराया न पड़ा था, *No one recognized what was his own, what another's.*

Occasionally, a writer is found using an additional Genitive sign. (It must be remembered that पराया is already a Genitive "*of another*"). Thus पराये की हिंसा अथवा निन्दा नहीं करते, *They do not injure or abuse another.* This is incorrect, unless the meaning of the writer be (which is quite possible) that they do not injure or abuse the people of another person's household. That would then equal पराये घर के किसी की हिंसा, etc.

RELATIVE, INTERROGATIVE AND CORRELATIVE PRONOUNS.

182. It may be well here to call attention to the fact that related groups of Pronouns, Pronominal Adjectives and Adverbs are characterized by initial letters which mark them off with considerable distinctness. ज indicates Relative; क both Indefinite and Interrogative;

य or a kindred vowel, Proximate Demonstrative; व or a kindred vowel, Remote Demonstrative.

According to the Paradigms printed in some Grammars, त might be taken as indicative of the Correlative; but all the paradigms must not be taken too seriously. Many of such forms are added to adorn the pages of the Grammer, but may be seldom met with in the pages of literature. The Demonstrative Pronoun and kindred words largely discharge the duties of Correlatives.

As Relatives under ज, may be noted जो, जितना, जब, जैसा, जहाँ.

„ Indefinite ... कोई, कुछ, कितना, कई, कहीं.

„ Interrogative ... कौन, क्या, कितना, कैसा, कहीं, कब.

„ Prox. Demonstr. ... यह, इतना, ऐसा, यहाँ, यहीं, अब.

„ Remote Demonstr. ... वह, उतना, वैसा, वहाँ, वहीं.

It is interesting to note that we find characteristic initial letters for similar groups of words in English. Thus, for Demonstrative "th," as in *the, this, these, those, them, then, there, thence, thither.* For Interrogative "wh," *who? what? whose? where? whence? when? why?*'

RELATIVE AND INTERROGATIVE PRONOUNS.

183. *Relative.* *Interrogative.*

	Relative.	Interrogative.
Sing.		
Nom.	जो, *who, which*	कौन, *who?*
	जिस ने	किस ने
Const. Base.	जिस	किस
Acc.	जो, जिसे, जिस को	(कौन), किसे, किस को
Dat.	जिसे, जिस को	किसे, किस को
Instr. / Abl.	जिस से	किस से
Gen.	जिस का, के, की	किस का, के, की,
Loc.	जिस में, *etc.*	किस में, *etc.*
Plural.		
Nom.	जो	कौन.
	जिन्हों ने, जिनने	किन्हों ने.
Const. Base.	जिन, जिन्हों	किन.
Acc. & Dat.	जिन्हें, जिन को, जिन्हों को	किन्हें, किन को, किन्हों को.

Instr. Abl.	जिन से, जिन्हों से	किन से, किन्हों से.
Gen.	जिन का, जिन्हों का, के, की	किन का, किन्हों का, के, की.
Loc.	जिन में, जिन्हों में	किन में, किन्हों में.

The plural forms of कौन are little used.

184. The Relative.

It has already been pointed out that, whereas in English the Correlative comes first, followed more or less closely by the Relative, in Hindi the Relative usually holds the first place, the Correlative coming later and in a separate sentence. Eng. *He who has been to a place knows what can be obtained there.* Hindi. जो कहीं गया हो वही जानता है कि वहाँ क्या मिल सकता है.

The Relative Pronoun जो must not be confused with जो used as a Conjunction, *e.g.*. जो आवें तब मालूम होगा, *If they come, it will be known*; but जो आवें सो जानें, *They who come will konw.* The Conjunction जो is often followed by तो or तब.

185. The Correlative. The one true Correlative is सो, *e.g.*, जो जानता सो कहे, *Let the man who knows speak.* Usually, the Correlative is a Demonstrative Pronoun: जो जानता है वही कहे, *Who knows let him speak.*

Occasionally, a Correlative is altogether wanting. जो मर गया हो क्या कर सकता, *What can a dead man do?* But this is not generally approved ; a Correlative of some kind is necessary.

In some Grammars is given a full paradigm of the various Cases of सो, singular and plural ; the stem of the sing. being तिस and of the pl. तिन, तिन्ह. As regards modern Hindi, such paradigms are largely fictitious. In old Hindi, however, and in poetry, forms moulded on these or similar stems occur, *e.g.*, for Rel. and Correl. in Acc. sing., we have in the Ramayan, जेहि, तेहि; for the Gen. जासु, तासु, Nom. pl. जे, ते, and Acc. pl. जिन्हहि, तिन्हहि,

186. The Interrogative. The various forms given in the paradigm are, by analogy, probably correct ; but some of them may be looked for in vain in modern literature. For the Nom. pl., the sing. is sometimes repeated, कौन कौन. This carries something of a distributive force as well as being for the plural. Some of the other pl. forms are also current.

कौन may be used alone as a Personal Pronoun, with the meaning, Who ?, or it may be used in conjunction with a Noun, कौन मनुष्य ऐसा करता है, *Wha man does so ?* कौन कौन मनुष्य ऐसा करते हैं, *What men do so ?*

कौन सा means, *What sort of ? e. g.*, **यह कौन सी स्त्री है,** *What sort of a woman is this ?* **इस पर्वत की कौन २ सी शोभा का मैं उल्लेख करूँ,** *Of which kind of the splendours of this mountain shall I write ?*

The Nom. form of **कौन** is sometimes found for Oblique Cases *e. g.*, **कौन कौन कारणों से,** *From what causes ?* **कौन काम करने और कौन न करने योग्य है,** *Which work is fit to be done and which is not ?*

Besides the purely interrogative use of this Pronoun, it is sometimes found carrying the meaning of a loose Relative Pronoun (with or without a Correlative). **कौन गया हो और किन २ लोगों के पास गया हो यह कोई नहीं जानता है,** *Who has gone and to which people he has gone, this no man knows.*

187. The Interrogative क्या. This indeclinable word should be considered in connection with **कौन,** as the uses of the two words overlap one another. The distinction between the two words is sometimes said to be that **कौन** is appropriate for persons, **क्या** for things (and animals.). This is largely true, but does not appear to reach the essential difference in the use of the two words. The real distinction seems to be that **कौन** individualizes, **क्या** is more indefinite and groups things, *e. g.*, **कौन आया है,** *Who has come ?* **यह कौन पुस्तक**

है, *What book is this?* यह क्या पुस्तक है rather suggests, *What class of literature does this book belong to? What is it about?* कौन काम वह करे ग्रौर कौन यह, *What work shall that man do and what this?* But वे क्या काम कर रहे हैं, *What work are they doing?*

Sometimes क्या is very vague. हम क्या करें, *What can we do?* At times, it is more of an exclamation than an interrogation. क्या ख़ूब, *How good!* Now and again, it conveys a relative force. वह क्या करेगा कोई नहीं जानता, *What he will do no one knows.* Sometimes, in writing, it simply expresses what would be done by a tone in speaking, or by the "?," in English. In printing, simply वे ग्रावेंगे, would not necessarily mean a statement *or* a question; it might mean either. If the context does not indicate which should be understood and a question be intended, then the sentence should be क्या वे ग्रावेंगे, *Will they come?* At the present time, it might often appear as वे ग्रावेंगे.

The following idiomatic use of two क्या's (or more) may be noticed. क्या ग्राज क्या कल क्या दस बीस दिन के बाद वे ग्रवश्य ग्रावेंगे, *Whether to-day or to-morrow or after ten or twenty days, come they surely will.*

The occasional use of such phrases as काहे का,

काहे वास्ते, *Wherefore?* are certainly not classical. They do not come within the range of Grammar.

188. The Indefinite Pronouns कोई and कुछ.

The Indefinite Pronoun कोई is thus declined :--

Nom.	कोई, किसी ने
Cons. base.	किसी
Accus. & Dat.	किसी को
Instr. & Abl.	किसी से
Gen.	किसी का, की, के
Loc.	किसी में, पर

This Pronoun has no plural form. To express the pl. कोई is sometimes doubled. कोई कोई मनुष्य स्त्रीशिक्षा के प्रतिकूल हैं, *Some men are opposed to female education.* यूरोप के कोई कोई विद्वान कहते हैं, *Some of the learned men of Europe say.* In this pl. use of the word, there is no small distributive force.

Somewhat similar in sound and use is कई or कई एक, *Several.*

Very frequently two कोई's are used in following clauses, meaning, "one"..........."another." कोई अपने देश में रहे, कोई परदेश चले, *One may remain in his own country, one may go to another country.*

Sometimes the two कोई's are used in the same

sentence without a plural meaning, but distinctly distributive, उस पर किसी किसी सखी का मुँह कुछ कुछ लटक गया, *Whereupon the face of this or that one of her companions began to droop somewhat.*

Somewhat similar is the use of the two कोई's, with न in between. The meaning is then, exactly, *if not one, then another.* कोई न कोई करेगा, *Someone or the other will do it.*

कोई followed by a negative equals the Eng. *no one.* किसी ने उसको नहीं देखा, *No one saw him.*

189. *The Indefinite* कुछ.

कुछ as a Pronoun means practically *a part,* more generally, *a small part*; as an Adverb, *partly.* Although principally applied to a part of a mass of *material,* it may also be applied to parts of masses of men· कुछ in both cases signifies some part of the whole. (cf. the Eng. "the one part were Sadducees," "of the Pharisees' part," Acts 23 : 6, 9.)

उसको भी कुछ देना चाहिये, *Give some to him also.* कुछ मनुष्य स्वीकार करना चाहते थे, कुछ विरोधी थे, *A part of the men desired to accept* (*the terms*), *a part was averse* (*to doing so*).

The following uses may be noted: कुछ नहीं, *nothing.* कुछ भी नहीं, *nothing whatever.* कुछ कुछ, *a very little.* कुछ न कुछ, *a very little,* or, *something or other.*

COMPOUND PRONOUNS.

190. Two Pronouns used together, or one closely connected with some other Part of Speech, often yield very idiomatic and useful meanings. A few such combinations are appended.

जो कोई	*Whoever.* In the Oblique, **जिस किसी को,** etc.
जो कुछ	*Whatever.*
और कोई	*Another* (Additional).
कोई और	... (Somewhat adversative).

Similarly, with **और कुछ** and **कुछ और**

सब कोई	*All.*
हर कोई	*Each one. Every one.*
सब कुछ	*The whole.* **बहुत कुछ,** *A great amount of.*
कोई दो चार	*Some few.* (lit., some two or four.)

CHAPTER IX.

PRONOMINAL ADJECTIVES.

191. Pronominal Adjectives of Quantity. **परिमाणवाचक.**

Pronominal Adjectives of Quality. **सादृश्यवाचक.**

The Pronominal Adjectives are, as the name signifies, Adjectives formed from the Pronouns. In many instances, they are used alone, with a Noun understood; in such cases, they are declined as Nouns, otherwise as Adjectives of two terminations. In not a few instances, these words are distinctly Adverbial in their use.

The first series of these Pronominal Adjectives indicate Quantity or Number, the second Quality. Their initial letters are characteristic of their meaning, in the same way as those of Pronouns, referred to in section 182.

192.

		Quantity or Number.		Quality.
Proximate Demonstrative.	**इतना**	This much, or this number.	**ऐसा**	This-like.
Remote Demonstrative.	**उतना**	That much, or that number.	**वैसा**	That-like.
Relative.	**जितना**	As much as, or as many as.	**जैसा**	Which-like

Correlative. तितना So much, or so many. तैसा Such-like.

(Generally supplied by उतना and वैसा).

Interrogative. कितना How much? or How many? कैसा What-like?

(कितना and कैसा have sometimes a loose Relative meaning).

193. *Pronominal Adjectives of Quantity or Number.*

When Quantity (*How much*), is referred to, the singular generally suffices; for Number, the plural form is necessarily required.

आप इतना डरते क्यों हैं? *Why do you fear so much?* उसे कितना मिला? *How much did he obtain?* क्या! दिन भर ऐसा परिश्रम किया और अब इतना देते हो, *What! I've laboured so the whole day, and now you give me just this much.* जितना मिला उतना लेकर जाओ. *Take what you have received, and go.* जिसका जितना भाग्य होता है, फल भी उसे उतना ही मिलता है, *Just what measure is written in the fortune of any one, that measure of fruit he obtains.* कितने पर मिला? *How much did you obtain it for?* जितने योधा थे उतनों को हार खाकर अपने अपने देश लौटना पड़ा, *All the warriors there were being defeated had to return, each one to his own country.* कितनी पुस्तक होंगी, *How many books do you suppose there are?* केवल इतनी, *Only so many.*

Sometimes कितना is used in the way of exclamation rather than in that of interrogation. कितने ही क्यों न हों, तौभी संतुष्ट न होंगे, *No matter how many there may be, they will not be satisfied.*

In colloquial speech, कितने is occasionally contracted into कै, and जितने into जै, *e.g.*, कै दिन हुए, *How many days have elapsed?* जै दिन वे रहे, उतने दिन सुख आनन्द से बीते, *The days they remained there passed in great comfort and happiness.*

The Adverbial use of these Pronominal Adjectives will be referred to in the Chapter on the Adverbs.

194. *Pronominal Adjectives of Quality.* The Hindi name, सादृश्य, *like to*, correctly describes the general scope of the meaning of this second class of Pronominal Adjectives. वह कैसा मनुष्य है? *What sort of a man is he?* When the idea of manner or method is more prominent than that of resemblance, the words are more strictly Adverbs. Probably in more than half the occurrences of these words they are Adverbs, *e. g.*, उस ने ऐसा किया. Here the idea is not that *he did something like something else (understood)*, but that *he did something in such and such a way.* Here the idea is distinctly Adverbial. Something further will be written on this matter in the Chapter on the Adverbs. Here only the Adjectival use will be dealt with.

The following sentence affords a good illustration: **जो बात मैंने जैसी देखी है वैसी ही कहूँगा**, *I will tell the matter just as I saw it.* That the words **जैसी** and **वैसी** are Adjectives, is indicated by the fact that they agree in Gender with **बात.** Had the words been Adverbs, they would have appeared as **जैसे** and **वैसे**

जैसा वह, वैसा उसका भाई, बरन उसके घर के जितने हैं वे सब के सब वैसे ही हैं, *His brother is just like him, in fact, every member of his household is like him.* **जैसे बोनी, वैसे भरनी**, *As is the sowing, so is the gathering.* **यह कैसा घोड़ा है,** *What sort of a horse is this?* This sentence might also mean, *What a fine horse!*

ऐसों पर दया न करनी चाहिये, *It is not fitting to shew mercy to such* (men).

The following sentences present special, but not uncommon, idiomatic uses of these words :—

...... **जनक जैसे महात्मा के घर हुआ,** (*That her birth) took place in the house of such a mahatma as Janak.* **वे जैसे के तैसे तीन साल तक रक्खे रहे**, *They* (the notes for a book) *were laid aside just as they were for three years.* **सन्नाटा फिर जैसे का तैसा हुआ,** *There became again just such a silence (as there was before).* **ऐसी वैसी बातों में दिल बहलाता है,** *He diverts his mind in such things.* **भगवन्तिया ऐसी वैसी स्त्री नहीं**

थी, *Bhagawantiya was no common-place woman.*

तुम्हारे ऐसा मित्र, *Such a friend as you.*

195. **Other Pronominal Adjectives.** A few other words may be given which *may* be regarded as Pronominal Adjectives, though, strictly speaking, the "Pronominal" should be omitted.

एक ... एक	cf. Eng. *One says (one thing), one another).*
एक ... दूसरा	......*One says (this), another (that).*
और ... और	यह तो और वह और, *This is one thing, that is another.*
अमुक	*A certain one.* About equivalent to "*such and such an one.*"
अनेक	*Several.* Lit., "*more than one.*"
प्रत्येक	*All*, with distributive force, *each one, one by one.*
कई, कई एक	*Several.*
बहुत, बहुत	*Many.* So also बहुतेरे,
सब के सब	*All.* "*The whole lot.*"
सकल, समस्त	*All.* With a collective force.
सारा	*The whole.* Used also in the plural, सारे
समूचा	*The whole* (of a thing, in the sense of unbroken, undivided).
आदि, आदिक	*And the other, the rest.*
इत्यादि	*Ditto, etc.*

CHAPTER X.

THE VERB.

196. Verb ...	क्रिया		
Transitive Verb	सकर्मक क्रिया		
Intransitive ,,	अकर्मक	,,	
Active ,,	कर्तृप्रधान	,, , or	कर्तृवाच्य
Passive ,,	कर्मप्रधान	,, , or	कर्मवाच्य
Impersonal ,,	भावप्रधान	,, , or	भाववाच्य
Causal ,,	प्रेरणार्थक	,,	
Compound ,,	संयुक्त	,,	
Past, Future, Present.	भूत, भविष्यत्, वर्तमान		

Tense. काल (काल means "*time.*") There are no "Moods" in Hindi Grammar. Generally, any part of a Verb is referred to as such and such a क्रिया (Verb), not such and such a काल (Tense).

Stem. For this, धातु or मूल is commonly given. Hindi Grammarians have been very loose in dealing with this matter. They very often use these words to signify the form of the word, when the ना termination of the Infinitive has been cut off. This is, however, not the "root" of the Verb, but only the "*stem*." Thus for "stem," there is no suitable equivalent in use. The words used, **धातु** and **मूल,** should be retained for their true meaning, *viz.*, Etymological root.

Infinitive.

(**खाना,** *to eat*) **क्रियार्थक संज्ञा,** *i.e.*, A Noun which gives a Verbal meaning.

Imperfect Participle. (**खाता** or **खाता हुआ,** *eating.*) **क्रियाद्योतक संज्ञा,** *i.e.*, A Noun (or Adjective) which displays a Verbal idea.

Perfect Participle.

(**खाया** or **खाया हुआ,** *having eaten, or having been eaten.*)

कर्मवाचक संज्ञा, *i.e.*, A Noun (or Adjective), indicating the idea of the Passive Verb.

Some confusion exists with reference to the name and function, or functions, of this Participle. Some would give two names, **कर्तृवाचक रूप कृदन्त** and **कर्मवाचक रूप कृदन्त,** the 1st for the Past Part. of Intransitive Verbs, which have often an Active meaning, and the 2nd for the Past Part. of Transitive Verbs, which have frequently a Passive meaning. Note the possible difference between **खाया हुआ** and **खिलाया हुआ** or **किया हुआ**. The first is Active, the second frequently Passive.

Conjunctive Participle.

(खाकर, **etc.,** ***Having eaten*****)** **पूर्वकालिक,** **Indicating that which is past or completed.**

Noun of Agency.

(खानेवाला, ***An eater*****)** **कर्तृवाचक संज्ञा,** **The Noun indicating** ***the doer.***

Contingent Future.

(खाए, ***He may eat*****)** **सम्भाव्य भविष्यत्,** **That which may possibly happen. A Contingent Future.**

Absolute Future.

(खाएगा, ***He will eat*****)** **सामान्य भविष्यत्,** **Ordinary Future.**

Imperative.

(खा, ***Eat*****)** **विधि,** **Injunction, command.**

Indefinite Imperfect.

(खाता, ***he eats*****)** **No general Hindi equivalent current.**

Indefinite Perfect.

(खाया, ***he ate*****)** **सामान्य भूत,** **Ordinary Past.**

Present Imperfect.

(खाता है, ***He is eating*****)** **सामान्य वर्तमान,** **Ordinary Present.**

Present Perfect.

(खाया है, ***He has eaten*****)** **आसन्न भूत,** **Proximate Past.**

Past Imperfect.

(खाता था,	*He was eating*)	अपूर्ण भूत, Incomplete Past.

Past Perfect.

(खाया था,	*He had eaten*)	पूर्ण भूत, Completed Past.

Contingent Imperfect.

(खाता हो,	*Should he be eating*)	सम्भाव्य वर्तमान, Possible Present.

Contigent Perfect.

(खाया हो,	*Should he have eaten*)	सम्भाव्यभूत, Possible Past.

Presumptive Imperfect.

(खाता होगा,	*He must be eating*)	संदिग्ध वर्तमान, Doubtful Present.

Presumptive Perfect.

(खाया होगा,	*He must have eaten*)	संदिग्ध भूत, Doubtful Past.

Past Contigent Imperfect.

(खाता होता,)	*Were he (at some past time) eating*)	अपूर्ण हेतुहेतुमद्भूत, Incomplete cause & effect Past.

Past Contigent Perfect.

(खाया होता,)	*Had he eaten*)	पूर्ण हेतुहेतुमद्भूत, Completed cause & effect Past.

197. PARADIGMS.

For future reference, Paradigms of the conjugation of some typical verbs will be given.

1. The two special Tenses of the Substantive Verb "to be."

2. Full Paradigm of the Verb होना, *to become.*

3. do. do. Intransitive Verb चलना, *to move, to go.* Stem ending in a consonant.

4. Concerning the Transitive Verb देखना, *to see.* Stem ending in a consonant.

5. do. Intransitive Verb आना, *to come.* Open stem, *i.e.,* ending in a vowel.

6. do. Transitive Verb दिखाना, *to shew.* Open stem.

7. do. do. देना, *to give.* Open stem.

8. do. do. करना, *to do.* Stem ending in a consonant.

9. Concerning the Passive Verb. **किया जाना,** *to be done.*

198. In reference to these Paradigms, a few explanatory notes are furnished.

1. **होना,** in the sense of "*to become,*" is complete in all its parts. This Verb serves, generally, also as the Substantive Verb "*to be,*" "*to exist*;" but for this latter, two special additional Tenses exist which do not appertain to **होना,** in the sense of "*to become.*" These two Tenses are a Present **है,** *he is* : **था,** *he was.* These are not interchangeable with the two corresponding Tenses of **होना,** *to become,* which are **होता है**, *he becomes* ; **होता था,** *he was becoming.*

है and **था** and certain parts of the verb **होना** are used as Auxiliaries in the conjugation of other Verbs.

2. It is worthy of notice that throughout the Tenses the 2nd and 3rd person singular are exactly the same in form, also the 1st and 3rd plural.

3. In some Grammars, 1st and 3rd persons are given under the Imperative. This appears to be incorrect. The Imperative can be used only in the 2nd person. The nearest approach to an imperative for the 1st or 3rd person is "*let me do so and so,*" "*let him do so and so.*" This is not Imperative but Optative, and the

forms of the Contingent Future meet the need. To print these forms a second time, under the Imperative, is misleading.

The only approach to a 3rd person under the Imperative are the special "respective" forms provided to use with the honorific आप. This has the 3rd person in construction, but with the meaning of the 2nd person.

4. In the Paradigms, the English translation is only given for one person, and that the 3rd person, this often being more simple and more commonly in use than the 1st person. The student will know that if the 3rd person be "he will go," the 1st and 2nd sing. and pl. will be "*I will go,*" etc., etc.

5. Full Paradigms are only given for होना and चलना. In the case of other Verbs, only the differences from the normal forms are referred to. As a matter of fact, the conjugation of the Hindi Verb is exceedingly simple, offering comparatively few exceptions to the general norm.

6. The so-called Adverbial Participle (चलते ही, *upon* (*his*) *going*, or some similar meaning) is not included in the Paradigms. This is merely one use of the Imperfect Participle, and has no claim for demanding separate mention in the Paradigm of the Verb.

199. (1). The two Tenses of the Substantive Verb "*to be.*"

Present.

	Singular.		Plural.	
1.	मैं हूँ	I am.	हम हैं	We are.
2.	तू है	Thou art.	तुम हो	You are.
3.	वह है	He is.	वे हैं	They are.

Past. He was.

1.	मैं था,	fem. थी	हम थे,	fem. थीं
2.	तू था	... थी	तुम थे	... थीं
3.	वह था	... थी	वे थे	... थीं

200. (2). The Verb होना, *to become.* This Verb is also used, in many of its parts, as the Substantive Verb "*to be.*"

Infinitive होना, *to become.*

Imperfect Participle. होता (fem. होती; pl. masc. होते,) *he who is becoming.*

Perfect Participle. हुआ (fem. हुई; masc. pl. हुए), *he who has become.*

Conjunctive Participle. हो, होकर, होके हो करके,* *having become.*

---

* Throughout these Paradigms, many alternative forms are given. Generally speaking, the earlier forms are the most common and the best approved. Each alternative form is not always repeated in each Tense and in each Paradigm, but in corresponding Tenses, etc., it may be understood.

Noun of Agency. होनेवाला, होनेहारा, होनेहार, होनहार (*f*...वाली, etc.), *he who is about to become.*

Tenses formed from the stem (हो).

Contingent Future. He may become.

1. मैं होऊँ	1. हम हों, होवें, होएँ, होंय
2. तू } हो, होए, होय,	2. तुम हो or होओ
3. वह } होवे	3. वे हों, होवें, होएँ, होयँ

Absolute Future. He will become.

1. मैं हूँगा, होऊँगा (*f*. गी)	1. हम होंगे, होएँगे, होवेंगे, होयँगे (*f*. गी)
2. तू } होगा, होएगा, होयगा, हो-	2. तुम होगे, होओगे (*f*. गी)
3. वह } वेगा (*f*. गी)	3. हम होंगे, होएँगे, होवेंगे, होयँगे (*f*. गी)

Imperative. Become.

2. तू हो	2. तुम हो

Respectful forms used as 3rd pl. with the honorific आप, हूजिये, हूजियेगा, हूजियो

TENSES FORMED FROM THE IMPERFECT AND PERFECT PARTICIPLES.

Indefinite Imperfect. *He becomes.*

1. 2. 3. मैं, तू, वह, होता (*f*. होती)	1. 2. 3. हम, तुम, वे, होते (*f*. होतीं)

Indefinite Perfect. He became.

	Singular		Plural
1. 2. 3.	मैं, तू, वह, हुआ (*f.* हुई)	1. 2. 3.	हम, तुम, वे, हुए (*f.* हुईं)

Present Imperfect. He is becoming.

	Singular		Plural
1.	मैं होता हूँ (*f.* होती हूँ)	1.	हम होते हैं (*f.* होती हैं)
2.	तू } होता है (*f.* होती है)	2.	तुम होते हो (*f.* होती हो)
3.	वह }	3.	वे होते हैं (*f.* होती हैं)

Present Perfect. He has become.

	Singular		Plural
1.	मैं हुआ हूँ (*f.* हुई हूँ)	1.	हम हुए हैं (*f.* हुई हैं)
2.	तू } हुआ है (*f.* हुई है)	2.	तुम हुए हो (*f.* हुई हो)
3.	वह }	3.	वे हुए हैं (*f.* हुई हैं)

Past Imperfect. He was becoming.

	Singular		Plural
1. 2. 3.	मैं, तू, वह, होता था (*f.* होती थी)	1. 2. 3.	हम, तुम, वे, होते थे (*f.* होती थीं)

Past Perfect. He had become.

	Singular		Plural
1. 2. 3.	मैं, तू, वह, हुआ था (*f.* हुई थी)	1. 2. 3.	हम, तुम, वे, हुए थे (*f.* हुई थीं)

The next six Tenses are given in Hindi; but no English translation is attempted. It seems impossible to give a bald translation of some of these Tenses which will yield any clear meaning, though in actual composition these Tenses, even in the Verb "*to become*," become distinctly possible, *e.g.*, take such a sentence as the following: **यदि वह यहाँ हुआ होता, तो उसे अवश्य दण्ड भोगना पड़ा होता,** *Had he been here, he would surely have had to endure punishment.*

Contingent Imperfect.

Singular	Plural
1. मैं होता होऊँ (*f.* होती होऊँ)	1. हम होते हों (*f.* होती हों)
2. तू } होता हो or होए, etc. (*f.* होती हो)	2. तुम होते हो or होओ (*f.* होती हो)
3. वह }	3. वे होते हों (*f.* होती हों)

Contingent Perfect.

Singular	Plural
1. मैं हुआ होऊँ (*f.* हुई होऊँ)	1. हम हुए हों (*f.* हुई हों)
2. तू } हुआ हो (*f.* हुई हो)	2. तुम हुए हो (*f.* हुई हो)
3. वह }	3. वे हुए हों (*f.* हुई हों)

Presumptive Imperfect.

Singular	Plural
1. मैं होता हूँगा (*f.* होती हूँगी)	1. हम होते होंगे (*f.* होती होंगी)

2. तू 3. वह	होता होगा (*f.* होती होगी)	2. तुम होते होगे (*f.* होती होगी) 3. वे होते होंगे (*f.* होती होंगी)

Presumptive Perfect.

1. मैं	हुआ हूँगा (*f.* हुई हूँगी)	1. हम हुए होंगे (*f.* हुई होंगी)
2. तू 3. वह	हुआ होगा (*f.* हुई होगी)	2. तुम हुए होगे (*f.* हुई होगी) 3. वे हुए होंगे (*f.* हुई होंगी)

Past Contingent Imperfect.

1. मैं 2. तू 3. वह	होता होता (*f.* होती होती)	1. हम 2. तुम 3. वे	होते होते (*f.* होती होतीं)

Past Contingent Perfect.

1. मैं 2. तू 3. वह	हुआ होता (*f.* हुई होती)	1. हम 2. तुम 3. वे	हुए होते (*f.* हुई होतीं)

201. (3) *Intransitive Verb* **चलना**, *to move, to go*

Stem ending in consonant.

Infinitive. **चलना**

Imperfect Participle. **चलता** or **चलता हुआ** (*f.* **चलती**; m. pl. **चलते**)

Perfect Participle. चला, or चला हुआ (*f.* चली; m. pl. चले)

Conjunctive Participle. चल, चलकर, चलकरके, चलके

Noun of Agency चलनेवाला, चलनेहारा (*f.* चलनेवाली)

Tenses formed from the stem (चल)

Contingent Future. *He may move* or *go.*

1. मैं	चलूँ	1. हम	चलें
2. तू	चले	2. तुम	चलो
3. वह	चले	3. वे	चलें

Absolute Future. *He will move* or *go.*

1. मैं	चलूँगा (*f.* चलूँगी)	1. हम	चलेंगे (*f.* चलेंगी)
2. तू	चलेगा (*f.* चलेगी)	2. तुम	चलोगे (*f.* चलोगी)
3. वह	चलेगा (*f.* चलेगी)	3. वे	चलेंगे (*f.* चलेंगी)

Imperative. *Move* or *go.*

2. चल 2. चलो

Respectful forms used as 3rd pl. with the honorific आप. चलिये, चलियेगा, चलियेा

Tenses formed from the Imperfect and Perfect Participles.

Indefinite Imperfect. *He moves* or *goes.*

1. मैं	चलता (*f.* चलती)	1. हम	चलते (*f.* चलतीं)
2. तू	चलता (*f.* चलती)	2. तुम	चलते (*f.* चलतीं)
3. वह	चलता (*f.* चलती)	3. वे	चलते (*f.* चलतीं)

Indefinite Perfect. *He moved* or *went.*

Singular		Plural	
1. मैं	चला (*f.* चली)	1. हम	चले (*f.* चलीं)
2. तू		2. तुम	
3. वह		3. वे	

Present Imperfect. *He is moving* or *going.*

Singular		Plural	
1. मैं	चलता हूँ (*f.* चलती हूँ)	1. हम	चलते हैं (*f.* चलती हैं)
2. तू	चलता है (*f.* चलती है)	2. तुम	चलते हो (*f.* चलती हो)
3. वह		3. वे	चलते हैं (*f.* चलती हैं)

Present Perfect. *He has moved* or *gone.*

Singular		Plural	
1. मैं	चला हूँ (*f.* चली हूँ)	1. हम	चले हैं (*f.* चली हैं)
2. तू	चला है (*f.* चली है)	2. तुम	चले हो (*f.* चली हो)
3. वह		3. वे	चले हैं (*f.* चली हैं)

Past Imperfect. *He was moving* or *going.*

Singular		Plural	
1. मैं	चलता था (*f.* चलती थी)	1. हम	चलते थे (*f.* चलती थीं)
2. तू		2. तुम	
3. वह		3. वे	

Past Perfect. *He had moved* or *gone.*

Singular		Plural	
1. मैं	चला था (*f.* चली थी)	1. हम	चले थे (*f.* चली थीं)
2. तू		2. तुम	
3. वह		3. वे	

Contingent Imperfect. *Should he be moving or going.*

1. मैं चलता होऊँ (*f.* चलती होऊँ)
2. तू } चलता हो or होये
3. वह } (*f.* चलती हो)

1. हम चलते हों or होएँ, etc. (*f.* चलती हों)
2. तुम चलते हो or होओ (*f.* चलती हो)
3. वे चलते हों (*f.* चलती हों)

Contingent Perfect. *Should he have moved or gone.*

1. मैं चला होऊँ (*f.* चली होऊँ)
2. तू } चला हो or होए
3. वह } (*f.* चली हो)

1. हम चले हों, etc. (*f.* चली हों)
2. तुम चले हो, etc. (*f.* चली हो)
3. वे चले हों, etc. (*f.* चली हों)

Presumptive Imperfect. *He will be moving or going.*

1. मैं चलता हूँगा (*f.* चलती हूँगी)
2. तू } चलता होगा
3. वह } (*f.* चलती होगी)

1. हम चलते होंगे (*f.* चलती होंगी)
2. तुम चलते होगे (*f.* चलती होगी)
3. वे चलते होंगे (*f.* चलती होंगी)

Presumptive perfect. *He will have moved* or *gone.*

Singular	Plural
1. मैं चला हूँगा (*f.* चली हूँगी)	1. हम चले होंगे (*f.* चली होंगी)
2. तू, 3. वह } चला होगा (*f.* चली होगी)	2. तुम चले होगे (*f.* चली होगी)
	3. वे चले होंगे (*f.* चली होंगी)

Past Contingent Imperfect. *Should he have been moving* or *going.*

Singular	Plural
1. मैं, 2. तू, 3. वह } चलता होता (*f.* चलती होती)	1. हम, 2. तुम, 3. वे } चलते होते (*f.* चलती होतीं)

Past Contingent Perfect. *Should he have moved* or *gone.*

Singular	Plural
1. मैं, 2. तू, 3. वह } चला होता (*f.* चली होती)	1. हम, 2. तुम, 3. वे } चले होते (*f.* चली होतीं)

202. (4) Transitive Verb **देखना,** *to see.* Stem ending in a consonant.

The only parts of a Transitive Verb differing from an Intransitive Verb having a similar stem, are the six Tenses formed from the Perfect Participle.

Something further will be explained about the rules of agreement between these Tenses of Transitive Verbs and their Accusatives, when the Nominative with **ने** is used, later on. For the present, the following statement may suffice.

When the Nom. with **ने** be used and the Accusative with **को**, then we have the following forms for the Tenses under consideration :—

Indefinite Perfect	**मैंने, तूने, उसने, हमने, तुम्होंने, उन्होंने.**	.... **को देखा**
Present Perfect	do. do. do. ...	**को देखा है**
Past Perfect	do. do. do. ...	**को देखा था**
Contingent Perfect	do. do. do. ...	**को देखा हो**
Presumptive Perfect	do. do. do. ...	**को देखा होगा**
Past Contingent Perf.	do. do. do. ...	**को देखा होता**

If the Accusative without **को** be used, that is, the Nominative form, then the Verb will agree with it in Gender and Number. **उस ने देखा, उस ने देखी, उस ने देखे**, and so on, to **उन्होंने देखा होता, देखी होती, देखे होते**, etc., etc.

203. (5). Intransitive Verb **आना**, *to come.* Open stem.

Infinitive **आना**

Imperfect Participle **आता**

Perfect Participle **आया**

Conjunctive Participle **आकर, आ, आकरके, आके**

Noun of Agency **आनेवाला,** etc.

Tenses from the Stem **(आ)**

Contingent Future **आवे,** *he may come.*

	Singular		Plural
1.	**मैं आऊँ**	1.	**हम आएँ, आवें, आयँ**
2.	**तू** } **आए, आय, आवे**	2.	**तुम आओ**
3.	**वह** } **आए, आय, आवे**	3.	**वे आएँ, आवें, आयँ**

Absolute Future. *He will come.*

	Singular		Plural
1.	**मैं आऊँगा** (*f.* **आऊँगी**)	1.	**हम आएँगे, आवेंगे,** (*f.* **आएँ, आवेंगी**)
2.	**तू** } **आएगा, आवेगा, आयगा** (*f.* **आए, आवे, आयगी**)	2.	**तुम आओगे** (*f.* **आओगी**)
3.	**वह** } **आएगा, आवेगा, आयगा** (*f.* **आए, आवे, आयगी**)	3.	**वे आएँगे, आवेंगे, आयँगे** (*f.* **आएँ, आवें, आयँगी**)

Imperative.

	Singular		Plural
2.	**आ**	2.	**आओ**

Respectful forms, used as 3rd pl., with the honorific **आप. आइये, आइयेगा, आइयो**

Tenses formed from the Imperfect and Perfect Participles.

The six Tenses formed from the Imperfect Participle **आता** are in every respect the same as those of **चलना,** already given. The six Tenses formed from the Perfect Participle are as follows:—

Indefinite Perfect. *He came.*

Singular	Plural
1. 2. 3. आया (*f.* आयी)	1. 2. 3. आये, आए (*f.* आयीं, आईं)

Present Perfect. *He has come.*

Singular	Plural
1. मैं आया हूँ (*f.* आयी हूँ, or आई हूँ)	1. हम आये हैं (*f.* आयी हैं)
2. तू } आया है (*f.* आई है)	2. तुम आये हो (*f* आयी हो)
3. वह }	3. वे आये हैं (*f.* आयी हैं)

Past Perfect. *He had come.*

Singular	Plural
1. 2. 3. आया था (*f.* आयी थी)	1. 2. 3. आये थे (*f.* आयी थीं)

Contingent Perfect. *Should he have come.*

Singular	Plural
1. मैं आया होऊँ (*f.* आयी होऊँ)	1. हम आये हों, etc. (*f.* आयी, or आई हों)
2. तू } आया हो or होए (*f.* आई हो)	2. तुम आये हो (*f.* आयी, or आई हो)
3. वह }	3. वे आये हैं (*f.* आयी, or आई हैं)

Presumptive Perfect. *He will have come.*

Singular	Plural
1. मैं आया हूँगा (*f.* आयी हूँगी)	1 हम आये होंगे (*f.* आयी होंगीं)

2. तू	आया होगा (f. आयी होगी)	2. तुम आये होगे (f. आयी होगी)	
3. वह		3. वे आये होंगे (f. आयी होंगी)	

Past Contingent Perfect. *Had he come.*

1. 2. 3. आया होता (f. आयी होती) 1. 2. 3. आये होते, (f. आयी होतीं)

204. The very common Verb, जाना, *to go*, is conjugated in the same way as आना, with the exception that the PerfectP articiple is irregularly formed, being गया, instead of जाया, as might be expected.

The six Tenses formed from the Perfect Participle are, of course, all affected by this, and we have गया, गया है, गया था, etc.

205. (6). Transitive verb दिखाना, to shew. Open stem.

This corresponds with the conjugation of आना, except in the six Tenses formed from the Perfect Participle. These are conjugated in the same way as the same Tenses in देखना (No. 4.), the Perfect Participle being दिखाया.

206. (7). Transitive Verb देना, *to give*. Open stem, ending in ए.

The closing vowel of the stem, *viz.*, ए, leads to some modifications. These modifications are noted below:—

Perfect Participle दिया.

Contingent Future. *He may give.*

1. मैं	दूँ, देऊँ	1. हम	दें, देवें
2. तू	दे, देवे	2. तुम	दो, देओ
3. वह	दे, देवे	3. वे	दें, देवें

Absolute Future. *He will give.*

1. मैं	दूँगा, देऊँगा (*f.* दूँ, देऊँगी)	1. हम	देंगे, देवेंगे (*f.* दें, देवेंगी)
2. तू	देगा, देवेगा (*f.* दे, देवेगी)	2. तुम	दोगे, देओगे (*f.* दो देओगी)
3. वह	देगा, देवेगा (*f.* दे, देवेगी)	3. वे	देंगे, देवेंगे (*f.* दें, देवेंगी)

Imperative. *Give.*

2. दे	2. दो, देओ

Respectful forms, used as 3rd pl., with the honorific आप. दीजिये, दीजियेगा, दीजियेा

The six Tenses formed from the Imperfect Participle देता, are quite regular.

The six from the Perfect Participle follow the same rules as apply to corresponding Tenses in देखा (No. 4.), excepting that the Perfect Participle is दिया, fem. दी, pl. दीं; plural masc. दिये.

207. (8). Transitive Verb करना, *To do.*

This Verb, though the stem ends in a consonant, like देखना, differs in the formation of its Perfect Participle, and respectful forms of the Imperative. The Perfect Participle is किया.

Imperative.

2. कर 2. करो

Respectful forms, used as 3rd pl., with the honorific आप. कीजिये, कीजियेगा, कीजियो

The six Tenses formed from the Past Participle are conjugated in the same way as those of दिया.

208. (9). The Passive Verb. The Passive Verb is formed by adding जाना to the Perfect Participle of the Active Verb. Thus देखना, *to see*, becomes देखा जाना, *to be seen*. It is conjugated exactly the same as जाना (see Sections 204 and 203). The form of the Participle changes with the change of the जाना, as regards Gender and Number. Thus देखा जाऊँ, देखी जाऊँ, देखे जाएँ, देखी जाएँ, देखा जाता है, देखी जाती है, देखे जाते हैं, etc.

209. CLASSIFICATION OF VERBS.

1. **Classification according to meaning and usage.**

The first point to engage our attention is this classification, according to the general scope of the meaning and uses. There are, at the very least, the following classes :—

(1) Transitive. (2) Intransitive. (3) Neuter. (4) Passive-Neuter. (5) Impersonal. (6) Passive. (7) Causal. (8) Compound.

(1). Transitive (सकर्मक). This class needs no special explanation. They are Active Verbs which require an object or Accusative (expressed or understood) to complete their meaning, *e.g.*, **तोड़ना,** *to break*; **फाड़ना,** *to tear*; **देखना,** *to see.* Apart from something to break, to tear, or to see, there can be little meaning of such words in a sentence.

(2). Intransitive **(अकर्मक)**. This name gives one particular phase of the classification, *viz*., that it has no object or Accusative. It may, however, be that the Verb indicates activity on the part of the Subject, *e.g.*, **वह उठा है,** *he has risen*; or, there may be involved a merely passive state, as **वह जीता है,** *he lives*; **उसका सिर पिराता है,** *his head is aching.*

(3). Neuter. A Neuter Verb is not only intransitive, but, strictly speaking, implies a state for which the subject is not responsible on account of any activity of his, *e.g.*, **वह सोता है,** *he is sleeping*; **वह वहाँ पड़ा है,** *It is lying there.*

(4). Passive-Neuter. The Verbs belonging to this class must be dealt with in a separate section, as they play a very important part in Hindi. They are Neuter, they are also truly Passive, but in structure and force distinctly differ from the ordinary Passive Verbs.

(5). Impersonal **(भावप्रधान क्रिया)**. Though this is not a very numerous class, it is of real importance.

and has special features. It demands a paragraph to itself, and one is given later on.

(6). Passive Verbs. These are much used in Hindi. They correspond very much with Passive Verbs in English, and require little notice. What would be the Object, with an Active Verb, becomes the Subject, and what would be the Subject, is thrown into the Instrumental Case, **करण**, *e.g.*, Act. **भगवानप्रसाद ने घर को देखा**, *Bhagawan Prashad saw the house*, becomes, **घर भगवानप्रसाद से देखा गया**, *The house was seen by Bhagawan Prashad.*

(7). Causal Verbs. These Verbs constitute a very large class, and will need careful and full treatment later. These Causal Verbs convey the idea of causing that to be done which is expressed by the simple Verbs from which they are formed. In English, we say, *The child eats, The mother feeds the child*; or, *The child fell, A man threw the child down*; or, *A man caused the child to fall.* In Hindi, the Causal Verbs meet all such cases in a very neat and effective way, *e.g.*, **लड़का रोटी खाता है**, *The child eats bread.* **मा लड़के को रोटी खिलाती है**, *The mother feeds the child with bread.* **लड़का गिरा**, *The child fell.* **एक मनुष्य ने लड़के को गिराया**, *A man caused the child to fall.*

(8). Compound Verbs. These are very numerous in

Hindi, and are made up in various ways. This matter also must receive full treatment later on.

210. 2. Classification according to form. The conjugation of the Hindi Verb is remarkably simple and regular. Apart from the changes effected in the structure of those six Tenses which are from the Perfect Participle, the irregularities are very few. Even in the case of the Passive Voice, the endings of all the parts are quite regular, conforming closely to the Active Verb.

As, however, some modifications do occur in the conjugation of certain Verbs, owing very largely to the final letter of the stem, some classification seems to be called for. The following division appears to fairly cover the ground :—

	Verb.	Stem ending in—	Example.	Paradigm.
1.	Intransitive	a consonant	चलना	3
2.	Transitive	do.	देखना	4
3.	Intransitive	a vowel	आना	5
4.	Transitive	do.	दिखाना	6
5.	General	the vowels ए, ई, ओ, ऊ.	देना	7
6.	Irregular	होना, जाना, करना, मरना	... ...	1.2.5.8.

7. Passive ... ... खोला 9
8. Passive-Neuter ... ... खुल जाना 9

Spread out in this way, the list may appear somewhat formidable; but any such impression will be dissipated on an examination of the very slight differences in the structure of the various classes given.

The only difference between 1 and 2 is that effected in the six Tenses formed from the Perfect Participle. Nos. 3 and 4 only differ from Nos. 1 and 2 in the formation of the Perfect Participle, या being added to the stem, instead of आ alone.

Under 5, the list of Verbs is not large. देना, *to give*; लेना, *to take*; खेना (or खेवना), *to row*; पीना, *to drink*; सीना, *to sew*; जीना, *to live*, रोना, *to cry*; सोना, *to sleep*; बोना, *to sow*; खोना, *to lose*; धोना, *to wash*; ढोना, *to carry*; छूना, *to touch*. These are probably nearly all the Verbs to be included in this class. Such modifications as occur, are few and simple. These modifications are mainly in the formation of the Perfect Participle.

In देना and लेना, we have दिया and लिया for the Perfect Participle; and in those parts of the Verb where the stem is followed by a vowel, the ए of the stem and the following vowel are compounded into one vowel. Thus, instead of देऊँगा, *i.e.*, दे, ऊँगा, we have often दूँगा; so दोगे for देओगे, etc. See Paradigm No. 7.

In खेना, the ए is not changed in this way, but remains ए. Frequently, the form खेवना for this Verb is used, in which case it comes under the rules for the conjugation of a Verb, the stem of which ends in a consonant.

Verbs, the stems of which end in ई, have the ई shortened into इ and a य inserted between this इ and the following आ, in the formation of the Perfect Participle. Thus पीना, पिया; जीना, जीया (not always shortened). The other parts are regular.

With Verbs, the stems of which end in ओ, a य is inserted between the final ओ of the stem and the आ, in the formation of the Perfect Participle. Thus रोना becomes रोया; सोना, सोया, etc. Here also the other parts of the Verb are conjugated regularly.

With छूना, the vowel ऊ is shortened in the formation of the Perf. Part.; thus we have छुआ.

The four Verbs mentioned under No. 6 are not very irregular. The full paradigm for होना is given (Paradigm Nos. 1 & 2). Particulars concerning जाना will be found under Paradigm No. 5 and Sect. 204. Those concernnig करना, under No. 8 Paradigm. मरना becomes मुआ for the Perf. Part. In the case of both करना and मरना, the forms करा and मरा are in use as well as किया and मुआ. This is especially true of मरा.

The conjugation of the Passive Verb has been already referred to under Paradigm No. 9.

When the Passive-Neuter Verbs have the जाना combined with them (and they very largely do), then they are conjugated in all respects in the same way as the Passive Verbs. The only difference between these and the Passive Verbs arises before there is any question of the conjugation of them. The Verbs come up for conjugation in a different form, *e.g.*, खुल जाना and खोला जाना ; उठ जाना and उठाया जाना. When जाना is not used with one of these Passive-Neuters, then it is conjugated as an ordinary Intransitive Verb, *e.g.*, खुलता है, खुला था, खुलेगा, etc., etc.

211. It will be noticed that the great majority of Verbs have a stem consisting of only one consonant and its vowel, or this plus one additional consonant. Thus गा—, खा—, पा—, पी—, ले; चल—, लग—, भाग,— बीत—, गिर—, etc., to which the ना is added to form the Infinitive. Some stems, however, have three consonants, *e.g.*, **टहलना,** *to walk to and fro* ; **छिटकना,** *to be strewed* ; **पुकारना,** *to call out* ; **बहलाना,** *to amuse, divert* ; **धकेलना,** *to push.* There is also quite a large class of Causal Verbs which have a second vowel (**आ**) added to the original stem. Thus **लगना, लगाना ; उठना, उठाना ; चलना, चलाना.** Sometimes an additional consonant is brought in : **खाना, खिलाना ; सोना, सुलाना.**

VERB : MOODS, TENSES, NUMBER, PERSON, GENDER.

212. *Moods.* That Moods are represented in Hindi, cannot be questioned, but the Tenses are not arranged with reference to any Moods, and there is in Hindi no equivalent for the word. The matter may therefore be dismissed from consideration.

Tenses. In Hindi, there is a term, **काल,** which corresponds in meaning with the English " Tense," but the word is not largely used. A Tense is generally referred to by the word **क्रिया,** *Verb.* Thus we have such terms as " *Imperative Verb, Possible-Future Verb, Absolute-Future* Verb, etc.

The order and nomenclature of the Tenses adopted is that found in Dr. Kellogg's Grammar, with the exception that, whereas Dr. Kellogg gives first the 6 Tenses formed from the Imperfect Participle and then the six formed from the Perfect Participle, the twelve Tenses are here given in six pairs, Indefinite Imperfect, Indefinite Perfect, etc. The names given to the Tenses well represent the functions of the respective Tenses, though for each one no single name could be found which would fully indicate the scope of its use.

Number, Person and Gender. The Hindi Verb has two Numbers, singular and plural; three Persons: and two Genders, masculine and feminine. In most parts of the Verb, the form is affected by Number, Person and Gender; but in some parts, the influence of one or more of these does not affect the form: *e.g.* The Infinitive may be affected by Gender and Number, but not by Person. The Contingent Future is affected by Person and Number, but not by Gender; so with the Imperative. The Conjunctive Participle is not affected by any of the three.

Attention is again called to the fact that the 2nd and 3rd Persons singular of each Tense assume the same form, also the 1st and 3rd plural. In the 6 Tenses, Indefinite Imperfect and Perfect, Past Imperfect and Perfect and the Past Contingent Imperfect and Perfect, all three persons of the singular are the same, likewise the three persons of the plural.

Generally, the subject of the Verb, is expressed by a Noun, Pronoun or some equivalent, but, in certain sentences, may be omitted, the person being indicated by the form of the Verb or by the context, *e.g.*, the English, "*Will you go? I will go,*" may be in Hindi **जाओगे? हाँ, जाऊँगा,** thus omitting both "*you*" and "*I.*"

213. *Tenses formed from the Perfect Participle, and the Nominative with* **ने.** This subject has already been referred to in sections 95 and 202. The construction only affects Transitive Verbs, and of these only the six Tenses in which the form assumed by the Perfect Participle occurs, *viz*:—

Indefinite Perfect, **देखा.** Present Perfect, **देखा है,** Past Perfect, **देखा था,** Contingent Perfect, **देखा हो,** Presumptive Perfect, **देखा होगा,** and Past Contingent Perfect, **देखा होता.**

No attempt will here be made to account for the origin of this peculiar construction. It may be that the Verb is, in this construction, really passive, and that what would ordinarily be the Nominative Case becomes the Agentive, and what would have been the Accusative is changed into the Nominative, and remains Accusative, or is the Dative. For all practical purposes, however, it may be understood that what was the Nominative with the other Tenses, remains still the Nominative, though with a special form, *viz.*, the addition of ने.

Sir George Grierson points out to me, and Dr. Kellogg takes the same view, that these Tenses have been formed from the Sanskrit Past Participle, and that the construction found came over with them from the Sanskrit into Hindi. In Hindi, however, the Passive force of the Participle appears to have been lost in these Tenses, and, on the whole, for practical purposes, it is simpler to treat this construction, as has been indicated above.

With these six Tenses, the use of this construction of the Nominative with ने is compulsory, but there is a choice in dealing with the Accusative. (1) the form with को may be used, in which case the Verb retains the form of the 3rd person, sing. masc. throughout, quite unaffected by the Gender, Number or Person of either subject or object, or, (2) the form of the Accusative without को (or, as some would prefer to say, the Nominative), may be used, and then the Verb will agree with this in Gender and Number.

Thus, whether the Nom. be मैंने, तूने, उसने; हमने तुमने, उन्होंने (or their equivalents), the form of the

Verb is quite unaffected, but will agree with the Accusative without को in Gender and Number, thus :—

... ने घर देखा, देखा है, देखा था, देखा हो, देखा होगा, देखा होता ॥

... ने पुस्तक देखी, देखी है, देखी थी, देखी हो, देखी होगी, देखी होती ॥

... ने घर (pl.) देखे, देखे हैं, देखे थे, etc.

... ने पुस्तकें देखीं, देखी हैं, देखी थीं, etc.

By the alternative construction, these would all be देखा. Thus... ने घर को देखा, etc. : पुस्तक को देखा; घरों को देखा, पुस्तकों को देखा.

As regards choice of these alternative constructions, nothing more definite can be stated than was given in considering the choice of the two alternative forms of the Accusative, in section 97.

214. There are just a few Verbs, with reference to which some uncertainty exists, as to whether this special construction should be used or not. One of these is समझना. Sometimes the ने is used, sometimes not, *e.g.*, मैं नहीं समझा, *I did not understand.* तुमने समझा नहीं, *You did not understand.*

With the following Verbs, this construction is not used, *viz.*—

बकना, *to chatter.* **बोलना,** *to make a sound, to speak.*

भूलना, *to forget.* **जनना,** *to give birth to.*

लाना, *to bring.* **लेजाना,** *to take.*

This last is not one Verb, but parts of two; it is the Verb **जाना,** preceded by the Conjunctive Participle of **लेना.** Thus, **वह लड़के को ले गया,** *He took off the boy,* is **वह लड़के को लेकर गया,** written in a contracted form. In the case of **लाना,** we have a similar construction, with this difference, however, that, whereas the construction of the rest of the sentence has been retained, the form of the Verb has been contracted in all its parts from **ले + आना** to **लाना.**

With reference to the two Compound Verbs... **ने देना,** *e.g.*, **करने देना** (Permissive Verbs), and... **ने पाना,** *e.g.*, **करने पाना** (Acquisitive Verbs), it should be noted that, in one case, this construction comes into use, in the other, not. With **देना,** the **ने** is used, but not with **पाना.** Thus **उसने उसको जाने दिया,** *He permitted him to go*; but **वह उसको देखने न पाया,** *He did not get a look at him.*

GENERAL VIEW OF THE TENSES.

215. *The Stem.* The Stem of the Verb is obtained by cutting off the ना of the Infinitive. Thus the stems of देखना, करना, देना, जाना are देख, कर, दे, जा. Stems ending in a consonent are called *closed*, those ending in a vowel, *open*. In a dictionary, a Verb is found under the form of the Infinitive.

216. Parts of a Verb. The verbal forms may be conveniently divided into three groups :

I. Those having the force of Verbal Nouns or Adjectives.

(1) The Infinitive. देखना, *to see.*

(2) The Imperfect Participle. देखता or देखता हुआ, *seeing*. This may be used as a Noun, *the person seeing*, or, as an Adjective, भूँकता कुत्ता, *the barking dog.* It is also used in the formation of six of the last twelve Tenses of the Verb.

(3) The Perfect Participle. देखा or देखा हुआ, *having seen*, or, *that which has been seen.* This is used in the remaining six of the twelve Tenses coming under No. III group.

(4) Conjunctive Participle. देख कर, etc., *having seen.* An explanation of the difference between the force of this " *having seen* " and the same words

given under No. (3) above, will be given later on.

(5) Noun of Agency. **देखनेवाला,** etc., *the one who sees.* This is generally used as a Noun, but may also be an Adjective.

II. This group of three obtains its forms from the stem of the verb, supplemented by Tense endings, indicating Person, Gender and Number in some places, but not in all.

(1) Contingent Future. **देखूँ,** *I may see.*

(2) Absolute Future. **देखूँगा,** *I shall see,* formed by the Addition of **गा, गी** or **गे** to the forms of the Contingent Future.

(3) Imperative. **देख,** *see.* The respectful forms are 3rd pl. in construction, but 2nd sing. in meaning.

III. Under this head come the six pairs of Tenses formed from the Imperfect and Perfect Participles, assisted in ten of the Tenses by parts of the Auxiliary Verbs **होना** and "to be."

The names of the Tenses are given in the Paradigms, and fuller explanations of their forms and meanings in the detailed examination of the various parts of the Verb which will be given in the following sections.

TENSES AND OTHER PARTS OF THE VERB.

217. We must now deal with the Tenses and other parts of the Verb, one by one, noting the forms they assume, their functions and idiomatic uses.

The Infinitive. क्रियार्थक संज्ञा.

218. The Infinitive is formed by adding ना to the stem of the Verb. The Infinitive is called by Hindi Grammarians क्रियार्थक संज्ञा, *i. e., a Noun giving the meaning of a Verb*, in other words, *a Verbal Noun*.

One of the Principal uses of the Infinitive is that of a Verbal Noun or Gerund. As such, it is liable to declension in the same way as other Tadbhava Nouns ending in आ, and has the same Case modifications. It is mostly used as a masculine Gerund, in the singular Number, but is also used in the fem. ...... नी, and the masc. pl. .... ने.

Sir George Grierson points out that this form in ना is not only an Infinitive, but also a Future Passive Participle. This may account for the fact that the idea of futurity is markedly present in some of the idiomatic uses of this form ending in ना.

As a Verbal Noun, it may sometimes be translated by the English Infinitive, *e.g.*, वहाँ जाना तुम्हारे लिये अच्छा नहीं, *To go there is not good for you.* In many instances, however, it is necessary to translate the Hindi Infinitive by one of the series of English words ending in "ing," such as *speaking, talking, singing, coming, going*, etc., these being equal to the Infinitive in meaning. In the above sentence, the English translation may be as given, or "*Going there is not good for you.*" In many instances, however, no such alternative is open in translating into English; *e.g.*, **लिखने से काम नहीं निकलेगा,** *The work cannot be effected by writing.* Here "*writing*" could not be replaced by "*to write.*" The form of the English Infinitive is not so pliable as that of the Hindi.

The uses of the Hindi Infinitive may be divided into three groups:

I. As a Verbal Noun. II. Compounded with other Verbs. III. As an Imperative.

219. I. As a Verbal Noun. As stated above, the Infinitive may be used as a Noun in all the Cases (except the Vocative).

Nominative. **ऐसा करना अच्छा नहीं मालूम होता है,** *To do thus does not seem good.* **इन के सच २ कह देने ने मेरे मन को ठंडा कर दिया,** *His utterance of the exact truth cooled down my mind.*

Accusative. **दूसरों के घर जाना उसने छोड़ दिया,** *He gave up going to other people's houses.*

Dative. **पहले वह ब्याह करने को राज़ी न हुई,** *At first she was not willing to marry.* The **को** is not infrequently omitted: **वह देखने गया,** *He went to see.*

Instrumental. चोरी करने से कुछ मिले तो मिले, पर अन्त में अपयश हो जाएगा, *By thieving something may perchance be obtained, but at the last disgrace will come.*

Ablative. वहाँ लेन देन करने से उसे बहुत धन प्राप्त हुआ, *By trading* (or money-lending) *there, he gained great wealth.* (Attention is again directed to the way in which the Instrumental and Ablative Cases overlap one another. In this latter instance, the Case might be regarded as Instrumental or Ablative, according to the working out of the exact meaning. If the wealth be regarded as having come *by means of* the trading, the Case would be Instrumental; if the trading be regarded as the *source* of the wealth, then the Ablative.)

Genitive. उसके आने जाने का यह परिणाम हुआ, *The result of his coming and going was this.* उसने कुछ देने की प्रतिज्ञा की, *He promised to give something.*

Locative. प्रार्थना करने पर उसने जाने की आज्ञा पाई, *Upon (her) entreaty, she obtained permission to go.*

The Infinitive is sometimes used in the fem. form. उनको सुनानी चाहिये, (You) must cause them to hear (this word). विदेशियों की शरण लेनी पड़ती है;

(We) have to take refuge with foreigners. दो बातें कहनी हैं, *There are two things to say.*

Also in the plural form. कौन २ गुण होने चाहियें ? *What qualities are needed?* उनको भी अनेक कष्ट उठाने पड़े, *They also had to endure great hardships.*

These feminine (sing. and pl.) and masculine plural forms have not uncommonly the idea of futurity in them, and may thus be connected with the Future Passive Participle, referred to by Sir George Grierson. Thus, नये नाटक की लीला करनी है, *There is to be the performance of a new play.* एक दिन सबकी यही गति होनी है, *One day this will be the condition of all.* इतने काम हम लोगों को अभी करने हैं, *Now we shall have to do so many kinds of work.*

Very closely connected with this use of the Infinitive, is its idiomatic use with चाहिये, in which futurity is necessarily implied. तुम को जाना चाहिये, *You must go.* अभी लड़ाई और होनी चाहिये, *It is necessary for more fighting to take place immediately.*

Though used as a Verbal Noun, the Infinitive still retains its verbal power to govern another Noun in the Accusative Case. यह सब विद्या प्रकाश कर देनी, *To display all this learning.* This might equally well have the form of the accus., with को; thus, इस सब

विद्या को प्रकाश कर देना. Or, the Genitive may be used with a similar meaning: thus, इस सब विद्या का प्रकाश कर देना. In the following sentence, we have both constructions. जो तू उस बात के जानने से जिसे अवश्य जानना चाहिये डरता नहीं, *If you are not afraid to know that matter which it is very necessary to know.*

220. II. Compounded with another Verb. The Infinitive, in its inflected or uninflected form, is found loosely compounded with other Verbs, especially in the Inceptive, Permissive, Acquisitive and Desiderative groups. As this use of the Infinitive will come up for consideration in the sections on Compound Verbs, the following summary may suffice here :—

a. With the Inceptives the inflected form is used. वह कहने लगा, *He began to speak.*

b. ......Permissives...................... वह कहने देता, *He allows (him) to speak.*

c. ......Acquisitives.............. वह कहने पाता, *He obtains permission*, or, *the opportunity, to speak.*

d. ......Desiderative...uninflected...... वह कहना चाहता है, *He desires to speak.* This sentence may also mean, *He is about to speak.* Formerly, the inflected form was used, वह कहने चाहता है; but it is now practically always used in the uninflected form. When the Verb चाहना is in the plural form, the previous Infinitive may assume the same form ; that is probably because both are made to agree with the plural Noun, *e.g.*, वे जाने चाहते हैं, *They are about to depart.* In the same way, both may be found in the fem. form, and probably for the same reason. Thus वह (*f.*) आनी चाहती है, *She is about to arrive.* Even in such sentences, however, the forms जाना and आना would often be found.

The use of the Infinitive with चाहिये was mentioned in sect. 219 and will be touched upon again in sect. 221.

221. III. As an Imperative. The Infinitive is often used as an Imperative. Its force lies somewhere between the other two forms generally in use. कीजिये is the very polite form, करो is an ordinary command. The Infinitive करना lies somewhere between the two. In some sentences, the element of futurity is stronger than in others. Of course, a measure of futurity must be involved in every order or request, by the nature of the case. In some sentences also there is a suggestion of continuity or repetition. The use of the Infinitive as an Imperative does not, however, necessarily carry the idea of either futurity or repetition.

वहाँ न जाना, *Don't go there.* आज नहीं कल करना, *Do it to-morrow, not to-day.*

What exact difference there is between करना and करना चाहिये it would be difficult to say.

IMPERFECT AND PERFECT PARTICIPLES.

222. Imperfect Participle. क्रियाद्योतक संज्ञा or कृदन्त, *i.e.*, the Noun setting forth the Verbal idea.

Perfect Participle. कर्तृवाचक or कर्मवाचक संज्ञा or कृदन्त, *i.e.*, the Noun which explains the doing, or that which is done or being done.

Possessing much in common, these two Participles, differ considerably. One very important difference is this that, while the Imperfect Participle is Active, the Perfect Participle, with हुआ, is often Passive, *e.g.*, सिखाई हुई बात, *the taught word.* Though, according to the form, this might be active, it is as unmistakeably passive as though it were written सिखाई गयी बात. In the following sentence, the Participle of the same form is very probably active. वह अपने पुत्रों को राज्य पाया हुआ देखकर प्रसन्न हुई, *She, seeing that her sons had obtained the kingdom, was pleased.* It may be safe to conclude that we have not here merely two different uses of one form, but two words which, though identical in form, are not so in origin, one having probably been a Sanskrit Passive Participle.

The Imperfect Participle is formed by adding **ता** to the stem of the Verb, the Perfect by the addition of **आ**. With both Participles, **हुआ** may be added. In the case of the Imperfect Participle, it changes the meaning but very little, if at all. Similarly, the addition to the Perfect Participle affects the meaning little in many cases; but, in some sentences, there is a distinctly passive meaning. Both Participles are declined like Adjectives of two terminations: masc. **आ**, pl. **ए**, fem. **ई**.

The names, Imperfect and Perfect, fairly represent the essential difference between the two Participles. The former, in **ता**, represents an act or state as in process of being done or experienced, *i.e.*, as not concluded. The Perfect Participle represents it as completed. **वह पत्र लिखते हुए बैठ रहा है,** *He is seated writing a letter.* **लिखे हुए पत्र उसके हाथ में देकर,** *Having given into his hand the letters which had been written.* The latter sentence illustrates also the tendency for the Perfect Participle to assume a passive meaning.

Mr. Platts, in his Hindustani Grammar (sections 418-427, in the 1904 edition), has an exceedingly carefully worked out note on the Participles, which, in the main, applies to Hindi as well as to Urdu. It may be doubted, however, if, in all cases, the exact force of the various uses of the participles, as there explained, can be maintained. It would rather seem that, frequently, the adoption of one or other of alternative forms or constructions,—the agreement of the Participle with its subject in Gender and Number, or its use in what is generally called its Absolute form, with हुआ or without, etc.—depends upon the fancy or taste of the writer or speaker, and not on any rigid rule, just as, in English, one writer may prefer to write, "*Going on his way, he was attacked,*" another chooses to write, "*As he went on his way, he was attacked.*"

223. *With* or *without* हुआ. *Agreeing with subject* or *in Absolute form.* A careful consideration of the numerous illustrations of the use of the Participles which will be found in the following sections, will, it is believed, tend to confirm the statement made in the last paragraph. Possibly, the forms with हुआ do tend to suggest something in the way of continuousness, but it is certainly not more than a tendency, and the same idea of continuousness is often present where the हुआ is not present, *e.g.*, मेरे लिये ख़र्च करते और मेरा सुख देखते तुम को बुरा लगता है, *Spending money on me and seeing me happy, displeases you.* The *spending* and *seeing him happy* refer not to one item of expenditure and one look at the happy youth, but to a continuous expenditure, etc.

With the Perfect Participle of a Transitive Verb, the हुआ frequently carries with it the passive meaning; but its use does not involve this, nor does it have any such effect on the Imperfect Participle.

The Participle may agree with the subject to which it refers, in Gender and Number, as मरती हुई माता को देख कर, *Seeing her dying mother.* Or, when used predicatively after an Accusative, with को, it may be in the form of the masc. singular, irrespective of the Gender and Number of the subject of the Participle, *e.g.*, अपने पुत्रों को राज्य पाया हुआ (see previous section). Or, it may appear in the masculine constructive form. This is frequently called the Absolute form, though, strictly speaking, this word ought, perhaps, to be confined to those cases in which the subject of the participle is not the same as the subject of the main Verb in the sentence, nor of an Accusative governed by that main Verb, *e.g.*, जब बहुत दिन राज्य करते हो गये, *When he had been reigning for a long time.*

It would be impossible, we believe, to formulate any rule or rules stating under what conditions one idiom would be more correct than another. Undoubtedly, in some sentences, certain constructions are preferable, in some probably absolutely necessary; but in many instances alternatives are open, and the choice depends not on rule, but on taste and custom. Different authors have their preferences.

224. *Various uses of the Participles.* Perhaps the following represent the main uses of the Participles :--

1. As attributive Adjectives.
2. As predicative Adjectives (see paragraph below).
3. As Nouns.
4. As Verbal Nouns.
5. Compounded with other Verbs.
6. Special uses and idioms.

Frequently, the Participles do not assume the functions of Adjectives, but retain their verbal force, *e.g.*, **मन्त्री ने उसको पापी समझते हुए कहा,** *The minister thinking him to be a sinful man, said.* Here it is **पापी** that is the Adjective, whilst the Participle, **समझते हुए,** can only be styled adjectival in a very loose sense. The Part. does not describe what sort of a man the minister was, but gives the thoughts which led him to say what he did say. The force of the Part. here is far more verbal than adjectival. The sentence might equally well have run, **मन्त्री समझते थे कि यह मनुष्य पापी है इस कारण उन्हों ने कहा.** Thus written, we have an ordinary Verb to express that which is expressed by the Participle in the other sentence.

As the idiomatic uses of the Imperfect and Perfect Participles differ considerably in some cases, it may be well to consider them separately.

THE IMPERFECT PARTICIPLE. क्रियाद्योतक संज्ञा.

225. To avoid multiplication of the divisions of our subject, we may now dismiss from consideration the question as to whether each Participle is attributive, predicative, or something else.

1. *The Participle in agreement with its subject in Gender and Number.*

(*a*) *With the Nominative.* रोती हुई लड़की घर पहुँची, *The weeping girl reached home.* इन सब कामों को करता हुआ मनुष्य धीरज धरे, *Doing all these things let the man remain steadfast.* इन कामों को करता हुआ मनुष्य घर में रहता हुआ भी भगवान की भक्ति से मुक्ति पा सकता है, *Doing these things, a man, even while living in his own house, by devotion to God, can secure salvation.* यह भी रोती चिल्लाती उनके पास दौड़ी, *She also weeping and crying ran out to them.* राजा की कीर्त्ति अब तक अपनी प्रजा को उपदेश देती हुई मौजूद है, *Up to the present time, the fame of the king abides, giving teaching to his subjects.* वे दोनों प्राणी जीते हुए भी मरे से हो जाते हैं,

They both, even while still alive, become as though dead. (Notice that with one participle the हुए is used not with the second).

(*b*) *With the Accusative and other Cases.* अग्नि को चमकता हुआ या दीपक जलता हुआ देखा, *(He) saw a fire shining or a lamp burning.* उसने सोते हुए निरपराध बालकों को मारा है, *He has slain the sleeping innocent children.* आप को हमने कभी कोई काम करते नहीं देखा, *I never saw you doing any work.* (करते is pl., to agree with आप).

In the two following sentences, the Participle in a very true sense has for its subject the subject of the principal Verb, and yet it is an Adjective belonging to the word समय, and, as such, agrees with it in Gender and Case. It is the construct. form, sing. masc., because समय is the Accuse. of time. स्त्री जाते समय बोली, *The woman at the time of her going away said.* चलते समय वह सोचने लगा, *At the time of his going, he began to think.*

2. *The Participle in its Absolute form, not agreeing with its subject in Gender and Number.*

(*a*) *With the Nominative.* किसी ने अपने गुरु की प्रशंसा करते हुए कहा, *Some one in praise of his religious teacher said.* The sentence is, literally, *praising his teacher said*, and *might* mean, *while he was praising his teacher, he said something about some other subject*; but the context would probably show that what he said was the very praising of the guru. **यह कहते कहते वह फिर रोने लगी,** *Saying this again and again, she once more started crying.* **अवधि पूरी होने आई,** *The limit appointed was reaching its completion.*

(*b*) *With the Accusative and other Cases.* **जब राजा ने उसको आते हुए देखा,** *When the king saw him coming along.* **शास्त्रों में लिखी हुई बातों पर विश्वास करना,** *Have faith in the words written in the holy books.* **उसने दोनों लड़कियों को सोते हुए पाया,** *He found both the girls asleep.*

3. Not infrequently, the subject of the Participle is not the same as the subject of the main Verb in the sentence. (This, of course, is also true of 2 *b*, but not in the same way). These instances correspond with the usually accepted meaning of the word "Absolute," as applied to the use of Parts of Speech.

कहते कहते उसकी बात रुक गई, *He went on talking, and then his words ceased.* Or, more lit., *He talking talking, his word stopped.* **ऐसे कहते कहते बुढ़ी का मन ईश्वर के ध्यान में मग्न हो गया,** *Talking on thus, the mind of* *the old lady became absorbed in the thought of God.* **जान पड़ता है कि मेरे लिए ख़र्च करते और मेरा सुख देखते तुम को बुरा लगता है,** *It appears to me that in spending money on my behalf and in seeing me happy you find unhappiness.* **जब बहिन को अकेली आते देखा,** *When he saw his sister coming alone.* **अपने साम्हने एक नयी बात होती हुई देख रही है,** *She sees a new state of affairs coming about before her very eyes.*

4. *The Imperfect Participle with* **ही**. This has sometimes been called the Adverbial Participle. It is, however, just one use of the Part., the **ही** conveying the idea that *at the very time that the act was taking place......e.g.,* **सुनते ही सबके सब दौड़े आये,** *As soon as ever they heard it, they all came running.* **मेरे मरते ही,** *Upon my death.* **यह सुनते ही जहाँगीर को बड़ा क्रोध आया,** *On hearing this, Jahangir became very angry.*

5. Occasionally, the Participle becomes about equal to a Noun or the Infinitive. The following sentences illustrate these and similar points :—

मैं अभी सोते से भी नहीं उठी हूँ, *I have not yet risen from sleep.* **मरता क्या न करता,** *What will not a dying man do?* **इसी के मिलते मुझे तेरी सुध आयी,** *On receiving it, the thought of you came to me.*

कैसे जाते बनता है, *How can you go?* करते भी सुना है, Has *(anyone) heard of (anyone) doing (it)* ?

6. Compounded with other Verbs. Sometimes, the Impferf. Part. is compounded with रहना or जाना, and then conveys the idea of continuativeness, *e.g.*, वे ऐसा करते रहते हैं, *They keep on doing so.* वह गिरता जाता है, *He keeps stumbling.*

There is one use of जाता रहना which is distinct from the above, being an idiomatic way of expressing the idea of something having come to an end, *e.g.*, चाँदी की सारी चमक जाती रही, *All the brightness of the silver passed away.*

THE PERFECT PARTICIPLE. कर्तृवाचक or कर्मवाचक संज्ञा.

226. As already stated, one principal difference between the Imperfect and Perfect Participles is that the latter have often a passive meaning. The Participles are so important in Hindi composition that illustrations of the use of the Perfect Participles are given even where the use does not materially differ from the use of the Imperfect Participle.

1. *a. The Perfect Participle agreeing with its subject in Gender and Number. Nominative.*

उनका मन तो ईश्वर में ही लगा हुआ था, *Their mind was set on God.* वह रावण से युद्ध करके मरा

हुआ पड़ा था, *He having fought with Ravan was lying dead.* वायु से उड़ाये हुए बादल जहाँ तहाँ घूमा फिरा करते हैं, *The wind-driven clouds are wandering around in various directions hither and thither.* (Notice that here the Part. is passive in meaning.) सिर पर हाथ रक्खे सिर झुकाये बैठे हैं, *He is seated with his hands to his head and bowed head.* (Lit., *having bowed his head*). दो चार मनुष्य हाथ में लाठी लिये बैठे देख पड़ते हैं, *Two or three men appear to be sitting there with long staffs in their hands.*

1. *b. The Participle agreeing with the Accusative, etc., in Gender and Number.* उन्होंने जटायू पृथिवी पर मरा पड़ा हुआ देखा. *They saw Jatayu lying dead on the ground.* वह तपाये हुए सोने के समान चमकता था, *It was shining like gold purified in the fire.* (Passive meaning of Part.). जब उसने प्राणों पर संकट आया जाना, *When he knew that calamity had come upon his life.* (Notice the use of the pl. प्राणों for "*life*"). यह अपने किये का फल आप भोगेगा, *This man will suffer the fruit of his own doings.* तब तक ईश्वर के दिये हुये भोगों को भोगेंगे, *Until then will they suffer the sufferings inflicted on them by God* (*Pass.*). राजा ने भी ब्राह्मण को अपने द्वार पर भिक्षा के लिए आया देख, *The king also having seen a Brahman who had come to*

his door for alms. दिन चढ़ा देख कर, *Seeing that the day had broken.*

It should be noted that, in addition to this use of the form of the Active Participle with a passive meaning, the true passive Participle is also used. आरम्भ किये गये किसी कार्य के सिद्ध होने का समय आ जाने पर, *When the time comes for any work that has been commenced to be completed.* अपने ऊपर किये गये अत्याचारों का वर्णन उसने किया, *He gave an account of the injustices which had been inflicted on him.*

2. *a. The Participle in the Absolute form, with a Nominative subject.* वह एक अनाथ बालक को लिये हुए घर में पड़ी है, *She stays in the house with an orphan child which she has brought.* मैं पाँव धोये बैठी हूँ, *Having washed my feet, I am sitting here.* अपनी बहिन के पास बैठे ही बैठे अत्यन्त श्रम होने के कारण सो गयी, *Sitting close to her sister, on account of her great weariness, she has fallen asleep.* वह कुमारिका राजा का हाथ पकड़े घूम रही थी, *The maiden was walking about, having laid hold of the king's hand.* जेठी कन्या लज्जा से अपना सिर नीचा किये हुए उसके पास आई, *The eldest girl, with her head bowed down on account of bashfulness, came to him.*

In the following sentence, the Participle is in the

singular, although the subject is plural. This is in accordance with the rule about an Adjective used predicatively and following an Accus. with को. इनको धूल माटी के बीच एक खेत में पड़ा हुआ पाते हैं, *We find them lying in a field amidst dust and dirt.*

2. *b. The Participle in the absolute form, with Accusative and other Cases.* उन्होंने अपने को एक कमरे में पलँग पर पड़े पाया, *He found himself lying on a bed in a room.* मार्ग भूले यात्री के लिये, *For a traveller who has lost his way.* उसे दर्शन घर बैठे मिले, *The vision came to him as he sat in his house.*

3. *The following sentence furnishes us with a good illustration of the full Absolute use of this form.* गले में फाँसी डाले हुए और नीचे को मुँह किये हुए अपने भाई को देख कर, *Having seen her brother with a halter thrown round his neck and with his face cast down.*

4. Sometimes, the Perfect Participle is found having much of the force of a Verbal Noun or of the Infinitive. बिना किसी के कहे वह घर का काम करने लगी, *Without any one telling her, she started to do the work of the house.* लड़े बिना इधर उधर भागने लगे, *Without fighting, they fled hither and thither.* लोगों के कहे कहाये हम उसके वैरी क्यों बनते हैं, *Why do we become his enemies just because of people's chatter.*

5. In some cases, the Participle becomes practically a Noun. मेरी कही नहीं सुनता, *He hears not my spoken (word), i.e., He does not obey me.* Words formed from a jingle on a Verb, in its simple form, and its Causative, are used in this way. सुनी सुनाई (बात) equals "*rumour*," "*hearsay.*" बना बनाया is, more strictly speaking, an Adjective rather than a Noun, the article referred to being understood. The word means *ready-made*, as contrasted with something made to order.

6. The Perfect Participle, or another word bearing that form, is used in the formation of Compound Verbs. It is found with चाहना and करना. With the first, we have, *e.g.*, वह किया चाहता है, *He wishes to do it*, meaning very much the same as वह करना चाहता है. With the second, वह किया करता है, conveying the idea of continuousness or repetition, *He keeps on doing it.*

Sir George Grierson and Dr. Kellogg consider that these forms are not Participles, but Verbal Nouns. दस बीस स्त्रियाँ मुनीश्व का दर्शन किया चाहती हैं, *Ten or twenty women are desirous of saluting the saint.* मैं उससे कुछ कहा चाहता हूँ, *I wish to say something to him.* गाड़ी आया चाहती थी, *The train was on the point of arriving.* रात दिन बहुत से लोग आया जाया करते हैं, *Day and night many people keep coming and going.* यह किया करो, *Keep on doing this.*

Note the following also. **तो क्या उसको वहीं पड़ा रहना चाहिये,** *What! ought he to remain there doing nothing?*

7. A few other sentences are given to illustrate some further uses of the Perfect Participle or of forms identical with those of the Perfect Participle.

a. **दस पन्द्रह बरस हुए यहाँ आकर रहने लगा,** *It is some ten or fifteen years since he came and took up his abode here.* This is a common and very useful idiom. **दस दिन हुए कि,** *It is ten days ago that...*

b. **वन में चले जाते हैं,** *They are going along in the forest.* **वह मरी जाती थी,** *She was (slowly) dying.* Probably, neither these nor the forms in the following sentences are Participles.

c. **वह चले जाता है,** *He is going along.* **मैं तुम से यह कहे देता हूँ,** *I say this to you.*

CONJUNCTIVE PARTICIPLE. पूर्वकालिक क्रिया.

227. Forms. The Conjunctive Participle may consist of the stem of the Verb alone, or may have added to it **कर, के,** or **करके.** Thus, from **जाना,** the forms are **जा, जाकर, जाके, जाकरके.** Sometimes forms are met with ending in **य, यके** and **इ,** *e.g.*, **जाय, जायके, करि.** These must be regarded as dialectical forms, rather than as standard Hindi.

Of the forms given, that terminating with **कर** is the one most widely and commonly used at the present time. The form with के was far more used some 40 or 50 years ago than at present. The simple stem form is by no means uncommon, and the करके form is occasionally found. If there be any difference in the use of these various forms, it is this, that the stem form is preferred when the Conjunctive Part is very closely related to the following Verb. In some cases, the two might be taken for a Compound Verb, *e.g.*, ले आना. This, we have seen, does become a Compound Verb in the contracted form लाना. Notice ले चलना, *having taken, go*; here, frequently, the meaning is, *Take (it) along*.

The main advantage of having these alternative forms is not to convey any difference in meaning or force, but to afford variety where there are more Conjunctive Participles than one in a sentence. The following well illustrates this point. एक दिन स्नान पूजा करि ब्राह्मणों को बहुत सा दान दे देवता पितरों को तृप्त करके ऋषि और पण्डितों को साथ लिये वैशम्पायन मुनि के पास जा दण्डवत कर खड़े हो हाथ जोड़ कहने लगे कि ...*One day, having bathed and performed worship, having given large gifts to the Brahmins, having satisfied deities and forefathers (by worship), taking saints and pundits (with him), having approached the holy Vaishampayan, having bowed down, having stood and clasped his hands, (he) began to speak, saying.........*

The Conjunctive Participle finds its main use in the avoidance of two Verbs in the same sentence. Where we should say, "*He went there, called a servant, and said,*" the Hindi would neatly express it by **वहाँ जा नौकर को बुलाकर कहा.**

228. Idiomatic Uses.

Temporal. The Hindi name, **पूर्वकालिक क्रिया,** *the verb which deals with past time,* is, on the whole, more correct than the English name, Conjunctive, for, generally speaking, the fact referred to in this Conjunctive Participle is something which precedes the action of the main Verb, not something which occurs at the same time, *e.g.*, **वहाँ जाकर उसने सब लोगों को इकट्ठा किया,** *Having gone there, he gathered them all together.* **घर में पहुँचकर उसने क्या देखा,** *Having gone into the house, what did he see?* **मन्त्री को बुलाकर पूछने लगा,** *Having called the minister, he began to enquire.* **जो कुछ तुम देख आये हो,** *Whatever having seen you have come.*

This is the more common force of this Conjunctive Participle, but at times it does indicate something which takes place contemporaneously with the act indicated by the main Verb, or in another way declares what is conveyed by the main Verb. Thus, **उसको समझा कर कहा,** *He gave him to understand.* It was by what he said that he tried to bring his hearer to his senses. उत्तर देकर बतलाया, *In his answer he explained.* He did not give him an answer, and then explain; the answer was the explanation.

229. Adverbial. The Conjunctive Participle is not infrequently used with Adverbial force. सावधान होकर करो, *Do it cautiously, or with great care.* निश्चय करके जानो, *Know assuredly.* विशेष करके, *Especially,* as in विशेष करके मैं ने यह पूछा, *I made enquiries specially about this.*

230. One idiom is worthy of notice, *viz.*, the use of बढ़कर, with the force of the comparative degree, *e.g.*, यह मुझ से कहीं बढ़कर है, *She is ever so much better than I.* इस से बढ़कर कोई कवि नहीं मिलेगा, *You will find no greater poet than he.* माँगने से बढ़कर कोई अधम काम नहीं है, *There is no meaner occupation than begging.*

A pleonastic use of करके, greatly affected by writers, now and again, especially some commentators, etc., is only noticed to warn the student against the adoption of it. धर्म करके युक्त असत्य का बहुत पाप नहीं है, *There is no great sin in a lie attached to the performance of one's duty.* Such ungrammatical affectations should be shunned.

Where a double Verb be used, जान बूझ, समझ

बूझ, etc., in this Conjunctive Participal form, the suffix is only added to the second Verb. जान बूझ कर उसने ऐसा किया, *He did it knowingly, i.e., deliberately.* खा पीकर वे सो गये, *Having eaten and drunk, they went to sleep.*

Two or more phrases, constructed in this way, may be used in the same sentence. In such cases, different forms are commonly employed, *e.g.*, रामचन्द्र ने उनके हाथ से धनुष ले सहज ही में उसकी प्रत्यंचा चढ़ाकर उस पर बाण खैंचा, *Ramchandra, having taken the bow from his hand and having strung it, fixed an arrow on the string.* Sometimes, however, the same form is repeated. यह चमत्कार देख परशुराम लज्जित हो उनकी बड़ी स्तुति कर चले गये, *Having seen this wonderful feat, Parashuram became ashamed, greatly praised him, and went away.*

The subject of the Conjunctive Participle is generally the same as that of the following Verb, but not invariably so. Such sentences as the following are found. यह सुनकर दया आई, *Having heard this, mercy came* (into his heart). यह सब देख कर उसका चेहरा फीका पड़ गया, *Having seen all this, his face became sallow* (with consternation).

THE NOUN OF AGENCY. कर्तृवाचक संज्ञा.

231. The form with हारा is not much used, that employing the suffix वाला is the one generally current. This suffix is added to the inflected form of the Infinitive.

The Noun of Agency, in the case of Active Verbs, indicates the "*doer*;" with Neuter Verbs, the one who experiences the state expressed by the Verb. This Noun of Agency is used for both persons and things, for masc. and fem., वाला and वाली. Thus, लिखनेवाला, लिखनेवाली, *a writer*; सोनेवाला, सोनेवाली, *a sleeper*.

Actually, these words are Adjectives of two terminatians, *e.g.*, उसके जानेवाले दास, *His servants who were going*. But, in common with many Adjectives, they may become Nouns, and are then fully declined as Nouns. These Nouns of Agency retain their verbal power of governing other Nouns in the Accusative Case, *e.g.*, अनेक देश की भाषा पहिरावा चाल व्यवहार जाननेवाले, *Those whe know the languages, dresses, manners and customs of many countries.*

One special use of this Noun of Agency calls for notice. It often carries with it the idea of immediate futurity. वह जानेवाला है, *He is about to go.* आप इसी मास में शिमले की यात्रा करनेवाले हैं, *He is about to make the journey to Simla this month.*

It may be mentioned here that वाला is not only added to the inflected Infinitives, but to Nouns also, *e.g.*, पश्चिमवाले, *Westerners.* वहाँवालों को, *To the people of that place.* वृन्दावनवाले, *that ... who lives at Brindaban.* उनके पीछेवाले ग्रन्थ, *His later books.* Some may not approve of these forms, but they are at times used by quite good writers.

होनहार (contraction for होनेहारा) is idiomatically used to express what must inevitably come to pass. It is also used of a person in the sense that, *he's a coming man, i.e.*, destined to become great.

THE CONTINGENT FUTURE. सम्भाव्य भविष्यत्.

232. This Tense is formed from the stem of the Verb, with the additional endings given in the Paradigms. With open root, य is often used instead of ए, *e.g.*, जाय, pl. जायँ, for जाए, जाएँ. The ऐ for ए, as in चलै, चलैं, is a somewhat dialectical form, but is in frequent use by some writers.

The Hindi name for this Tense, सम्भाव्य भविष्यत्, *the Possible Future*, well represents its general character. It expresses that which *may be.*

Its main uses are probably included in the following division. It may express :—

1. A condition.
2. A possibility.
3. A wish.—Optative.
4. An interrogation.

5. With the force of an Absolute Future.

In modern Hindi, there is a very marked tendency to use either two Contingent Futures or two Absolute Futures in a sentence where logical exactness would demand one Contingent and one Absolute Fut., *e.g.*, **आवें तो देखेंगे**, *If they come, they will see.* The **आवें** is conditional and quite problematical. This uncertainty is rightly expressed by the Contingent Future, but the statement made, that if this conditition be fulfilled "they will see," has no uncertainty involved; and therefore in this case, the use of the Absolute Future seems perfectly correct. Most writers, however, at the present time would in this sentence use either two Cont. Futures, **आवें तो देखें**, or two Abs. Futures, **आवेंगे तो देखेंगे**. One is led to compare the corresponding disinclination in England to employ the Subjunctive, *e.g.*, *If he comes, I will see him*, instead of, *If he come, I will see him.*

233. 1. *Conditional.* The conditional clause may be introduced by **यदि, जो**, *if*; **जब**, *when*, or some similar word, or may stand alone. **यदि जाए तो उसे मालूम होगा**, *If he go, he will ascertain.* **जब आवें मुझे ख़बर दो**, *When he arrives, let me know.* **जाऊँ तो देखूँ**, *If I go, I shall see.*

This Contingent Future in the *protosis* may be followed in the *apodosis* by an Imperative, an Absolute

Future, or by another Cont. Future. अगर बोलने में इन पाँच बातों का विचार रक्खेा तो बहुत आफ़तों से बचे रहो, *If in speaking you be careful about these five things, you will be saved from many troubles.* (Notice that the second Cont. Fut. is equal in meaning to an Absolute Fut.). यदि तुम्हारा क्रोध शान्त न हो तो अपने मन से कहो, *If your anger does not calm down, then say to yourself,* कहूँ तो क्या कहूँ, *If I speak, what shall I say?* जब तक उसको पकड़ कर नाश न करें तब तक सुख से दिन न कटें, *Until he seize and destroy him, the days will not pass happily.*

Sometimes, the conditional clause comes second in the sentence. इस लिये दूसरों के साथ वैसा ही बरताव करो जैसा कि तुम चाहते हो कि वह तुम्हारे साथ करे, *Therefore deal with others as you desire that they should deal with you.*

234. 2. *Possibility.* That which *may* happen. मैंने ऐसा कौन पुण्य कर्म किया है कि सुख से कालक्षेप करने की सम्भावना करूँ, *What righteous deed have I performed that I should have the possibility of passing my time in happiness?* राजा उसका प्राण लेले, *The king may take his life.* चाहे आज आवें चाहे दो चार दिन के बाद, *Whether he come today or after a few days.* हो न हो. *Whether it be so or not.* सम्भव है कि पण्डित

आवें, *It is possible that the pundit may come.* बात खुल जाए, This may mean, *Should the matter become manifest.* or, it may about equal the force of the Absolute Future, and mean, *The matter will out.* जहाँ तक बन पड़े, *As far as possible.*

235. 3. *Optative.* मैं चाहता हूँ कि पुत्र यशस्वी हो, *I desire that my son may become illustrious.* मैं नहीं चाहता कि उसकी उन्नति रुक जाय, *I do not wish that his progress should be hindered.* यह तथा हमारी अन्य त्रुटियाँ यदि क्षमा की जाने योग्य हों तो क्षमा की जायँ, *This and my other failings, if they be fit to be forgiven, then may they be forgiven.* जितने दिन तुम अपने भाई बन्धुओं से अलग रहोगे उतने दिन देवता तुम्हारे साथ साथ फिरें और तुम्हारा कल्याण करें, *As long as you remain separated from your kith and kin, so long may the gods be with you in your wanderings and prosper you.* जो काम करे विवेकपूर्वक करे, *Whatever work he do, let him do it with discrimination.*

236. 4. *Interrogative.*

हम कैसे करें, *How shall we do it?* हम तुम्हें अकेली कैसे छोड़ दें, *How can I leave you alone?* उसकी क्या शक्ति है जो यहाँ तक आ सके, *What power has he that he should be able to come here?* मैं क्या संदेश लिख भेजूँ, *What news shall I write and send?* मैं कहूँ, *Shall I speak?* अब वह जाए, *May he now go?*

237. 5. *Equal to Absolute Future.* It has been stated above that the Contingent Future is very largely employed in the apodosis where the Absolute Future might be expected, and where the meaning is that of the Absolute Future. There are other cases also where the Contigent Future appears to carry the force of the Absolute Future. मिले तो मैं दूँ, *If I get (it), I will give* (*it to you*). हम मिलकर धन कमावें, *We will join together and acquire riches.* (Unless this be taken as Optative, *Let us acquire wealth).*

In some instances, an immediate future appears to be indicated. जो बुरा न मानो तो एक बात कहूँ, *If you will not take it ill, I will speak one word.* मैं जा कर देखूँ, *I will go and see.*

THE ABSOLUTE FUTURE. सामान्य भविष्यत्.

238. This Tense also is formed from the stem of the Verb. गा, *masculine singular,* गी, *feminine,* and गे, *masculine pl.*, are added to the forms of the Contingent Future.

The uses of this Tense may be grouped as follows :—

1 The Definite Future.

2 The Interrogative.

3. The Conditional.

4. Special use of होगा.

239. 1. The Definite Future. Little explanation is needed concerning this. It is the simple statement that a certain thing will happen. Necessarily, there is uncertainty about the future, but when this is intended to be made prominent, it is generally indicated by a subordinate phrase, *e.g.*, मैं जानता हूँ कि वे कल आवेंगे, *I expect he will come tomorrow.*

One or two illustrations are given. यदि लोग मेरी ओर देखेंगे तो मैं उसे न कर सकूंगा, *People will look at me* (lit., *in my direction*), *and then I shall not be able to do it.* हम तुम्हारे साथ चलेंगे, *We will go with you.* हम सेना के वीरों से युद्ध करेंगे, *We will fight with the warriors of the army.* बेकार लोगों के लिये काम ढूँढ़ने की चिन्ता दूर हो जाएगी, *For people out of work, anxiety in seeking work will be far removed.*

Generally, where this form is used to express the presumptive Future, the presumption is expressed in some way. यह जानकर कि आप को क्लेश होगा, *Understanding that you will be grievously troubled.* This might also mean, *Thinking that you must be in trouble.*

240. Interrogative. The simple interrogative calls for little in the way of illustration. वे क्या करेंगे, *What will they do?* वह कब आएगी, *When will she come?*

इतने पर मिल सकेगा ? *Can it be obtained for that?*

Often, the use of the interrogatory form indicates a strong negative to the question asked. राजा ऐसा करेंगे ? *Will the king do such a thing?* The intended meaning is, *Certainly not.* ऐसे शूरवीर भाग जाएँगे ? *Will such doughty warriors fly? Never.* भरत जैसा भाई जगत् में मैं कहाँ पाऊँगा ? *Where shall I find a brother like Bharat in the whole world?* The implied answer is "Nowhere."

241. 3. **The Conditional.** This use of the Absolute Future has been referred to in treating of the Contingent Future (Sect. 232). यदि कोई उस समय उन्हें देखेगा तो उन्हें बिलकुल ही जंगली समझेगा, *Should anyone see them at that time, he will regard them as altogether uncivilized.* मैं जब तक जीती रहूँगी छोटी बहिन की तरह तुम्हारी सेवा करूँगी, *As long as I live, I will take care of you as I would of a little sister.* In both these sentences, the meaning of the first Future is that of the Contingent Future.

242. 4. **Special use of होगा.** The form होगा is frequently used with the force of the Presumptive Imperfect or Perfect. Often it may be considered as a contracted form of one of these Tenses. देरी होने

का कोई कारण तो होगा, *There must be some reason for the delay.* देश देश में ऐसे कंगाल होंगे, *Such poor people there must be in many countries.* उसके समान कोई दूसरा विद्यावान् न होगा, *No other man of learning can be his equal.*

Not infrequently, होगा is used in an answer with similar force, *e.g.*, वह घर में है ? होगा, *Is he in the house? He will be, i.e., I expect he is.* क्या किसी दूसरे देश में ऐसे पापी होंगे ? होंगे· *Will there be such sinful beings in any other country? Yes, there will be.*

IMPERATIVE. विधि.

243. This also is from the stem of the Verb. The simple stem for the singular जा, *go*, for the pl. ओ, is added, जाओ, *go*.

It has been pointed out that the forms often given in Grammars for the 1st and 3rd persons do not belong to the Imperative. They are simply the forms of the Contingent Future copied out. They belong to the Contingent Future, not to the Imperative, being hortatory, not imperative in their force.

The respectful forms, कीजिये, कीजियेगा, कीजियो, though rightly included in the Imperative, are, strictly speaking, not imperatives. They convey not a command, but a request. In कीजिएगा, there is apparent affinity with the simple Future as well as with the Contingent Future form, suggesting a comparison with such an English phrase as "*Will your honour be pleased to do so.*" All three respectful forms presuppose the use of आप, or some similar title of respect.

What has been written about the use of the Pronouns applies fully here, and practically covers the matter of the use of these Imperative forms. The 2nd singular may be wisely neglected as regards using it, although, as already stated, among Indians themselves, it is often used with children, pupils and others, as indicating affection and paternal regard rather than conveying any idea of contempt. The plural करो may be used in addressing servants and others in a similar position. Of the respective forms, कीजिये is the one most commonly used; कीजिएगा is generally reserved for persons of great dignity; कीजियेा is but little used. In form, it suggests a 2nd person plural, and appears to be sometimes used in addressing numbers of people together. It is by no means, however, confined to this. I find it used by a girl to her elder sister, *and with* तू. तू भी चलियेा, *You go (with me) also.* Again, it is used by a king to his prime minister, and with him also तू is used, evidently indicating familiarity and regard, the forms दीजियेा and रहियेा being used.

and One or two illustrations of the other forms are

given. जब आप का जी चाहे चल दीजिएगा, *Be pleased to go whenever you are inclined to.* नाव पर चढ़िये, *Be pleased to go on board.*

A servant speaking to his royal master says, आप सुन लीजिएगा, *Hear me.* मेरी कठोर बातें के लिये मुझे क्षमा कीजिएगा, *Pardon me for my harsh words.*

It should be remembered that the 3rd plural of the ordinary Contingent Future is also used hortatively. आप मेरी सहायता करें, *Render me help.*

The Infinitive is also used as a gentle Imperative. यह करना, *Do this, please.*

With कर and करो, and corresponding forms of all the Verbs, for the negative, मत is used. With the respectful forms, न is the correct word, though मत is occasionally found.

THE TWELVE TENSES FORMED FROM THE PARTICIPLES.

244. We have now to consider the twelve Tenses formed from the Imperfect and Perfect Participles, six from each. These twelve Tenses naturally fall into six pairs, the first of each pair representing the act as incomplete (the Imperfect Participle), the second as complete (from the Perfect Participle). In either case, the time referred to may be past, present or future, but the action is either complete or incomplete, respectively, at the time referred to. The point can be easily illustrated by English sentences. *He was making it; He is making it; He will be making it; He had made it; He has made it; He will have made it.* These sentences in Hindi would be rendered by Tenses formed from the Imperfect and Perfect Participles, though, as a matter of fact, there is no Tense in Hindi exactly corresponding with the English Future-Perfect. It is true there is a *literal* equivalent, **उसने उसको बनाया होगा**, and the literal translation of this might deceive one and give the impression that we had here an exact equivalent. The literal translation of the sentence is, "*He will have made it,*" not, however, with the meaning of the Future-Perfect, but of the Presumptive Perfect. The sentence does not mean in Hindi that at some future time he will be in the position of one who has done the work, but that the conviction of the speaker is that he has already made whatever is being spoken about. This point is thus elaborated to make the student realize that the Hindi Tenses do not always exactly correspond in meaning and scope with English Tenses which are their nearest equivalents. The student will, however, find that Hindi is capable of giving very full and exact expression, through its Verb, of many niceties, as regards time, etc. When not capable of expression by the Tenses of the ordinary Verb, there are always available various Compounds, very pliable and effective. Take an illustration. We wish to say that a person is coming, meaning that he has already left his house and is actually on the way. वह आता है, *He is coming*, might express this, but does not necessarily do so, as the sentence is ambigucus, as ambiguous as the English, "Christmas is coming." The Hindi *may* might express what we wished it to, but might also mean that, *he is about to come*, or that, *he is in the habit of coming*. We have, however, only to use the phrase, वह आ रहा है, and all is clear as daylight. This means that the *coming* has been started and is still proceeding—he is actually on the road.

As we consider the twelve Tenses one by one, it will become manifest that each one does not exactly carry out the functions which are arranged for it in the admirable scheme presented. The symmetry is not quite so exact as at first appears, *e.g.*, the Past Perfect is not exactly equivalent to the English Pluperfect, "he had gone," etc. It *may* mean that, often it does *not*. Recognizing these facts, the statement may still be maintained that the Hindi Verb is very scientific in its arrangement and most efficient. The twelve Tenses under consideration may be thus tabulated :

From the Imperfect Participle.	*From the Perfect Participle.*
Indefinite Imperfect.	*Indefinite Perfect.*
वह खाता, *he cats.*	**उसने खाया**, *he ate.*
Present Imperfect.	*Present Perfect.*
वह खाता है, *he is eating.*	**उसने खाया है**, *he has eaten*
Past Imperfect.	*Past Perfect.*
वह खाता था, *he was eating.*	**उसने खाया था**, *he had eaten*
Contingent Imperfect.	*Contingent Perfect.*
वह खाता हो, *should he be eating,*	**उसने खाया हो**, *should he have eaten.*
Presumptive Imperfect.	*Presumptive Perfect.*
वह खाता होगा, *he must be eating·*	**उसने खाया होगा**, *he must have eaten.*
Past Contingent Imper fect.	*Past Contingent Perfect.*
वह खाता होता, *had he been eating.*	**उसने खाया होता**, *had he eaten.*

THE INDEFINITE IMPERFECT.

245. That difficulties exist with reference to this Tense may be inferred from the fact that Indian Grammarians appear to be unable to agree about its name. Much of the difficulty possibly arises from this, that the form of this Tense is often used as a contraction for other Tenses.

Some Hindi scholars have gone so far as to take the position that there is no such Tense as the Indefinite Imperfect, but that this form is always a contraction to express some other Tense and that its place is only assigned to it in the scheme of Tenses, for the sake of symmetry. We shall, however, see that the Tense is a real one and quite a serviceable one.

The Tense refers to an action (or experience) as actually proceeding, still unfinished, but contains no reference to the time *when* the action takes place; it might have been going on in the past, it may be proceeding in the present, it may belong to the future. An English sentence may help to show how reference may be made to an action as actually proceeding, with no reference to the time of its occurrence. "*A man speculates, he becomes involved in financial difficulties, he grows desperate, he blows his brains out.*" It is a suppositious case of what may have happened, what may be happening, what may happen at some future time. Somewhat similarly with this Indefinite Imperfect, but with important difference. It is seldom used in a sentence like the above; the Hindi has two clauses, the first conditional, the second indicating something in the way of the outcome from the condition referred to in the first clause, the Indefinite

Imperfect being used in both clauses. जो जाता वही जानता, *He who goes knows.* There is no reference to time, let the condition be carried out, *at any time,* let a man "*go,*" and the *knowledge* will be gained. It is in such sentences that this Tense is mostly employed; the application may be to universal truths or to circumstances arising in the life of an individual.

जो जन अपने राजा को हितोपदेश नहीं करता वह मित्र नहीं (होता understood in the second clause, but unexpressed, unnecessary with नहीं), *He who does not give his king sound advice, is not his friend.* In the following sentence it is not a general truth that is given but the circumstances in an individual life. इनको जो अच्छा पण्डित मिलता उसी से ये यह प्रश्न करते, *Whenever he comes across a good pundit, he asks him this question.* A man speaking of the trouble that "clever" people bring about says, संसार में बुद्धिमान् बहुत न होते तो संसार के कितने काम सुगम हो जाते, *If there were not so many clever people in the world, how many matters would become easy.*

In the following there may be a reference to the past; if so, the Indef. Imperf. would be used for the Past Contingent, but the statement is fairly general and the Tense is probably the Indef. Imperf.; it means, *on your doing so and so, such and such a result would come about.* यदि आप कुछ भी उद्योग करते तो शत्रु सब तरफ़ से विपत्तियों के फन्दे में फँसे बिना न रहते, *If you only make the slightest effort, then the enemies will not escape from being entangled in a network of difficulties from all directions.*

Not infrequently, the sentence does refer to some special time, but the indications of that reference are not contained in this Tense, but conveyed in some other way, *e.g.*, उन पिछले दिनों के कर्तव्यों में यदि न चूकते अथवा यों कहो कि उस समय को व्यर्थ न खोते तो आज पछताना न पड़ता, *If in the doings of past days he had not failed, or, let us say, had not wasted the time, then there would not be the repenting of to-day.* Here the fact that the reference is to past days is contained in पिछले दिनों, etc., not in चूकते, खोते, पड़ता.

The use of ता,...ता, in sentences similar to the above, is very common.

Occasionally, this Tense is used to express an earnest wish. हे ईश्वर, मैं भी यदि उनके सदृश हो जाता, *Oh, God, if I also could become like him.*

246. Sometimes the force of this Tense is not altogether unlike that of the Contingent Future, the writer evidently having in his mind something which has reference to the future and not to a matter which has no reference to any particular time. यदि हमारा बस चलता तो हम आज ही तुमको सुखी कर देते, *Had I the power, I would make you happy this very day.* यदि तुम्हारा थोड़ा भी लाभ होता तो हम बिना कुछ कहे तुम को जाने देते, *If it would be of the slighest advantage to you, I would, without anything being said, let you go today.*

247. Sometimes it is equivalent in meaning to the Present Imperfect. It should be noticed that sometimes the form practically stands for the Present Imperfect, because there is a नहीं in the sentence, and with नहीं the है may be idiomatically omitted. उससे जिसको मारते वह तुरंत टुकड़े टुकड़े हो जाता, *Whoever he smites with this that man is immediately shivered to atoms.* सत्संग से कौन बड़ा नहीं हो जाता और कुसंग से कौन नहीं बिगड़ जाता ? *By companioning with the good, who does not become great, and who does not go astray who companions with the bad ?*

248. Now and again it is about equivalent to the Past Imperfect. तब तो जिधर से ताड़का की आवाज़ पाते उधर ही वे तीर चलाते, *Then from whichever direction they were hearing sounds of Taraka, thither they were shooting their arrows.* जूता बनाकर अपना

गुज़र करते और जो समय उस काम से बचता था उसे भगवतभजन में लगाते, *He was earning his living by making boots, and the time that was left him from his work he was devoting to the worship of God.*

249. Sometimes, the Indefinite Imperfect is equal to the Past Contingent Imperfect or Perfect in force. यदि वह चाहता तो कोई अप्रिय बात न करता, दूसरे लोगों की तरह वह भी मीठी २ ठकुरसुहाती बातें कहता, *Had he so desired, he would not have given utterance to unpleasant words but, like others, would have said sweet things that would please his master.* यदि उस समय कोई ऐसा लेखक होता तो अवश्य अपनी भाषा में कुछ न कुछ लिखता और हमें उस समय की भाषा का कुछ नमूना मिलता, *Had there been such a writer at that time, he would surely have written something or the other in his own language and we should have possessed a specimen of the current language of that time.* यदि मेरे राजा उसे न मार डालते तो यह तुम्हीं को अपना शिकार बना डालता, *Had not my king slain him, he (this one) would have made you his prey.* यदि मैं जानती तो मैं भी वैसाही करती, *Had I known, I also would have done likewise.*

250. Occasionally, this Tense becomes almost equal to an Infinitive or Verbal Noun. दो ही उपाय थे, या

तो मेल करते, या दण्ड देते, *There were two expedients, either to conciliate or to punish (them).*

251. Very often, when the Past Contingent Future is used, the full form is not repeated in the second clause ; this Indefinite Imperfect takes its place. This will be illustrated under the Past Contingent Perfect Tense.

INDEFINITE PERFECT. सामान्यभूत

252. The most common use of this Tense is to express the simple fact that something was done, or that something occurred, in the past, without any indication as to the exact time when it occurred. The Tense might well be called "The Vague Past Tense." Any information about the *time when*, is indicated not by this Tense, but by some additional words of the sentence, *e.g.*, सुनते ही उसने कहा, *Upon hearing (this) he said.* The Tense equals such English phrases as "*he went,*" "*he did it,*" "*he said,*" etc.

The uses of the Tense may be given as below:

253. 1. *Indefinite Past.* वहाँ बहुत से लोग मर गये, *Many people died there.* किसी ने कहीं कहा, *Somewhere or other some one said.* अपने २ घर छोड़ कर भाग गये, *They left their houses and fled.*

Definiteness if often given by other words in the

sentence. वह कल चला गया *He went yesterday.* दस बरस हुये राजा ने चढ़ाई की, *It is ten years ago that the king went up (against him).*

254. 2. Sometimes this Tense about equals the Present Perfect. आप ने कब से जाना कि रामानन्द आने वाले हैं? *Since when have you know that Ramanand was coming?* The meaning is quite evidently, "*have you known?*" not "*did you know?*" क्या मेरी आज्ञा तुमने मानी, *Have you obeyed my order?*

255. 3. Sometimes it bears a meaning in which the force of the Contingent Perfect plays some part. It really becomes a kind of Future Contingent Perfect, indicating the possibility of something that will have happened in the future. यदि कहीं मिल भी गया तो बिना भक्ति स्थिर नहीं रहता, *If in any way it should have been obtained, apart from devotion it will not remain firm.* और जब ऐसा मत हुआ तो अज्ञान आही गया, *And when such a religious position shall have come about, then ignorance will have come in.* यदि राजा हुए तो कोई चूँ तक भी न करेगा, *Should he have become king, then no one will make the slightest fuss.*

256. 4. Closely akin to the above, is the use of the Tense as found in Proverbs and similar pithy sayings. The force then is, should such and such a thing have taken place. **जीत लिया तो हार गया, हार गया तो मर गया,** *If a man has won he has lost, if he has lost he's a dead man* (referring to the fate of those who go to law).

THE PRESENT IMPERFECT. सामान्य वर्तमान

257. In the case of perhaps all these Tenses which are formed from the combination of a Participle and some auxiliary, a consideration of the two parts separately often renders considerable help in understanding the exact force of the Tense. Take the present, *e. g.*, **वह लिखता है,** *i. e.*, **वह है + लिखता हुआ,** *i. e., He is.* What is he doing? *writing.* He is the man who is at present writing.

With Neuter verbs, caution is necessary as to the exact meaning. **वह जाता है** may be correctly translated, "*he is going,*" but what exactly does this mean? In English, the general meaning would be, "*he is about to go,*" and it *might* be, *he is actually moving on his way.* In Hindi, the latter is the true idea involved in the Tense, though it *might* mean the former. **वह जाता है** may mean (1) He is actually on his way (2) He is in the habit of going (3) He is about to go.

The following uses may be noticed. One sentence

to illustrate each may suffice, as this is a very simple Tense.

1. The Actual Present. (The action going on at the present moment). **वह सोता है,** *He is sleeping*

2. The Habitual Present. **वह क्या नौकरी करता है?** What work does he do?

3. The Imminent Future. **मैं आगे चलता हूँ, तुम सेना लेकर आओ,** *I am going ahead; you collect the army and follow.*

4. The Historic Present. **उन्होंने क्या देखा कि एक यह कहता है, एक वह, और सब के सब आपस में झगड़ा करते हैं,** *What did he see? One is saying this, another that, and they are all quarrelling among themselves.*

Very occasionally, the Present Imperfect is loosely used for the Contingent Imperfect, *e. g.*, **जो तेरा गुरु सब जानता है तो** ... *If your guru knows everything then*......(**जानता है** is evidently equal to **जानता हो**).

THE PRESENT PERFECT. आसन्नभूत.

258. Little need be said about this Tense; its use is quite simple. It has not the same variety of idiomatic uses which are common with some of the Tenses.

It is equivalent to the English Perfect. मैं आया हूँ, *i.e., (Here) I am, having come, i.e., I have come.* जो उसने लिखा है सेा यही है, *This is what he has written.* आप की सब बातें उन्होंने मानी हैं, *They have obeyed all your words.* राजा अब आये हैं, *The king has now come.*

Occasionally, this Tense is used where we might expect to find the Indefinite Perfect. व्यास वाल्मीकि के बाद हुए हैं, *Vyas came after Valmiki.* As Valmiki passed away many centuries ago, one might have expected to find हुए not हुए हैं. Similarly, हम इन से दो एक बार कानपुर में मिले हैं, *I met him once or twice in Cawnpore.* We should, however, notice here that, in English, we might use this, *e. g., I have met him once or twice,* instead of *I met him once or twice.* Probably, the reason of the construction, both in the Hindi sentence and in English, is this that the point under consideration is not the actual meetings, but the present slight familiarity with the man that rests on the fact of having met him once or twice. The मिले has more of its distinctly participial force than is usual in the Present Perfect.

In many sentences in which the form at first sight appears to be the Present Perfect, a little consideration will show that it is actually a Participle with the Present Tense of the verb "to be." Thus, घर के साम्हने पाँच आदमी बैठे हैं. This is not, *Five men have seated themselves before the house*, but. *There are five men sitting* (बैठे हुये) *in front of the house.* यह पुस्तक किस की लिखी है, *By whom was this book written?* उसने पुस्तक लिखी है, *He has written a book.* In the first sentence, लिखी is the Participle (लिखी हुई). The sentence really means, यह किस की लिखी हुई पुस्तक है? In the second sentence, we have the true Present Perfect.

THE PAST IMPERFECT. अपूर्णभूत

259. This is perhaps the simplest and clearest of all these twelve Tenses. It bears two shades of meaning.

1. वह यह करता था, *At some past time he was actually doing it.*

2. The same sentence may mean, *He was in the habit of doing it.* This would be more distinctly expressed by वह यह किया करता था.

Probably, all the uses of this Tense are included in the above, though sl ght modifications of meaning or force may be introduced by means of other words in the sentence, *e. g.*, **वह कब किसी को कुछ देता था?** *When did he ever give anything to anybody?* The force of the Participle is here very weak, the meaning being that never did he do a generous act to anyone.

THE PAST PERFECT. पूर्णभूत.

260. According to the scheme of the Tenses, this ought to equal the English Pluperfect. As the Past Imperfect represented the subject of the verb in the past as actually engaged in the action indicated by the verb, so this Past Perfect should represent him as being in the position of one who had already completed the action, *i. e.*, Past Imperfect, *he was + writing*, *i. e.*, *he was writing*; Past Perfect, *he was + having written*, *i. e.*, *he had written*. The Hindi **पूर्णभूत**, however, does not definitely, express this; it does not, generally, as does the English Pluperfect, express the fact that something had been completed before another event occurred, but simply states the fact that something did occur in the past. The main difference between this Tense and the Indefinite Perfect (**सामान्यभूत**) is this that this **पूर्णभूत** indicates a more remote past. This Tense may, and at times does, equal the English Pluperfect, but does not do so as a rule.

The following sentence illustrates the use ot this Tense as a full Pluperfect. उनको बड़ा आनन्द हुआ क्योंकि जब से रामचन्द्र जनकपुर में आये थे तब से उन्हें देखकर सभों की यह लालसा हुई थी कि किसी तरह जानकीजी का ब्याह रामचन्द्र के साथ हो, *They greatly rejoiced, for, since Ramchandra had come to Janakpur, having seen Ramchandra, the desire of all had been that in some way or other Janki might be married to Ramchandra.*

In the following sentence, the addition of चुकना indicates that the writer recognizes that the Past Perfect alone does not necessarily carry the force of the Eng. Pluperfect. यद्यपि उसके मार डालने से चाणक्य की प्रतिज्ञा पूरी हो चुकी थी किन्तु उसने सोचा..., *Although by killing him, the promise of Chanakya had been fulfilled, nevertheless he considered that......*

In the following, the Tense is evidently used as about equivalent to the ordinary Indefinite Perfect. We have, उन्होंने उनको समझाया था, and then, as the reply, उन्होंने कहा था कि हे नाथ. Evidently, both indicate simply a somewhat remote past. *He explained to her... She said...* Again, उसको हमने पढ़ा था और उसका ढंग भी हम को बहुत पसन्द आया, *I read that book, and its style gratly pleased me.* The पढ़ा था and आया are apparently synchronous, and are evidently both the simple past. सीतापुर में उत्पन्न हुए थे, the context shows that, *was born in Sitapur*, is the right translation, not *had been*. So with the following: देवताओं ने प्रसन्न होकर वह धनुष राजा जनक के पुरखाओं को दिया था, *The gods having been pleased, gave that bow to King Januk's ancestors.* "*Gave,*" not "*had given,*" is the meaning. Let one more illustration suffiice. जिस समय असंख्य बीरों ने कट कट कर अपने प्राण छोड़े थे, उस समय ऐसा जान पड़ा था, *At the time when countless warriors were cut to pieces and yielded up their lives, at that time it seemed to me as though...* Quite clearly, *yielded up* and *seemed*, not, *had yielded up*, and, *had seemed.*

CONTENGENT IMPERFECT. सम्भाव्य वर्तमान.

261. The Hindi name, "the Possible Present," admirably expresses the functions of this Tense. The component parts,—the Imperfect Participle and the Contingent Future,—clearly indicate its general force; the action indicated by the Participle *may* be taking place. Whereas the Contingent Future more often refers to the future than the present, this Contingent Imperfect more frequently has reference to something that may be occurring at the present time. वह देश पवित्र समझना

चाहिये जहाँ भगवान के भक्त रहते हों, *Regard that country as holy where God's devotees may be living.* In simple English, *where God's devotees are living.*

The principal uses of the Tense are as follows:—

1. It may refer to an action as possibly taking place now or in the future. The Dubious Tense.

2. With a force closely akin to the Present Imperfect.

1. **यदि मेरे प्राण देने से पति का मंगल होता हो तो मैं प्राण देने को तैयार हूँ,** *If by the giving of my life my lord's good may be effected, then I am willing to give my life.* **यह विचार तक मन में नहीं आता कि वे सूरदासजी का कुल तक न जानते हों,** *I cannot frame the thought in my mind that they should not have even known what caste* (or *family*) *Sûrdâs belonged to.* **चाहे वह आप उस पर न चलता हो,** *Even though he should not be walking according to that* (*rule*) *himself.* **विरोध न होता हो,** *If it be not contrary to......*

2. Sometimes, the Contingent Imperfect is used in Hindi, where in English we should use the Present Imperfect. **ऐसे शब्द न आने पावें कि जिन का व्यवहार हिन्दी में न होता हो,** *That no such words may obtain a place the use of which may not exist in Hindi.* We should say, in English, *does not exist.*

THE CONTINGENT PERFECT. सम्भाव्यभूत

262. This Tense sets forth the possibility of something having been done in the past, not of *being done*, as with the Contingent Imperfect, but as *having been done*. In the second place, as we have seen that the Contingent Imperfect sometimes about equals the Present Imperfect, similarly the Contingent Perfect in some sentences is about equivalent to the Present Perfect.

1. Dealing with the possibility of something having happened in the past. **सम्भव है कि उन्हों ने साहित्य-लहरी सूरसागर के कुछ ही पीछे बनाई हो और सूरसारावली बनाने का विचार उनके चित्त में बहुत दिन पश्चात् उठा हो,** *It is possible that he may have composed the Súrságar shortly after the Sáhitya-lahari and that the thought of writing the Súrsárávalí arose in his mind a long time later.* **यह नहीं कहा जा सकता कि यह परिवर्तन एकाएक हुआ हो,** *This cannot be said that this change may have come about suddenly.* **जो कभी किसी ने देखे सुने भी न हों,** *Which (wonderful deeds) no one may have ever seen or heard of.* **इस काम को उन्हों ने शायद पसन्द किया हो,** *Perhaps he may have approved of this work.*

2. Very frequently this Tense occurs with similar force in conditional sentences. **जो भाव उसके चित्त में**

भरे हों उन्हीं का वह वर्णन करे *The sentiments which may have filled his mind, of these he may give a description.* यदि उसके किनारे सीढ़ियाँ बना दी गई हों, *If steps had been made by its side then.....* उसका चाहे जितना बड़ा अपकार हो गया हो, *No matter how great his wrong may have been.* उन्हों ने इस तरह की बातें यदि कही भी हों, *Should he even have uttered words of this character.*

3. Occasionally, the Contingent Perfect about equals in meaning the Present Perfect. कोई बात ऐसी नहीं रह गई जो उसने न सीखी हो, *There is no subject left which he has not learnt.*

THE PRESUMPTIVE IMPERFECT. संदिग्धवर्तमान.

263. This Tense and the Presumptive Perfect express the inference that something is occurring, or has occurred. The two Tenses might be called the Inferential Present and Inferential Past Tenses.

Naturally, the presumption may vary in degrees of assurance, ranging from, *I cannot but infer that.....* to *I am utterly sure that.........* अब राजा आते होंगे, *The king will be coming just now.* वह सोती होगी, *She will be sleeping.* वहाँ पहुँच कर वे आज बहुत दुःख उठाते होंगे, *They will have arrived there and to-day be enduring great troubles.*

THE PRESUMPTIVE PERFECT. संदिग्धभूत.

264. The explanation with reference to the use of this Tense has been given above (Sec. 263).

कोई जीव-जन्तु मार कर खा गया होगा, *He must have killed some living creature and eaten it.* **यह सुन कितना दुःख हुआ होगा,** *Having heard this, how great must have been the grief.* **ईसा के छठे शतक के पहले ही विद्यमान रहे होंगे,** *He must have lived before the sixth century of the Christian era.* **इसी से उसे दुःख पहुँचा होगा,** *From this he must have suffered great trouble.* **अब आप लोगों की समझ में पैसे की महिमा आ गयी होगी,** *Now the might of money will have reached your understanding.* **कोई बीस बरस का अर्सा हुआ होगा,** *An interval of something like twenty years must have elapsed.* **किसी ने सुना होगा,** *Some one must have heard.*

Slight modifications of the force of this Tense occur when found in interrogative sentences and in various other circumstances, but the above illustrations fairly cover the general scope of the uses of this Tense.

THE PAST CONTINGENT IMPERFECT. अपूर्णहेतुहेतुमद्भूत.

THE PAST CONTINGENT PERFECT. पूर्णहेतुहेतुमद्भूत.

265. These two Tenses are conditional in their general use. In the protasis, the Tense is used to express the condition, and in the apodosis to indicate what would have been the result had the condition been, or not been, fulfilled. In the apodosis, the form of the Tense is frequently contracted and sometimes another Tense may be used. To illustrate :—

यदि वह न देखता होता तो क्यों ऐसा घबराया होता (or, it might be घबराता alone), *If he had not been looking, then why should he have become so disturbed?* Or, if the न be omitted, *If he had been looking, then why should he have become so disturbed?* Or, in the Perfect, यदि उसने देखा होता तो ऐसा घबराया न होता, *If he had looked, he would not have been so disturbed.*

These Tenses are apparently only used when the condition is represented as not having been fulfilled (or if there be a negative in the conditional clause, then having been fulfilled.) In the protasis, यदि or some similar word, expressed or understood, will be found.

266. Illustrations of the Past Contingent Imperfect.

मेरे समान जो तुम घर के लोगों को छोड़ दूसरों के साथ रहते होते तो तुम को जान पड़ता कि दो महीने दो बरस से बीतते हैं, *Had you left your own people and been living with others as I have, then you would have thought that the two months passed like two years.* यदि वह उस समय जागता होता तो अपनी बहन के पीछे छाया की तरह अवश्य चला जाता, *Had he been awake at that time, he would assuredly have followed his sister like her shadow.*

267. Illustrations of the Past Contingent Perfect.

यदि पुण्य किया होता तो मेरा घर इस तरह क्यों नष्ट होता! *Had I done good deeds, then why should my house have thus been ruined?* यदि केशवदास ने केवल विज्ञानगीता बनाई होती तो हम उन्हें दूसरे दर्जे का कवि कहते, *Had Keshavadas only written the Vigyán-gítá, we should have called him a second-rate poet.* पर मर गया होता तो बैठा कैसे रहता! *But if he had died, how could he remain in a sitting posture?* यदि मेरी उम्र ढल न गई होती तो आज तुम्हारा यह सुन्दर मुँह देख कर अपनी जान न्यौछावर कर देता, *Were I not such an old man, having to-day seen your pretty face, I would give my life a sacrifice for you.*

Occasionally, neither the Past Contingent Perfect, nor an equivalent, is used in the apodosis. यदि कहीं उसकी यह इच्छा भी पूरी हो गयी होती तो फिर क्या कहना था ! *If in any way this desire of his had also been fulfilled, then what was there to say ?*

Now and again, the Past Contingent Perfect is not fully written in the protasis. अगर मैं चाहता तो आज तक कभी का उसे यमलोक पहुँचा दिये होता, *Had I desired, there would have been for him an arrival in the realms of death long enough ago.*

THE IMPERSONAL VERB. भावप्रधान क्रिया.

268. The Hindi Impersonal Verb does not correspond with the English verb bearing that name, but cannot be denied a right to being so called.

In form, it is the same as the Passive Verb, the main verb assuming the form of the Perfect Participle and being followed by the Verb जाना. As there is no Nominative for the Participle or Verbal ending to agree with, the Verb always remains in the form of the 3rd person, singular, masculine. Practically, the participal part of the Verb is the subject, and is equal to a Verbal Noun. उससे खाया नहीं जाता, *By him eating cannot be done.*

A few illustrations of the use of this Impersonal Verb will probably be more helpful than further explanation. मुझसे यहाँ बैठा नहीं जाता, *I cannot sit here.* (Lit. *By me sitting here cannot be endured*). रात भर तीनों से नहीं जागा जाता, *The three of them cannot keep awake the whole night.* निर्बल हो कर उससे न उठा जाता न सहा जाता है, *Being very weak, he can neither rise nor can he bear (the pain).* हम से नहीं चुप रहा गया, *I could not keep silence.* मुझसे नहीं रहा जाता. Practically, this comes to "*I can't stand it.*" उससे चला नहीं जाता, *He cannot walk.*

This construction with the Impersonal Verb is not a *very* common one, but cannot be called very uncommon. It is a construction which the student ought to be familiar with.

THE PASSIVE-NEUTER VERB.

269. We venture to give this name to a very numerous class of Hindi Verbs which are *Passive*, forasmuch as the state of the subject of the Verb is brought about by something other than any action on the part of that subject, and yet forasmuch as the instrument of the action is not generally stated, or indicated, the Verb is not a *true Passive*, in the ordinary acceptance of that term, but has more affinity with a *Neuter* Verb.

e.g. For the true Passive, we may have पेड़ हिलाया जाता है, *The tree is being shaken.* It may be mentioned, or not mentioned, that it is shaken by the wind or by some person, but the Verb is Passive and the indication clearly made that the shaking is caused by some person or thing; but in the sentence, पेड़ हिल जाता है (or हिलता है), the form of the Verb is the Passive-Neuter, and attention is drawn only to the simple fact that the tree shakes. It may be logically inferred that the shaking did not originate without some cause, but the Verb makes no reference to any cause and has no concern with the fact as to whether there was a cause or not. The one single import of the Verb is to set forth the fact that the tree shakes. In English, there are a few Verbs which are both Transitive and Intransitive, and thus lend themselves to a similar double use, e.g. *The pipe burst.* (No reference to, *how.*) *The pipe was burst* (suggesting that this was due to a sudden thaw, or something of the kind). Again, *The papers were burnt*; Passive, the mind of the reader naturally gathering that some one burnt them, or that in a general fire they had been burnt, or something of a similar character. *The fire was burning.* Here we have a pure Neuter Verb.

In Hindi, we need not use the same Verb in two

ways, forasmuch as a very large number of Verbs is provided for which there are two forms, an Active form, of which the Passive form can be used, and, from the same root as the Active, a Passive-Neuter form. Thus खोलना and खुलना. Using the first, we may have the sentence खिड़की खोली गयी, *The wicket was opened.* We infer that some one opened it. खिड़की खुल गयी, *The wicket opened.* Here the thought is in no way directed to any consideration as to how the opening occurred, the one fact to which the attention of the writer and the reader is directed is that the wicket became open. So, again, लकड़ी जलायी गयी, *The wood was burnt* (Passive). लकड़ी जल गयी, *The wood burnt* (Neuter). यह बात छिपायी गयी, *This matter was concealed.* यह छिप गया, *This* (*man*) *was hidden.* Attention is simply drawn to the fact that the man disappeared; no reference is made or suggested as to his being concealed by anyone.

With the one series of Verbs, the forms, construction and meaning are those of the true Passive Verb; in the other, the meaning has close affinity with the true Neuter Verbs, and the form and construction are not Passive.

One special feature of these Passive-Neuter Verbs demands notice. जाना is generally added to the Verb, though it is not invariably used in all the Tenses. With this जाना, however, the form of the Perfect participle is not used (as is the case with the Passive Verb) but the stem, e.g., जल जाना, not जला जाना. Thus we may have the two forms for the Passive-Neuter खुलना or खुल जाना, *to open.* In the Indefinite Perfect, the form would almost invariably be खुल गया, but in the Future the form खुलेगा would probably be more frequently found than खुल जाएगा. But take another Verb, फटना or फट जाना, the Indefinite Perfect would almost invariably be फट गया, but in the Future फट जाएगा would be far more frequent than फटेगा. Speaking generally, we find that the जाना is very much used with the Past Tenses, not *so* much with the Future.

It may be asked, Why this addition of the जाना at all? Some might state, and do state, that the जाना is *intensive.* A careful consideration of a large number of sentences in which this जाना occurs with these Passive-Neuters, will make it evident that, in most cases, this suggestion about *intensity*, has no support whatever. A more plausible suggestion is that, as जाना is indicative of the Passive, its addition to these Verbs is appropriate, forasmuch as they are in one respect Passive. This appears to be a reasonable suggestion. The question still remains, How is it that sometimes the जाना addition is used, sometimes not? To this question, the only safe and sound answer appears to be, "Because it is." It is a matter of usage. Why is it that in English we may say "*a big house,*" "*a large house,*" but, while allowed to say "*a big girl,*" the phrase "*a large girl*" is not idiomatic (in England)?

A few illustrative sentences of the use of these Passive-Neuter Verbs will now be given.

वह नीचे गिर जाती है, *It falls down.* (Were it Passive, it would be, **गिरायी जाती है**, *is flung down*). **स्वभाव सचमुचही नहीं छूटता**, *One's natural disposition, of a truth, does not leave one.* **उन्हें शीघ्र ही स्त्री-पुत्र की चिन्ता घिर आई**, *Immediately the thought of wife and son possessed him.* The Neuter **घिरना** is used in preference to the Active **घेरना,** because thoughts come involuntarily. **हाय, मेरा सर्वस्व लुट गया**, *Alas! my all has gone.* **उस की सूरत पल भर भी उस के मन से नहीं टलती,** *Her form does not for a single moment pass from his mind.* **वह भँवर की ओर खिच गयी**, *She was drawn towards the whirlpool.*

So general has become the use of these Passive-Neuter Verbs that they are sometimes found where the Passive would be more appropriate, as distinct reference is made to the cause of the state referred to, *e.g.*, पसाते वक़्त उसके हाथ पाँव माँड़ से जल गये, *At the time of skimming (the water in the cooking-pot), her hands and feet were scalded by the rice-water.* Here, however, one can see a measure of appropriateness in the use of the Passive-Neuter, forasmuch as the instrument was not a conscious instrument. She suffered *through* the water, the water did not *inflict* the suffering. जो अन्य जाँच से भी ठीक जँचता है, *Which is proved to be right by other proofs.* Here, again, we notice the instruments are not conscious instruments.

Another indication of the favour which these Passive-Neuter forms obtain is found in the fact that some Verbs which are already Neuter assume a shortened form, more characteristic of the Passive-Neuters, *e.g.*, जागना and जगना, *e.g.*, जब वह सोती है तब भी उसके हृदय में यह आशा जगी रहती है, *When she sleeps this hope remains awake in her heart.* So with भागना and भग जाना, *to flee.* भाग गया and भग गया are both used.

No attempt can be made to give a complete list of all these Passive-Neuter Verbs: their name is legion. A few, however, are given below, showing the Active Verb from the same stem, the Passive form of which can be used instead of the Passive-Neuter, when preferred. In considering the Causal Verbs an Active Verb may often be referred to as the Causal Verb from one of these forms, *e.g.*, **बनाना**, *to make*, the Pass.-Neut. form being **बनना**, *to be made, to become made*, this, of course, being distinct from the true Passive, *to be made*, **बनाया जाना**. This matter will be referred to again in the section on Causal Verbs.

270. Passive-Neuter.		Active.	Passive.
उखड़ जाना,	to be rooted up.	**उखाड़ना**	**उखाड़ा जाना**
बँट जाना,	to be distributed.	**बाँटना**	**बाँटा** ,,
सुधर जाना,	to be put right.	**सुधारना**	**सुधारा** ,,
रुक जाना,	to be stopped.	**रोकना**	**रोका** ,,
रुँध जाना,	to be shut in.	**रुँधना**	**रुँधा** ,,
कट जाना,	to be cut.	**काटना**	**काटा** ,,
उलझ जाना,	to be entangled.	**उलझाना**	**उलझाया** ,,
उठना,	to rise.	**उठाना**	**उठाया** ,,
घुल जाना,	to be dissolved.	**घोलना**	**घोला** ,,

Passive-Neuter.		Active.	Passive.
पिघल जाना,	to melt.	पिघलाना	पिघलाया जाना
चेतना,	to return to consciousness.	चिताना	चिताया ,,
छिद जाना,	to be pierced.	छेदना	छेदा ,,
छिन जाना,	to be picked out.	छीनना	छीना ,,
जित जाना,	to be conquered.	जीतना	जीता ,,
बच जाना,	to be saved.	बचाना	बचाया ,,

This list could be greatly extended. A little observation in the course of regular reading will show what a very important place this class of Verbs takes in Hindi. As indicated by one or two illustrations given above, the use of the Pass.-Neuters is not *always* sharply distinguished from the use of Passives, but, generally speaking, where the attention of the reader is directed to the state itself, and not to the means by which it is brought about, the Passive-Neuter form is used, the Passive thus being left for cases in which the agents are to have attention directed to them. Thus, यह किस से बिगाड़ा गया, *By whom was this ruined?* But यह बिगड़ गया है वह कुछ काम का नहीं, *This is ruined, it's fit for nothing.*

CAUSAL VERBS. प्रेरणार्थक क्रिया.

271. The first point to notice in considering the Causal Verbs is that many Verbs which are causal in form are not, strictly speaking, Causal Verbs, *e.g.*, पिलाना is a true Causal, it means, *to cause to drink*, the first form of the Verb being पीना, *to drink*; but it is a misuse of language to call छीलना, the Causal of छिलना or छिल जाना. The former is an Active Verb, meaning, *to pare, to scrape, to peel*; and there is a Passive-Neuter form of the Verb छिल जाना, which means, *to be pared, etc.* The true Causal Verb indicates the causing of another to do something, instead of doing it oneself, *e.g.*, करना (Trans.), *to do*, कराना (Causal) *to cause another to do*; but to call a Verb a Causal because it signifies that something is caused to take place, is rather a twisting of language and likely to cause confusion. बनाना is Causal *in form*, but not so in meaning; it simply means, *to make*. From the same stem there is a Pass.-Neut. Verb, बनना or बन जाना, *to be made*. बनाना is actually an ordinary Active Transitive Verb. And the Causal of this is बनवाना, *to cause another to make, to have something made by another*.

As in the present section, our chief concern is with the *form* of these so-called Causal Verbs, bearing in mind what has been written above, we may accept the loose nomenclature and speak of Causal Verbs, even though they are not strictly so in meaning. We should, however, recognize that even as regards form it might be as correct, or more correct, to regard बनना, *to be made*, as a shortened form of बनाना, as to insist on the latter being the Causal form from बनना. For convenience of treatment, however, we accept the latter course and note the changes of form on that basis.

272. For the sake of clearness, with reference to the force and meaning of these different classes of Verbs, it is suggested that the student might do well in the course of his reading to work out a tabulated list of Verbs on somewhat the lines adopted in the following table.

Neuter †, or Passive-Neuter * Verb.	Active Intransitive.	Active Transitive.	Ordinary, Act. in meaning; Causal in form.	Genuine Causal.	2nd Causal.
* **सोना,** *to sleep.*	... ...	... ...	... ...	**सुलाना,** *to cause another to sleep.*	**सुलवाना,** *to cause another to cause a third person to sleep.*
	चलना, *to move.*	... ...	... ...	**चलाना,** *to cause another to move.*	**चलवाना**
		करना, *to do.*	... ...	**कराना,** *to cause another to do.*	**करवाना**
* **बनना** *to be made.*	... ...	... ...	**बनाना,** *to make.*	**बनवाना,** *to cause to be made.*	

Neuter †, or Passive-Neuter * Verb.	Active Intransitive.	Active Transitive.	Ordinary, Act. in meaning; Causal in form.	Genuine Causal.	2nd Causal.
		खाना, *to eat.*	... ...	**खिलाना,** *to cause another to eat.*	**खिलवाना**
	बैठना, *to sit.*	... ...	... ...	**बैठाना,** *to seat.*	**बिठवाना**
* **पिटना,** *to be beaten.*	...	...	**पीटना,** *to beat.*	**पिटवाना,** *to cause to be beaten.*	
	भागना, *to flee.*	... ...	... ...	**भगाना,** *to cause another to flee.*	**भगवाना**
* **बिगड़ जाना,** *to be spoilt.*	... ...	... ...	**बिगाड़ना** or **बिगड़ाना,** *to spoil.*		
* **घिर जाना,** *to be surrounded.*	... ...	... ...	**घेरना,** *to surround.*	**घिराना**	

273. The most simple form of the Causal Verb is in the case of a Verb, the stem of which ends in a consonant preceded by a short vowel; the Causa is often then formed by adding **आ** to the stem for the First Causal and **वा** for the Second Causal. Thus:—

चढ़ना, *to ascend.* **चढ़ाना,** *to cause to ascend.* **चढ़वाना,** *to cause another to cause a third person to ascend.* **उठना,** *to rise.* **उठाना,** *to make another rise.* **उठवाना.**

As will be shewn, other stems, and even the stems spoken of above, may have the Causal form formed in other ways.

In not a few instances, the idea expressed by the Causal form may be expressed by a single word in English, *e.g.*, **पढ़ना,** *to read*; **पढ़ाना,** *to cause another to read*, that is, *to teach*; **जागना,** *to wake up*; **जगाना,** *to wake* (another person).

With some Verbs in the Causal form, the meaning of the Verb is modified in other ways, besides being causal. *e.g.*, **बोलना,** *to speak*, or, *to utter a sound*; Causal, **बुलाना,** means *to call* (**उस को बुलाओ,** *call him*); **समझना,** *to understand*, **समझाना** *may* mean simply *to explain*, but probably more often carries somewhat of the force of our slang phrase, "*knocking a little sense into anyone.*"

Second Causals are not in use with all the Verbs. It will be noted that, what appears as a Second Causal *in form*, may only be a First Causal in *meaning*, *e.g.*, बजवाना, बनवाना; the earlier forms, बजाना and बनाना are not truly Causals in meaning, but Active Transitive Verbs, meaning *to play* (an instrument), *to make.* बजवाना therefore, simply means, *to cause another to play*: बनवाना, *to cause another to make.* That is, they are, *in meaning*, only First Causals.

The question sometimes arises with regard to some of these Causals as to the Cases governed by them, *e.g.*, in the sentences, लड़के को रोटी खिलाओ, or पानी पिलाओ, do खिलाना and पिलाना take two Accusatives, or only one? If only one, which is the Accusative, what case is the other word? रोटी and पानी are the Accusatives; लड़के को is Dative. The *bread* is the Accusative, whether I eat it or cause another to eat it. The use of another Causal Verb may help to clear this matter. मैं घर को देखता हूँ, *I see the house*; मैं लड़के को घर दिखलाता हूँ, *I shew the house to the boy.*

The idiomatic use of मारना involves a similar difficulty. *We* speak of striking a horse *with* a whip;

making the horse the Accusative. In Hindi, the *whip* is the Accusative, the *horse* Dative. वे घोड़ों को चाबुक मारते थे, *They were beating the horses with whips.* The idiom really works out—*They were striking the whips to the horses.* Almost invariably, in Hindi, it is the instrument with which the striking is done, that is in the Accusative, the person struck in the Dative.

274. The changes made in forming these Causal forms will now be noticed and examples given. Again, the attention of the student is directed to the fact that it is the Causal *forms* that are now to be dealt with, not the *meanings*.

1. Some of the Verbs, the stem of which ends in a consonant, preceded by a short vowel, form the First Causal by the addition of आ to the stem, the Second Causal by the addition of वा to the stem.

बनना	बनाना	बनवाना
to be made	*to make.*	*to have made.*
सुनना	सुनाना	सुनवाना
to hear	*totell*	*to cause another to tell.*

Other examples, जलना *to burn*, मिलना *to meet*, करना *to do*, उड़ना *to fly*, उठना *to rise*, गिरना *to fall.*

In the same way, words with an extra syllable.

पकड़ना	पकड़ाना	पकड़वाना
to lay hold of.	*to cause another to seize.*	*to cause to have seized.*

So also **समझना** *to understand,* **भटकना** *to go astray,* **बदलना** *to change,* **चिपकना** *to stick* (*Neut.*) **चमकना** *to shine.*

There are exceptions to this rule, *e.g.*:—

कहना	कहलाना *or* कहाना	कहलवाना
to speak.	*to cause to speak, to name, to be named.*	*to be called or named.*

275. 2. **Other Verbs, with root ending in a consonant preceded by a short vowel, form their First Causal** by lengthening the vowel of the root. For the second Causal, the long vowel is again shortened and the usual **वा** added to the root.

कटना	काटना	कटवाना
to be cut	*to cut*	*to cause to be cut.*
बँटना	**बाँटना**	**बँटवाना**
to be divided	*to distribute*	*to cause to be distributed.*
पिसना	**पीसना**	**पिसाना**
to be ground	*to grind*	*to cause to be ground.*
बिनना	**बीनना**	**बिनवाना**
1. *to be woven*	*to weave*	*to cause to be woven.*
2. *to be picked*	*to pick*	*to cause to be picked.*

छिदना	छेदना	छिदवाना
to be pierced	*to pierce*	*to cause to pierce.*

So also :—

बँधना	*to be bound*	बाँधना	बँधवाना
पिटना	*to be beaten*	पीटना	पिटवाना
डुलना	*to move*	डोलना	डुलवाना
खुदना	*to be dug*	खोदना	खुदवाना
खुलना	*to be opened*	खोलना	खुलवाना
घुलना	*to be dissolved*	घोलना	घुलवाना
फिरना	*to be turned*	फेरना	फिरवाना
मिटना	*to be effaced*	मेटना	मिटवाना
		or मिटाना	
खिँचना	*to be drawn*	खींचना	खिँचवाना
		or खैँचना	
फिँकना	*to be flung*	फेँकना	फिँकवाना
			or फेँकवाना
दबना	*to be pressed*	दाबना	दबवाना
		or दबाना	
तुलना	*to be weighed*	तोलना	तुलाना *or*
		or तौलना	तौलाना

Similarly, words with an extra syllable :—

उखड़ना	*to be rooted up*	उखाड़ना	उखड़वाना

बिगड़ना *to go bad*	बिगाड़ना or बिगड़ाना	बिगड़वाना

So उतरना, *to descend*, निकलना, *to be turned out, to go out*, सम्भलना, *to be supported or strengthened.* बटुरना, *to be collected* (Caus. बटोरना).

दीखना or दिख जाना *to be seen*; देखना *to see*; दिखाना or दिखलाना or देखाना *to cause to see*; with a second Causal दिखलवाना

276. 3. Verbs with root ending in a consonant, preceded by a long vowel

The Vowel shortened for both First and Second Causals, and आ and वा added to this modified root in the usual way.

जागना or जगना	जगाना	जगवाना
to awake (*Neut.*)	*to arouse* or *awaken*	*to cause to be aroused.*
बोलना *to speak*	बुलाना or बोलाना	बुलवाना
बीतना *to pass (of time)*	बिताना	बितवाना
जोतना *to yoke*	जुताना	जुतवाना

Some of these verbs do not shorten the vowel, some insert ल before the आ and वा, others have no first Causal in use (or, it would be more correct to say that the First Causal takes the form of the Second Causal) Other irregularities also occur.

Examples.

दौड़ना *to run* दौड़ाना दौड़वाना
फैलना *to spread* फैलाना फैलवाना
बैठना *to sit* बैठाना, बिठलाना, *or* बैठालना
खेलना *to play* खेलाना *or* खिलाना खेलवाना
बोना *to sow* बोआना.
भेजना *to send* भिजवाना *or* भेजवाना
डालना *to throw* डलवाना
मारना *to strike* मरवाना

Etymologically, मारना is First Causal from मरना *to die.* ख़ीजना *to be angry* खिजलाना *or* खिजाना

277. 4. Verbs with an open root.

For the formation of the Causal forms, the vowel is shortened, and commonly ल is inserted before the आ and वा. Many of these Verbs present some little irregularity.

पीना *to drink* पिलाना पिलवाना
सोना *to sleep* सुलाना सुलवाना
देना *to give* दिलाना दिलवाना

More or less irregular.

खाना	*to eat*	खिलाना	खिलवाना
बोना	*to sow*	बोआना	
लेना	*to take*	लिवाना	
रोना	*to weep*	रुलाना *or*	रोलाना
सीना	*to sew*	सिलाना	सिलवाना
छूना	*to touch*	छुवाना *or*	छुलाना

278. 5. Some few Verbs undergo a modification of one of their consonants when changed into Causals.

छूटना *or* छुट जाना	*to be set free*	छोड़ना	छुड़ाना, छुड़वाना
टूटना	*to be broken*	तोड़ना	तोड़वाना *or* तुड़वाना
फटना	*to be rent or torn*	फाड़ना	
फूटना	*to be broken*	फोड़ना	फोड़वाना
बिकना	*to be sold*	बेचना *or* बिकाना	बिकवाना *or* बेचवाना
धुलना	*to be washed*	धोना	धुलाना

The total number of Causal Verbs is very large. Probably most of the methods of their formation are illustrated in the rules given above; but it is more than possible that some few may not conform to any of them.

VERBS FORMED FROM NOUNS, ETC.

279. Some few Verbs are found in Hindi formed from Nouns and other Parts of Speech. These Verbs are formed by the addition of **आना**, and remind one of such a phrase in English as "*the play was staged,*" for "*putting on the stage.*"

These Verbs are found most largely in colloquial speech or in verse, but must certainly be regarded as part of the language. A few of them are given below.

दुःखना *or* दुखाना	*To pain* or *to cause pain.*	From	दुःख
दृढ़ाना	*To strengthen, establish.*	"	दृढ़
अलगाना	*To separate.*	"	अलग
अपनाना	*To make one's own.*	"	अपना
नियराना	*To draw near.*	"	नियर
नगिचाना	do.	"	नगीच
	(a corruption of नज़दीक		
पीड़ाना	*To pain.*	from	पीड़ा
गरमाना	*To become hot*, or *angry.*	"	गर्म
शरमाना	*To feel shame*, or *make ashamed.*	"	शर्म

ONOMATOPOETIC VERBS.

280. Onomatopoetic words are abundant in Hindi. The Verbs are formed by the addition of **आना** to some word, or sound, representing the cry of an animal or some other sound. In this class of Verbs should be placed also the Verbs which do not attempt to imitate some sound, but seek to suggest by sound some special appearance, *e. g.*, **चमचमाना,** *to glitter ;* **डहडहाना,** *to glow ;* **सटपटाना**, *to be in a flutter*, or *fluster.* (Compare the similar English attempts in such words as, sparkle, glitter, dazzle, etc.). To what extent these words convey through the ear what is seen by the eye, may depend in some measure on the imagination of the hearer. Indians seem to possess a perfect genius for inventing onomatopoetic words. **फुसफुसाना** strikes one as a very successful attempt to produce an imitative Verb for, *to whisper*. So with **बड़बड़ाना** or **कुड़कुड़ाना,** *to grumble.*

It is interesting to note how nearly identical some of these Hindi and English onomatopoetic words are, *e.g.*, **मरमराना** in Hindi for expressing the *murmuring* of the wind in trees; in **हिनहिनाना**, we have the *neigh* of English, only the " n " and " h " are in reverse order. As this is a Grammar, not a Dictionary, no attempt will be made to give a list of the Onomatopoetic Verbs so numerous in Hindi. A few are appended as illustrations.

चहचहाना, *To twitter*, of birds.
खटखटाना, *To rap at, to rattle*, a door.
भूँकना, *To bark.*
घड़घड़ाना, *To rumble* (as thunder).
सनसनाना, *To whistle* or *whizz.*
झनझनाना, *To clang.*
थरथराना, *To shiver.*
चिंघारना, *To scream*, or *shriek* (*also of the trumpeting of an elephant*).
गुर्राना, *To growl* (of a tiger).
टपटपाना, *To patter* (as rain).
कड़कड़ाना, *To crackle*, or *cackle.*

COMPOUND VERBS. संयुक्त क्रिया.

281. Compound Verbs abound in Hindi. They vary greatly in their formation and use, but it is not difficult to broadly classify them.

I. In the first division may be included all those Compound Verbs in which two words are joined, giving, generally, one Verbal idea. The first Verb makes the main contribution to that idea, but the second may modify the force in some way. Of the earlier Verb only the stem is used. This is subject to no changes throughout the conjugation, and thus the Compounded Verb becomes, both as regards meaning and conjugation, one compound word. Examples, **मिटा देना,** *to obliterate, to blot out*; **मान लेना,** *to obey*; **जल उठना,** *to flare up,* either literally, as a fire, or metaphorically, in a rage.

This class may be called Close Compounds.

II. The second class may include those Compounds in which each Verb retains, more or less fully, its own proper meaning. The earlier is often used in its Infinitive form (inflected or uninflected), or the stem alone, the second member of the Compound only being subject to the usual inflectional changes. Examples, **जाने देना** *to permit to go*; **रोने लगना,** *to begin to weep*; **कह चुकना,** *to finish speaking*; **उठ सकना,** *to be able to rise.*

This second class may be called, Loose Compound Verbs.

III. The third class includes those Compounds in which the first member is a Noun, or, occasionally, an Adjective, Adverb or Postposition. Examples, **क्षमा करना,** *to forgive*; **दिखाई देना,** *to appear*; **पीछा करना,,** *to follow*; **पीछे करना,** *to put behind*; **अच्छा करना,** *to heal, make well.*

This third class may be called Noun-Verbal Compounds.

I. CLOSE COMPOUND VERBS.

282. Whether the origin of these Compounds must be placed side by side with that love of doubling a word which is a characteristice of Hindi, is a question which we need not attempt to decide. Certain it is that these doubles are widely prevalent in Hindi. The second member of the Compound may tone the force of the earlier word, or somewhat modify its sense, but it seldom makes any distinct difference to the meaning. In the partnership, the first word supplies the capital, the second is the working partner; for, although the first dominates the meaning and power of the Compound, the conjugational changes fall entirely on the latter. Perhaps the nearest parallel in English to this class of Compounds is in such colloquial phrases as, *I'll give a look at it*; *I'll take a walk*; *I'll have a swim*.

Dr. Kellogg takes the form of the first word in these Compounds as the Conjunctive Participle. It seems, however, simpler and safer to regard it as the simple stem, as there is nothing of the force of the Conjunctive Participle in the use of the first word. This may be illustrated by the following. **खा आओ** has two possible meanings, 1. *Having eaten, go.* Here **खा** is the Conjunctive Participle, but the two Verbs do not constitute a Compound Verb. 2. *Eat away.*

This is the Compound Verb, and in this there is no suggestion of the Conjunctive Participle.

Sometimes, the second member of the Compound may strengthen, intensify, or otherwise affect the force of the earlier word, but in many cases it does not, but can only be regarded as an alternative way of saying what would be expressed by the simple Verb. In Compounds with **डालना**, and **उठना**, the difference is frequently very apparent. *e.g.*, **वह बोला**, *He said* ; but **वह बोल उठा**, *He spoke up*, or, *spoke out*. Take the following sentence also : **रघुपति मारे क्रोध के आग बबूला होकर बोल उठे**, *Raghupati perfectly furious with anger burst out.* In the following sentence, however, who can say that **लेना** adds any additional force ? **इसका वह पहले ही ठीक २ विचार कर लेता है**, *He gives, in the first place, a very careful consideration to this matter.* **विचार करता है**, would give just the same meaning.

283. Some examples of these Close Compound Verbs will now be given, and, where possible, a suggestion as to the force indicated by the addition of the second Verb.

1. and 2. **देना** and **लेना**. These roughly convey

the ideas of, *giving out*, and, *taking*, repectively. **लौटा देना** and **लौटा लेना** are good illustrations. The first means, *to return a thing*; the second, *to receive a thing back again.*

दे देना,	*to give.*	ले लेना,	*to take.*
कह देना,	*to say.*	सुन लेना,	*to listen.*
गाड़ देना,	*to bury.*	मान लेना,	*to obey.*
गिरा देना,	*to throw down.*	लौटा लेना,	*to take back.*
डाल देना,	*to throw away.*	ताड़ लेना,	*to find out.*
भेज देना,	*to send.*	छीन लेना,	*to sieze.*
चल देना,	*to go.*	पकड़ लेना,	*to lay hold of.*
कर देना,	*to do.*	कर लेना,	(the meaning depends on the context.)
छोड़ देना,	*to leave.*	पहचान लेना,	*to recognize.*
सुना देना,	*to cause to hear.*	समझ लेना,	*to understand.*
मिटा देना,	*to efface.*	लूट लेना,	*to sack, to rob.*
जमा देना,	*to collect.*	बना लेना,	*to put right.*
खिला देना,	*to feed.*	पिला देना,	*to give to drink.*

पहिना देना, *to clothe.*

284. 3. **जाना.** In some instances, this may have a slightly intensive force, but its use in the Passive Verb probably accounts for its general combination with the Passive-Neuter Verbs already referred to. To say that **गल जाना** is "intensive of, or equals, **गलना**" appears to be somewhat futile. **गल जाता है, गल गया, गल जायगा,** will almost always be the forms found; it would be difficult to find **गलता है, गला, गलेगा.** The use of **जाना** differs somewhat with different Passive-Neuter Verbs, being invariably used with some, not so invariably with others.

With Verbs other than the Passive-Neuters, the addition of **जाना** may suggest intensity, but not necessarily so.

Examples :—

जान जाना	*to get to know.*	**भूल जाना**	*to forget.*
मिल जाना	*to meet with.*	**मर जाना**	*to die.*
हो जाना	*to become.*	**आ जाना**	*to arrive.*
सो जाना	*to go to sleep.*	**पी जाना**	*to drink.*

With such Verbs, the **जाना** is more frequently used with some than with others, *e.g.*, **मिला,** *It is obtained*, is quite common; with **मरना** the **जाना** is generally used, **मर गया**, not **मरा.**

No examples of Passive-Neuter Verbs have been given. They may be seen in sufficient numbers in sections 269, 270.

285. 4. **डालना.** This Verb, meaning, *to throw, to fling*, is compounded with Verbs with which the idea of throwing, or of the addition of force, is appropriate.

फेंक डालना	*to fling away.*	फोड़ डालना	*to smash.*
मार डालना	*to kill.*	फाड़ डालना	*to rend.*
खो डालना	*to squander.*	काट डालना	*to cut, to hack.*
तोड़ डालना	*to smash.*	दे डालना	*to give away (lavishly).*
खा डालना	*to devour.*		

286. 5. **पड़ना.** The word **पड़ना** means, *to fall, to happen* (*cf.*, the English, *befall*, or " it fell out "), also, *to lie*. These meanings are echoed in Compounds formed by the addition of **पड़ना.**

समझ पड़ना	*to be understood.*
सुन पड़ना	*to be heard.*
देख पड़ना	*to come into view.*
बन पड़ना	*to be made.*
आ पड़ना	*to arrive.*
जान पड़ना	*to be known.*
हँस पड़ना	*to fall to a laughing.*
गिर पड़ना	*to fall.*

21

287. 6. **उठना.** Associated with the idea of, *rising up*, comes also that of *suddenness*.

चिल्ला उठना	*to cry out.*	जाग उठना	*to awake.*
बोल उठना	*to speak up or out.*	चौंक उठना	*to start up.*
रो उठना	*to break out crying.*	काँप उठना	*to begin suddenly to tremble.*
जल उठना	*to break out into anger.*	धधक उठना	*to blaze out.*

288. 7. **बैठना** suggests the settling down to something.

रो बैठना *to give way to grief.*

बिगड़ बैठना *to persistently go astray.*

पूछ बैठना *to set to work to interrogate someone.*

बन बैठना *to become something, and to remain so.*

289. 8. 9. 10. **रखना. आना** and **निकलना.** These three are somewhat similarly used in such Compounds, but are not so common as those given above.

रखना. उठा रखना *to take up (responsibility).*

रोक रखना *to stop.*

सज रखना *to arrange (a room, etc.)*

समझ रखना *to understnd.*

लगा रखना *to affix.*

आना. निकल आना *to come out.*
लौट आना *to return.*
बन आना *to be made.*
हो आना *to become.*
निकलना. आ निकलना *to come out.*
जा निकलना *to go out.*
चल निकलना *to start off.*

The Compounds with रहना will be noticed under Class II. Some of them belong to this Class I, but it may be well to consider them all together.

290. Synonymous and Alliterative Compound Verbs.

There may be mentioned under this Class I the Verbs Compounded of two stems, having similar meanings or similar in sound. Those brought forward here are generally used with the second stem having the addition of the sign of the Conjunctive Participle. It bears the *meaning* of this Participle also, and has Adverbial force in a sentence. Sometimes such Verbs are used in the Imperfect Participial form, and then the Participial termination is used with both stems, *e.g.*, कूदते फाँदते, *i.e.*, leaping and bounding along.

1. Two stems indentical or similar in meaning.

जान बूझकर, *knowingly, deliberately.*

देख भालकर,	*cautiously, looking carefully.*
सोच समझकर,	*with understanding, having thought it over.*
सिखा पढ़ाकर,	*having instructed (them) carefully.*

2. Sometimes, similarity of sound, especially in the way of alliteration, is combined with similarity of meaning.

समझ बूझकर,	*Understandingly.*
समझा बुझाकर,	*Having fully explained (to them).*
तोड़ फोड़कर,	*Having broken and smashed things.* (The Hindi of, "a bull in a China shop.")

291. Causal Compound Verbs. Somewhat similarly we find an ordinary Verb followed by its Causal form, the two thus combined conveying a comprehensive and general meaning, *e.g.*, **दे दिलाना, कर कराना,** thus **शरीर रहेगा तो कुछ प्रायश्चित्त कर कराके फिर शुद्ध हो लेंगे,** *If I remain alive (lit., if the body remain) then, having performed or effected some expiation, I shall again become (ceremonially) clean.*

In such instances, the Causal is not usually pleonastic, the meaning intended and expressed being, whether *done by the person himself or through another.*

LOOSE COMPOUND VERBS.

292. These Verbs differ widely from those just considered, as regards their structure. The two Verbs in these Compounds are closely associated rather than compounded, and not only as regards structure but as far as meaning also is concerned, the union is not so close. One might say that each of the two Verbs retained its own full meaning, were it not for the fact that some of the Verbs used in these Loose Compounds do not possess or retain their definite meaning outside of those Compounds. **सकना** cannot be used alone, **लगना** with its very wide range of meanings does not include "to commence," except in these Compounds, **चुकना** in its Passive-Neuter form **चुक जाना,** is used in the sense of "*to be finished,*" but is far more used in the compounded form than alone.

293. In considering the Verbs used in these Compounds, we will at the same time note any other uses which are special to the words. The following Verbs will be considered.

Verb.	Form in which the associated Verb is used.	Name given to the Compounded Verbs.
(1) सकना	With the stem.	Potentials.
(2) चुकना	ditto.	Completives.
(3) लगना	Inflected Infinitive.	Inceptives or Inchoatives.
(4) देना	ditto.	Permissives.
(5) पाना	ditto.	Acquisitives.
(6) करना	With Gerund (in the form of the Perfect Participle.)	Frequentatives.
(7) रहना	With the Imperfect or Perfect Participle.	Continuatives.
(8) जाना	ditto.	Progressives or Continuatives.
(9) चाहना	Uninflected Infinitive or Gerundive form.	Desideratives.

294. (1). **सकना,** *Potentials.* **सकना** is added to the stem of the Verb with which it is associated, the earlier Verb remaining unchanged throughout, in the same manner as with the Close Compounds. **सकना** yields the meaning, *to be able,* and is conjugated as an ordinary Intransitive Verb.

यह क्या कर सकता है, *What can he do?* **वे नहीं चढ़ सकेंगे,** *They will not be able to go up.* **उसकी स्त्री नहीं जा सकी,** *His wife was not able to go.* **उसी से यह नहीं किया जा सकता है.** *This cannot be done by him.*

Occassionally, the inflected form of the Infinitive may be found used in this Compound, but this is antiquated and should not be adopted. **वह नहीं निकलने सकता,** *He is not able to get out.*

295. (2). **चुकना,** *Completives.* A Passive-Neuter Verb **चुक जाना,** *to be used up,* is in use, also the Causal **चुकाना,** but the use of **चुकना** is mainly confined to use in these so-called Completives, **चुकना** being added to the stem of the earlier Verb. The Compound thus formed becomes an ordinary Intransitive Verb, and indicates the completion of the act signified by the first word of the Compound.

वह खा चुका, practically, *He has finished his meal.* अब वे कर चुके होंगे, *They will have finished doing (it) by now.* मैं कह चुका हूँ, *I have said my say.* In many instances, the English "finished" represents a more definite statement than the Hindi चुकना often carries. It is frequently used where we might use a simple past tense of the earlier Verb, *e.g.*, मैं सुन चुका हूँ, would often mean only, *I have heard (it).* हो चुका, *It's done.*

296. (3) लगना, *Inceptives,* occasionally called *Inchoatives.*

लगना is not used alone, with the meaning of "*to begin.*"

In these Compounds, the exact meaning is not, *to begin*, but, *to become engaged in.* The inflected form of the Infinitive with which it is used, is probably the Locative Case, with the में unexpressed, and therefore वह पढ़ने लगा equals वह पढ़ने में लग गया, *He became occupied in reading.*

These Compounds, in common with the two already mentioned, are conjugated as Intransitive Verbs, *i.e.*, the Nominative with ने is not used with them.

In not a few sentences, the लगना though used quite idiomatically and correctly, is somewhat redundant, no special force being indicated. In Hindi, **कहने लगा**, is often found where we should say, *He said*, not, *He commenced to say*. In the majority of instances, however, it does convey some idea of the commencement of some act, and in some cases has the full force of "*commenced to.*" *e.g.*, **तब से लोग आने जाने लगे**, *From that time people began to come and go, i.e., to visit*, some person or place.

297. (4 and 5) **देना** and **पाना**, *Permissives* and *Acquisitives*. These two sets of Compounds, though in one sense contrasted, have much in common, and may conveniently be considered together. They are used with the inflected Infinitive. This may be regarded as the Dative Case, with the **को** or **के लिए** unexpressed. Thus **उसने उसको जाने दिया**, might be more fully written, **उसने उसको जाने के लिए......दिया**, *He gave (permission) to him to go*, and so **वह जाने पाया** might, similarly, be more fully written' **उसने जाने को** (or **जाने के लिए**) ...**पाया**, *He obtained (permission) to go*.

An unexplained inconsistency is found in the use of these two Verbs, whereas the Nom. with **ने** is used in the case of **देना** with Tenses formed from the Perfect Participle, **पाना** is treated as an Intransitive Verb, though, in meaning, it is as transitive as **देना**, and takes the same construction when not in a Compound. We find **तुमने अर्थ-गौरव को हाथ से नहीं जाने दिया,** *You have not allowed profundity of meaning to escape from your hand*, i.e., *You have not allowed your fluency to carry you away*, but **रचना किसी स्थान पर शिथिल नहीं होने पाई,** *The composition has not in any place allowed slovenliness to obtain a place.*

298. (6) **करना,** *Frequentatives* or *Continuatives.*

In this Compound, **करना** is used with the Gerund having the form of the Perfect Participle. **वे नित यह कहा करते हैं,** *They always go on saying this.*

Frequentatives is a better name than Continuatives for this class of Compounds for even where the idea of continuity is present it is generally a continuity of repetition, *e.g.*, **वह घर पर आया करती है,** *She is in the habit of coming to the house.* **आप मुझे सब बातों में योंही रोक दिया करते हैं,** *In everything you thus go on crossing me.*

299. (7). **रहना,** *Continuatives.*

This may be used with the Imperfect or Perfect Participle of the accompanying Verb. **वह साल भर**

पढ़ता रहता था, *He kept up his studies during the whole year.* वह बैठी रहेगी, *She will remain seated.*

The question has been raised as to whether these are, strictly speaking, Compound Verbs, and not rather the ordinary use of रहना in close proximity to the preceding Participle. The question is one deserving consideration; but, on the whole, the application of the word, Compounds, does seem justifiable; there is not only proximity, but very close connection. In the sentence, वह घबराता हुआ चला जाता है, *He goes on his way greatly perplexed*, there are two distinct verbal ideas, namely, *he is perplexed*, *he goes on his way*, he might do either alone. But in, वह चलता रहता है, *He continues his journey*, no such separation is possible: the two Verbs have combined in one idea. If the two were separated, we should have the meaning, *he goes, he remains.*

Two or three examples of the use of this Compound are given. उसके उपरान्त ये महाराज गऊघाट पर रहते रहे, *After this, the Brahman continued living at Gaoghat.* भगवान तुम्हारा धर्म बनाए रहें, *May God continue to maintain your righteousness.* शरीर का निबाह होता रहे, *That there remain sufficient support for the body.* उसके पीछे २० बरस जीती रही, *After that she remained alive for twenty years.*

300. रहना *in Close Compound Verb.* Here may be noticed the use of रहना in a Close Compound Verb. As regards construction (*viz.*, with the stem of the preceding Verb), it is a Close Compound, but in meaning it is somewhat akin to the Loose Compounds, as the रहना retains its very distinct force. It indicates that the action referred to in the earlier Verb continues,—it has commenced, it is still incomeplete. वह आ रहा है, *He is coming, i.e.*, is actually on his way, has started but not yet arrived. वह मर रही है, *She is dying.* राजा कह रहे थे, *The king was actualy speaking when......*

In some sentences, the force of रहना is weaker than in others, but the idea of continuation is generally present. क्यों जी क्या सोच रहे हो, *My dear Sir, what are you thinking about?*

301. (8). **जाना**. *Progressives or Continuatives.*

With जाना, the preceding Verb is joined in its Participial form, Imperfect or Perfect, and agrees with it in Number and Gender. It is not easy to distinguish the exact difference in meaning between a Compound in which रहना is the second Verb and one in which जाना is used. It may be that with the former the emphasis, if emphasis there be, is on the continuation of the act or the condition, with the latter there may be an underlying hint of persistence, something like the difference between *The child continued crying, The child cried and cried.* Examples. वह बैठे २ काम करता जाता है, *While seated he goes on working away.* वह उसको मारती जाती और लड़का चिल्लाता जाता है, *She goes on beating the boy and he goes on crying out.* वे देते जाएं ये लेते जाएं, *They will go on giving and these will go on taking.*

302. (9). **चाहना,** *Desideratives.* The Verb compounded with **चाहना,** may be, 1, in the uninflected form of the Infinitive, or, 2, the Gerund having the form of the Perfect Participle. Formerly it was common to use the inflected form of the Infinitive, वह सुनने चाहता था, but of recent years the uninflected form is preferred, वह सुनना चाहता था.

Very often this **चाहना** with the other Verb forms a Compound rightly designated a Desiderative, but sometimes it is imminence, not desire, that is indicated, *e.g.*, मेरा लड़का मरा ही चाहता है, *My child is at the point of death.* एक बहुत बड़ी बुराई होना चाहती है, *A great evil is about to happen.*

The Infinitive may be in the feminine form, उन लोगों ने कुछ बिनती करनी चाही, *Those people wished to ask for something.* **इसने क्यों आज आप पर छुरी चलानी चाही थी,** *Why did this man wish to thrust a knife into you to day?* (Lit., *get his knife to work on you*). It is, however, more generally in the macs. sing. **उसने चलना चाहा,** *He desired to go.* **वे लेना चाहते हैं,** *They desire to take it.* **मैं सुनना चहता हूँ,** *I* (fem.) *desire to hear it.*

Very occasionally, an Infin. with **को** is used before **चाहना,** but this cannot be considered a very approved idiom. **मेरा जी इन बातों के जानने को चाहता है,** *My heart longs to know these matters.*

This **चाहना** is also used with the Perf. Participle form, or Gerund. **मैं आप का जी दुखाया नहीं चाहती.** *I* (fem.) *do not wish to trouble your life.* **वह...लिखाया चाहता था,** *He was wishing to get* (something) *written* **वह तुम्हें फँसाया चाहता है,** *He wishes to entangle you.*

303. Reference has already been made to the use of **चाहिये** as an Impersonal Verb. It is a common and useful construction. The Infin. may be in the masc. or fem. form and also in the plural form. **तुम को पढ़ना चाहिये,** *You must study* (*It is necessary for you* *to study.*) कब उसके साथ सन्धि करनी चाहिये, *When is it necessary to make a treaty with him?* तुमको अपने ग्रन्थ पढ़ने चाहियें, *You must read your own books.*

Sometimes a Verb is added after this चाहिये, *e.g.*, मुझे कुछ भी न बोलना चाहिये था, *It was not necessary for me to say anything.*

304. To complete the references to the special uses of चाहना, we may repeat that चाहे ...... चाहे ... ... is used for, *whether......or*...Thus, विद्वानों का मत है कि चाहे काम छोटा हो चाहे बड़ा, *The view of the wise is that whether it be a little matter or a great matter.*

NOUN-VERBAL COMPOUND VERBS.

305. These Verbs are also called Nominal Compounds. They are formed by adding a Noun, or other Part of Speech to the Verb करना (or to some other Verb). As in English, we can say, *to do penance*, *to do justice*, *to do homage* or *obeisance*, so in Hindi they can say, *to do worship*, पूजा करना; or आराधना करना; *to do mercy*, दया करना; *to do protection*, रक्षा करना; *to do food*, भोजन करना; and innumerable other do's.

These Compounds are of two kinds. In one Class, the Noun and Verb are so fully compounded that they become one Verb and can govern another Noun in the Accusative Case; in the second Class, the compounding is less effectively carried out, and the Noun remains related to the other Nouns in the sentence as though it were not compounded with the Verb, and is itself governed by that Verb. This distinction may be well illustrated by वर्णन करना, which is used in both ways. As fully compounded, we find, उसने अपना और पिशाच का वृत्तान्त वर्णन किया, *He related the story of himself and the goblin.* Here वर्णन and करना have become one Verb, and this Verb governs अपना और पिशाच का वृत्तान्त in the Accusative (without को). More generally, however, वर्णन करना is not fully compounded, and we should then have उसने अपने और पिशाच के वृत्तान्त का वर्णन किया, In the first case, we have, "*he related the story,*" in the second, "*he did a relation of the story.*"

A few of these Compounds are used in both ways, *e.g.*, स्वीकार करना. We find भाइयों ने महर्षि की आज्ञा स्वीकार की, *The brothers accepted the saint's command.* Here the Verb is a true Compound and is fem., because of आज्ञा. In the following sentence, इस ग्रन्थ का स्वीकार करें, *Let them accept this book*, the Verb is not fully compounded, and so does not govern ग्रन्थ in the Accus. The sentence runs literally, *Let them do acceptance of this book.*

Another illustration from an actual occurrence of sentences in a book is given, as it is most important to have a clear grasp of the differences of construction in the use of these two classes of Compound Verbs. इस पुस्तक के गुणों को हम कहाँ तक वर्णन कर सकते हैं, *How far can I describe the excellences of this book?* Here वर्णन करना is a full Compound and governs गुणों को in the Accus. But in the following, from the same book and within a line or two of the previously quoted sentence. यदि उसके गुणों का पूरा वर्णन किया जाए, *If a full description of its excellences should be given* (lit, "*made*"), the Verb is not fully compounded with वर्णन; otherwise the sentence would run यदि उसके गुण......वर्णन किये जाएं. The किये जाएं would be plural, agreeing with गुण. As it is, it is sing., agreeing with वर्णन.

It is only a few of these Compounds which are used in both forms. पालन करना is another of them. We may have उसने लड़के को पालन किया, *He nurtured the child.* Or, उसने लड़के का पालन किया, *He did nourishment of the child.* So also, प्रजा का पालन करूँगा, *I will cherish my subjects.*

त्याग करना, *to forsake* ; आरम्भ करना, *to commence*, and some others are used in both forms, but generally the Compound is either close or loose and used consistently in one way or the other.

ग्रहण करना, *to receive,* or *accept.* बिदा करना, *to farewell, to dismiss,* क्षमा करना, *to forgive,* are examples of the first Class, the fully Compounded Verbs.

In the case of the great majority of the Verbs now under consideration, the compounding is not fully carried out; the Noun which is more or less joined to the करना is related to other Nouns in the sentence, as though it were not an integral part of the Verb, and in truth it is not so.

Among such *not* fully Compounded Verbs come words like दया करना, *to display mercy*: रक्षा करना, *to afford protection*; पूजा करना, *to offer worship*; सहायता करना, *to render help.* In English, we have what we consider an appropriate Verb to use with each Noun; but, in Hindi, in spite of its wealth of words,

करना may be used with countless Nouns; and so we have above, *to do mercy, to do protection, to do worship, to do help*.

Other Verbs are used in these Compounds, such as देना, लेना, होना, खाना, मारना, but करना is the favourite Verb for these Compounds.

Not only are Nouns joined up in this way; occasionally, an Adverb, or Adjective, or even Postposition may be joined up, *e.g.*, अच्छा करना, *to heal*; भला करना, *to do good*; शीघ्र करना, *to hasten*; पीछे करना, *to put behind*; पीछा करना, *to pursue*.

No attempt will be made to give lists of these Compounds. Dr. Kellogg, in his Grammar, gives quite long lists of some of them, with the right constructions (in sections 450-465), and Mr. F. Pincott, in his Hindi Manual, similarly, gives useful lists (pp 49-59 in the edition of 1882).

It is very important that the student should learn which form is correct of these numerous Compounds, and also what is the right construction. Possibly, seeing the phrase, मुझ पर दया कीजिये, *Have mercy on me*, it might be concluded that दया करना was a full Compound, and that therefore उसने मुझ पर दया किया,

would be correct; but it is not so. **दया करना,** is not a full Compound, and the sentence should therefore be, **उसने मुझ पर दया की.**

306. दिखाई देना, etc. One small class of Compounds demands a separate notice. A few Abstract Nouns, notably **दिखाई,** *a seeing,* **सुनाई,** *a hearing* (and a few others formed on the same principle), are formed with **देना** into Compound Verbs which are treated as Neuters, but have somewhat the force of Passives. Occasionally, **पड़ना** is found instead of **देना.**

तब चन्द्रगुप्त का राज गया सा दिखाई देता है, *Then Chandragupt's kingdom appears as though it had passed away.* **वे जानवर से क्या दिखलाई देते हैं,** *What are those (things) like animals which are visible?* **जब कोई पुरुष दिखाई न दिया,** *When no man appeared.* **जय शब्द सुनाई पड़ा,** *The shout of "Victory!" was heard.* **चाणक्य बैठा हुआ दिखाई पड़ता है,** *Chanakya, seated, comes into view (i. e., when the curtain is lifted).*

SYNTAX OF THE VERB.

307. The matter of agreement between the Verb and its Nominative and Accusative, has already been dealt with in sections, 142-144, and the position of the Verb, in the sentence in section 147. Many other points have also come under consideration in the various sections on the Tenses, etc. One or two other points, more or less related to Syntax, may now be noticed.

Subject of the Verb unexpressed. The omission of the subject is more common in Hindi than in English. This is natural when it is remembered that in many parts of the Verb the Verb itself indicates whether the subject is sing. or plural; masc. or fem. With those Tenses of Transitive Verbs which are formed from the Perfect Participle this is not the case. Another disability under which Hindi suffers is the lack of a 3rd personal Pronoun. **वह** and **यह** have to serve for *he, she* and *it*.

In the English sentence, *Will you go? I will*, the Pronoun is used in the reply, the Verb is not repeated; in Hindi, the Verb is repeated, but (often) no Pronoun is used; **तुम जाओगे ? जाऊँगा.** For the English, *People say*, the Hindi will be, in many cases, simply, **कहते हैं.** In the following sentence, the Pronoun, *you*, is omitted in Hindi. **विवाह होने पर सास ननद की बात जानेगी,** *When (you) are married, (you) will know about mother-in-law and sister-in-law.*

Such omissions are quite common in Hindi.

The position of the subject and Verb often does not

correspond with the position common in English sentences. *e.g.*, *The king pondered over it and became much perplexed.* **सोचते सोचते राजा बहुत घबरा गये.**

308. The use of a Participle instead of a second principal Verb. A Conjunctive Participle, or ordinary Participle, very generally supplies the place which a second Verb would occupy in a corresponding English sentence. Eng. *He stood up in the assembly and said.* Hindi. **सभा में खड़े होकर उसने कहा.** Eng. *They kept walking on and became very weary.* Hindi. **चलते २ वे बहुत थक गये.** Eng. *He went to the shop, examined the cloth, asked the price and came away without purchasing anything.* Hindi. **दूकान पर जा कपड़ा देख और दाम पूछ कर बिना कुछ लिये चल निकला.**

309. Omission of Auxiliary. It has already been mentioned that, with some of the Tenses, the Auxiliary is sometimes omitted.

Again, one Auxiliary often does service for two or more Verbs. **रोज़ रोज़ वह घर जाता और बहुत चेष्टा करता था कि ...** *He went day by day to the house and tried hard to ......*

310. Omission of है with नहीं. In a sentence in which **नहीं** occurs, the **है** is often, perhaps we may say generally, omitted. Some are of the opinion that **नहीं** is a form **न** plus **है**. **मैं यह नहीं कहता कि**, *I do not say this that.....* So **वह कहीं नहीं जाता**, *He does not go anywhere.*

311. **है**, *not an Auxiliary.* Not, infrequently what at first sight may be regarded as a Present Imperfect Tense, etc., proves, on closer consideration, to be part of the Verb **होना**, preceded by a Participle. Thus, **वे वहाँ बैठे हैं**, will generally prove to be, not, *They have seated themselves there,* but, *They are there, having seated themselves, i.e.,* **बैठे हुए हैं**; and so with other Verbs.

312. Repetition of a Verb. The repetition of a Verb generally indicates either repetition of an act, continuation of the action expressed by the Verb, or intensity. It is most commonly a Participle or the Conjunctive Participle that is repeated, not one of the ordinary Tenses.

Implying Repetition. **करते करते वह निपुण हो गया**, *Doing it again and again he became very clever* (at it). **पूछते २ उसको मालूम हुआ कि**, *By asking many questions he became aware that........*

Implying Continuation. **स्नान करते २ इसी प्रश्न को सोचने लगे**, *As he went on bathing, he thought over* *this question.* चलते २ दो पहर रात वह घर पहुँचा, *Going right on he reached home at midnight.*

Implying Intensity. पैर की आहट बचा बचा कर चलने लगे, *They went forward, taking great care that the sound of their footsteps (should not be heard).* घोर अन्धकार में टटोल टटोल कर सीढ़ी पर पाँव रखते हुए नीचे जाने लगे, *In the thick darkness, feeling very carefully as they placed their feet on the ladder, they began to descend.* चुपके चुपके कुछ बात कर रहे थे, *They were speaking very very softly.*

Sometimes, in the repetition of the Verb, its form is slightly altered the second time. नाव को खींच खाँच कर आगे बढ़ा ले गये, *Dragging the boat this way and that, they carried it forward.*

Chapter XI.

PREFIXES AND SUFFIXES.

VERBAL AND OTHER COMPOUNDED NOUNS.

313a. **उपसर्ग**, Prefix.

प्रत्यय, Suffix.

कृदन्त, Nouns formed from Verbs.

तद्धित, Nouns formed from other Nouns by the addition of a suffix.

This subject is a large and important one. To deal with it fully would not be possible in such a Grammar as this, as many difficult and intricate questions of etymology would have to be investigated. All that can be attempted is to give some of the more important and common prefixes and suffixes, to state their general force and meaning, and to illustrate this by giving a few examples of words thus compounded.

PREFIXES. उपसर्ग.

313b. These are arranged, *in the main*, in alphabetical order, but, where there are two or more prefixes having similar meanings or cases in which they pair off in the way of opposition or contrast, they are brought together for the sake of comparison.

Prefix.	Meaning.	Examples.
अ अन	*negation.*	अधर्म, *unrighteousness.* अनुचित, *unseemly.* अनमोल, *priceless.*
अन्तर	*inner, mind, soul.*	अन्तर्यामी, अन्तर्जामी, *pervading the spirit.* अन्तरज्ञानी, *Knower of the heart.*
बे	*negation.*	बेकाम, *without work.* बेकारण, *without cause.*
अति	*excess.*	अतिशक्त, *very powerful.*
अप	*defect.*	अपमान, *disgrace.* अपगति, *ill-conduct.*
अद अध आध अर्ध	*half.*	अधपक्का, *half-cooked, half-ripe.* अधमुआ, *half-dead.* अधखिला, *half-blown (of a flower.)* अर्धांगी, *a paralytic.*
अनु	*inferior, after, according to,*	अनुगामी, *a follower, a disciple.*
अभि	*superior, before.*	अभिमुख, *in the presence of.* अभिमान, *pride.*
अधि	*superiority.*	अधिराज, *a great king.*

Prefix.	Meaning.	Examples.
प्रति	*opposition, substitution, repetition.*	**प्रतिकर्म**, *retaliation.*
		प्रतिफल, *recompense, requital.*
		प्रतिदिन, *day by day.*
		Compare **अनुकूल**, *in accordance with*, and **प्रतिकूल**, *contrary to.*
		This **प्रति** has various meanings.
अन्य	*another.*	**अन्यदेशी**, *a foreigner.*
अल्प	*little.*	**अल्पज्ञ**, *one possessing little knowledge.*
अव	*diminution.*	**अवगुण**, *a defect, a vice.*
		Compare **अवगति**, *going down, deterioration*, and **उन्नति**, *rise, progress.*
उद्, **उत्**	*superiority, excess.*	**उत्कृष्ट**, *superior.*
		उद्वेग, *perturbation.*
उप	*inferiority, nearness (also excess.)*	**उपवन**, *a garden, artificial forest.*
		उपकारी, *a helper.*
कु	*bad.*	**कुमार्ग**, *an evil course.*
दुर्, **दुस्**, **दुष्**, **दुः**		**दुर्भाग्य**. *ill-fortuned.*
		दुश्चरित, *ill-behaviour.*

Prefix.	Meaning.	Examples.
		दुःशील, *of bad disposition or conduct.*
		दुस्तर, *difficult to be crossed.*
सु	*good.*	सुशील, *of good disposition or conduct.*
निर, निस, निः निष नि	*negation.*	निर्बल, निबल, *powerless.*
		निस्सन्तान, *without offspring.*
		निःसन्देह, *without doubt.*
		निष्कपट, *without deceit.*

This must not be confused with another नि, an intensive particle.

Prefix.	Meaning.	Examples.
पर	*distant, ulterior, exceeding, beyond.*	परदेशी, *a foreigner.*
		परलोक, *the next world.*
		परब्रह्म, *the Supreme Being.*
परा	*intensive, the reverse.*	पराक्रम, *power.*
		पराजय, *defeat.*
परि	*around, excess.*	परिक्रमा, *circumambulation.*
		परिताप, *great heat.*
प्र	*excess, intensive.*	प्रयत्न, *great effort.*
वि	*disjunctive, intensive.*	विदेश, *foreign country.*
स	*conjunctive.*	सबल, *strong.*
		सफल, *fruitful.*

Prefix.	Meaning.	Examples.
		Compare **विधवा**, *widow*, and **सधवा**, *a woman whose husband is alive;* also **वियोग**, *separate* and **संयोग**, *united*.
सम	*equal like.*	**सम्दर्शी**, *impartial, one who looks equally on all.*
सह	*with.*	**सहगामी**, *a fellow-traveller.*
		सहकर्मी, *a fellow-labourer.*
सर्व	*the whole, cf.* **सम**	**सर्वज्ञानी**, *the Omniscient.*
स्व = **अपना**, *one's own.*		**स्वदेश**, *one's own country.*

SUFFIXES. प्रत्यय

314. In dealing with Suffixes, it may be better to use another method than that adopted in the section on Prefixes. There we pursued the alphabetical order. It is proposed to throw the Suffixes into groups, so that some light may be thrown upon the systematic formation of the Compounds, which will now be considered, *viz.*, Nouns and Adjectives (some of them used as Nouns) formed from a Verb or Noun base, by the addition of a Suffix.

There are two main groups: I, called by Indian Grammarians **कृदन्त**, which have a Verbal base, and II, **तद्धित**, which have a Noun as a base.

Indian Grammarians have worked out the divisions and sub-divisions with great elaboration and much ingenuity. Pundit Mádhava Prasád Páṭhak, in his " Hindí Bálbodh Vyákaran, " has done a very useful piece of work in this special section, and I gratefully acknowledge the help I have derived from him in the order here adopted.

It has not been thought necessary to work out the details of the euphonic changes which often take place in the original word in adding the suffixes. They are interesting, but not absolutely necessary, for the student, who will hardly be expected to enter on the task of forming new words, but, for a time, at least, will content himself with ascertaining the meaning and use of those already formed.

Many of the changes, and the suffixes themselves, are Sanskrit, but they belong to Hindi, forasmuch as the words are widely current in Hindi, and new words are being formed from time to time.

VERBAL NOUNS. **कृदन्त**

315. These words are formed from a Verbal base, supplemented by what is called a **कृतप्रत्यय**, *i.e.*, a Suffix which conveys a further verbal force to the word with which it is united. These **कृदन्त** are also called **क्रियावाचक संज्ञा**, *i.e.*, Nouns setting forth verbal ideas.

Five classes are given.

I. **कर्तृवाचक संज्ञा.** Nouns which indicate the *Doer.*

II. **कर्मवाचक संज्ञा.** ....*Act done.*

III. **करणवाचक संज्ञा.** ....*that by which the act is accomplished.*

IV. **भाववाचक संज्ञा.** ....*the doing itself.*

V. **क्रियाद्योतक संज्ञा** ....*the doer in the doing of the act.*

II. and V. need no further explanation; they are the Perfect and Imperfect Participles, respectively, being formed from the stem of the Verb, by the addition of **आ**; fem. **ई** and pl. masc. **ए**, for the Perfect Participle; and **ता, ती,** and **ते** for the Imperfect Participle. These have been dealt with in Chapter X.

We have, therefore, now to consider classes I. III. and IV.

Class I. **कर्तृवाचक संज्ञा.** Nouns indicating the *Doer.*

Under this head come the Nouns of Agency, formed by adding **वाला** or **हारा** to the inflected Infinitive. These have been explained in the chapter on the Verb, Chapter X.

Other Compounded Nouns are formed by the addition to the stem of the Verb of such suffixes as **क, इया, वैया,** etc.

पालक, *a preserver.* **कारक,** *a doer.*

जड़िया, *a setter of jewels.*

छवैया, *a thatcher.* **गवैया,** *a singer.*

Class III. **कर्णवाचक संज्ञा.** Nouns indicating the *Instrument.*

Formed from the Infinitive by changing **ना** to **नी.**

घेरनी, *a handle for turning a spinning-wheel.*

धौंकनी, *bellows.*

खोदनी, *a spade.*

Class IV. **भाववाचक संज्ञा.** Nouns indicating the *action itself.*

Some of these indicate the action, some the abstract idea of the action, and not a few words are found, formed in the same way, which stand for the price paid for work done.

a. The stem alone. **बोल,** *sound, utterance.* **दौड़,** *running, a race.* **समझ,** *understanding.*

b. The stem lengthened. **चाल,** *walk.* **पाठ,** *reading* (from **पठना, पढ़ना,** *to read.*)

c. The stem with **आव,** or **आऊ, बढ़ाव,** *progress, increase.* **भुलाव,** *deception* (fr. **भुलाना,** meaning *to deceive.*) **दिखाव,** *shew, display.* **खिलाऊ,** *serving food.*

d. The steam with आई. सिलाई, *sewing*; बोआई, *sowing*; बिनाई, *weaving*; जोड़ाई, *joining, especially of bricks in masonry*: बनवाई, *making*.

Many of these words are also used to signify the price for such work.

e. The stem with वट or हट. बनावट, *make*; सजावट, *adornment*; बुलाहट, *calling, summons*; चिल्लाहट, *outcry*.

NOUNS (AND ADJECTIVES) COMPOUNDED OF A NOUN AND A SUFFIX. तद्धित.

316. The word तद्धित is from तत, *that*; *i.e.*, the original Noun, and हित, *that which relates to, or suits*; तद्धित is applied to those Compounded Nouns which are formed from an original simple Noun, to which a suffix has been added.

Such Nouns have been divided into five Classes.

I. अपत्यवाचक. This word is from अपत्य, *offspring*, and therefore is somewhat equivalent to the English, *patronymic*. In Hindi, however, this group not only includes *descendants*, but *followers*. Names indicating nationality, also, are included under this head.

II. कर्तृवाचक. In this group are contained the Compounds indicating "*doer of*" and names identified with the workers in different trades and crafts.

III. **भाववाचक.** Abstract Nouns expressing the nature or character of a person or thing.

IV. **गुणवाचक.** These are, as the name indicates, adjectival in character, describing persons by the qualities they possess. Some adjectives, not used as Nouns, must also be included in this group.

V. **ऊनवाचक.** From **ऊन,** *deficient.* Diminutives.

317. I. **Patronymics, etc.** These may be formed by—

a. Lengthening the vowel, *e. g.*, **शैव,** a worshipper of Shiva, fr. **शिव. वैष्णव,** a worshipper of Vishnu, fr. **विष्णु. पाण्डव,** the descendants of **पाण्डु. बौद्ध,** a follower of **बुद्ध.**

b. Adding **ई. गोरखनाथी,** *a follower of* **गोरखनाथ; यदुवंशी,** *belonging to the tribe of* **यदु; पंजाबी,** *one born in the Punjab.*

c. Adding **इया** or **वाल** *e.g.*, **भोजपुरिया,** *a resident* of **भोजपूर; अगरवाल** or **अगरवाला,** *an important caste,* descendants of **अगर.**

318. II. A large class, indicating *doer of.* These names are closely connected with trades and occupations, though, as has already been pointed out, a man often enjoys the caste name, when no longer following the occupation special to that caste.

The Noun of Agency ending in वाला or हारा has been included in the previous section, कृदन्त; but some words formed from a Noun, by the addition of वाला or हारा, belong to this group. रोटीवाला, *a baker*; दूधवाला, *a milkman*; पनहार or पनहारा, *a water-carrier*.

(*b*). Formed by adding such terminations as इया, क, वान, आर, आरी, पाल, दाता, etc. The last two are perhaps rather words than suffixes.

लोनिया, *a seller of salt*; मखनिया, *a dealer in butter*; उपदेशक, *a preacher or teacher*; गाड़ीवान, *a carter*; सुनार or सोनार, *a goldsmith*; लोहार, *a blacksmith*; जुआरी, *a gambler*; द्वारपाल, *a gate-keeper*; अन्नदाता, *a giver of grain*.

319. III. Abstract Nouns, relating to both persons and things.

Formed by adding the suffixes, ता, त्व, ई, पन, पा, व or आव, *e.g.*, पवित्रता, *holiness*; उत्तमता, *excellence* (These Abstract Nouns ending in ता are very common): मनुष्यत्व, *manhood*; दासत्व, *serfdom*; चौड़ाई, *breadth*; चतुराई, *cleverness*; बचपन, *childhood*; बुढ़ापा, *old age*; गौरव, *weightiness, dignity*; गहिराव, *depth*.

320. IV. Adjectival Nouns and Adjectives. These describe the persons or things by the qualities they possess.

Formed by the addition of such suffixes as **वान**, **मान**, **वत**, **वन्त**, **ल**, **लु**, **लू**, **आ**, **एला**, **नीय**, **अक**, **इक**, **ई**, **इष्ठ**.

दयावान, *merciful*; **धनवान**, *wealthy*; **बुद्धिमान**, *wise*; **पशुवत**, *animal-like, bestial.* **बलवन्त**, *an athlete, strong man*; **कृपाल** and **कृपालु**, *compassionate*; **दयालु**, *merciful*; **झगड़ालू**, *a brawler, quarrelsome person*; **भूखा**, *hungry*; **प्यासा**, *thirsty*; **घरेला** or **घरैला**, and **बनेला** or **बनैला**, *domestic and wild animals*; **विश्वासनीय**, *worthy of trust*; **प्रशंसनीय**, *worthy of praise*; **मासिक**, *monthly*; **दैनिक**, *daily*; **अनर्थक**, *injurious*; **अलगाई**, *aloofness*; **घनिष्ठ**, *very dense (of a forest)*; **बलिष्ठ**, *very strong.*

Many other words and suffixes might be added, *e.g.*, **ऐत**, in such words as **लठैत**, **भालैत**, wielder of a **लाठी** or of a **भाल** *spear*: **इत** in words like **शोकित**, *grieved*; **हर्षित**, *glad.*

There are many suffixes also which are more akin to words than simple suffixes, *e.g.*, **मय**, *full of*; **आनन्दमय**, *joyful*; **दाई**, *giver of*; **पूर्वक**, *with*; **भर**, *full of*; **मात्र**, *just, only*; **युक्त**, **भीत**; **आतुर**, etc.

321. V. Diminutives. With a final ई, replacing आ, etc.

रस्सी, *a rope*, smaller than रस्सा; दौरी, *a basket*, smaller than a दौरा; with the termination इया, *e.g.*, लड़किया, a little girl; खटिया, *a small bedstead.*

The lists of the suffixes given above are by no means complete, and lists of words have not been attempted, only a few illustrations given. The whole subject is a wide and important one. In Sanskrit, compounding is carried out to an extravagant extent, and that more than traces of this should have come into Hindi is not surprising. Many long Sanskrit Compounds are brought bodily into Hindi; others are manufactured. Tulsi Das' "विनयपत्रिका" affords many illustrations of long Sanskrit Compounds.

CHAPTER XII.

ADVERBS.

322. Adverb. **क्रियाविशेषण.**

Adverb.		**क्रियाविशेषण.**
,,	of time.	**कालवाचक.**
,,	,, place.	**स्थानवाचक.**
,,	,, manner.	**भाववाचक.**
,,	,, quantity or degree.	**परिमाणवाचक.**

323. The Hindi **क्रियाविशेषण** corresponds very largely with the English word Adverb: it means the word which qualifies the Verb. As in English so in Hindi, the Adverb in use covers more than its name signifies. **हाँ** and **नहीं**, as affirmative and negative, words indicating time and place, such as **यहाँ, वहाँ, अब, तब,** do not appear in any special manner to qualify the Verb, and yet these and many other words do furnish information closely connected with that which the Verb conveys. To be informed when and where an act is done, is certainly related to the act itself.

Perhaps the use of the Adverb in which it is most true to its essential character is that in which the English words ending in ... *ly* are found, setting forth how an act is performed, *e.g.*, *He fought bravely*. But particulars connected with the verbal idea may be largely widened, and thus we meet with Adverbs of Time and Place, and even a whole sentence, called an Adverbial Extension.

It will be noticed that some words appear in lists of Postpositions which have already appeared as Adverbs, and some of these same words are Nouns also. Day is a Noun, and yet in the sentence, "*He did it day by day,*" (daily), it is truly an Adverb. Words do thus change in their character, as they are used in different ways. In उसके नीचे क्या है, *What is under it?* नीचे is a Postposition. In the sentence, वह नीचे गिरा, *It fell down,* it is an Adverb. So, in आगे चलो, *Go forward,* आगे is an Adverb. In उनके आगे घर और विश्राम दोनों हैं, *Ahead of them are both home and rest,* it is a Postposition.

As in English so in Hindi, we may have :—

1. A simple Adverb. वह धीरे चलता था, *He was walking slowly.*
2. Another word used as an Adverb. वह आनन्द-पूर्वक रहता था, *He lived joyfully,* or *with joy.*
3. An Adverbial sentence. वह इतनी शीघ्रता से चलता था कि कोई उसको नहीं पकड़

सकता था, *He was going along so quickly that no one was able to lay hold of him.*

324. Adverbs may be noticed under three headings:

1. Pronominal Adverbs.
2. Adverbs.
3. Adverbial Phrases.

I. PRONOMINAL ADVERBS.

We have already noted the series of Pronominal Adjectives in which the characteristic letters of the Pronouns appear and modify the meaning. In a similar way, we have a series of words adverbial in their force, and these have been suitably denominated Pronominal Adverbs.

In the following lists, it will be observed that, 1. are related to the Proximate Demonstrative Pronoun यह. 2. to the Remote Demonstrative Pronoun वह. 3. to the Relative Pron. जो. 4. to the Correlative सो, under its somewhat obsolete inflected form तिस. 5. to the Interrogative कौन. and 6. to the Indefinite कोई.

In some cases, not all the members of the series are in use.

a. Of Place.

1. यहाँ, यहीं *here.*
2. वहाँ, वहीं *there.*

3. जहाँ *where, (relative).*

4. तहाँ *there, (correlative).*

5. कहाँ *where?*

6. कहीं *anywhere.*

b. **Of Direction.**

1. इधर *hither.*

2. उधर *thither.*

3. (जिधर) *whither* } For जिधर and तिधर,

4. (तिधर) *thither.* } जहाँ and तहाँ are

5. किधर, *whither?* almost invariably used.

6. ——— Even for इधर, उधर,

and किधर, यहाँ, वहाँ, and कहाँ are commonly used. Even as, in English, *where are you going?* is far more commonly used than, *whither are you going?*

c. **Of Time.**

1. अब *now.*

2. तब or उस समय,

3. जब *when.*

4. तब *then.*

5. कब *when?*

6. कभी.

d. **Of Manner.**

1. यों, यूं *thus.*

2. वों *obsolete, supplied by* उसी तरह.

3. ज्यों, ज्यूं *as.*		These are generally used of time, *Just as,..... at that moment.* For manner, जिस तरह, उसी तरह are more common.
4. त्यों *so.*		

5. क्योंं, क्यौं, क्यूं *how? why?*

6. ——

Some of these Pronominal Adverbs are treated somewhat as Nouns, becoming subject to declension, by the use of Postpositions, *e.g.*, यह कहाँ का है, *Of what place is this (man)?* यहाँ से जाओ, *Go away from here.* कब तक रहोगे, *Until when will you remain?* यहाँ के भीतर, *In here.* अब के लिये, *For the present.*

By repetition and combination, these Pronominal Adverbs yield other modifications of meaning; जहाँ जहाँ......तहाँ तहाँ, *wherever......in those places.* जब जब......तब तब, *whenever......then.* कब कब, *whenever.* कभी कभी, *sometimes.* ज्यों ज्यों......त्यों त्यों, *just as...so also* (especially in reference to succession in time.)

जहाँ का तहाँ, *Just the same as it was.* उनका काम जहाँ का तहाँ रह गया, *Their work remained just as it was.* उत्तम ग्रन्थ जहाँ के तहाँ पड़े रहते हैं. *Excellent books remain as they are* (i.e., either unpublished or unsold)

कभी न कभी, or **कभी कभी**, *occasionally.* **कहीं न कहीं**, or **कहीं कहीं**, *somewhere or other.* **यहाँ, वहाँ**, *here and there.* **जहाँ कहीं**, *wherever.* **इधर उधर**, or **इधर विधर**, *hither and thither.* **अब तब**, *now and again* (**अब तब करना** is idiomatically used for "*to procrastinate*"). **जब तब**, *occasionally.* **ज्यों त्यों**, or **ज्यों का त्यों**, *exactly in the same state or condition.*

2. ADVERBS.

325. A. Adverbs of Place and Direction.

आगे *forward*, or *forwards.*

पीछे *backward*, or *backwards.*

ऊपर *upward*, or *upwards.*

नीचे *downward*, or *downwards.*

दहिने *to the right.*

बाएँ *to the left.*

बाहर *outward*, or *outwards.*

भीतर *inward*, or *inwards.*

पार, *on the other side.* Used after a Noun, followed by **के** *or* **से**, this word has very much of a prepositional force, but with a Demonstrative Pronoun in the construct. state, it has an adverbial force. **इस पार**, *this side*; **उस पार**, *that side.*

वार *on this side.*

वार पार } *right through.* Spoken, *e.g.*, of cutting
आर पार } right through anything.

अनत (prop. अन्यत्र) *in another place, elsewhere.*

एकत्र *in one place*, or *together.*

सर्वत्र *in all places, ubiquitous.*

निकट *near*, पास *close to*, दूर *far*, are not properly Adverbs, though sometimes used with an adverbial force.

326. B. Adverbs of Time.

Under these will come words indicating different parts of the day, and different periods of time, *e.g.*, आज to-day, कल to-morrow. The more common of these are mentioned in Chapter XVI.

आगे *before.* According to the context, this may stand for *past* or *future* time, *formerly* or *hereafter.* The English word "before" is somewhat analogous, *e.g. They used to do this before*, i.e., previously. *In the years that lie before let us not do so.*

पहिले *before, previously.*

पश्चात *subsequently.*

निदान *finally.*

एकदा *once upon a time.*

इतने में *meanwhile*

नित or नित्य *continually, always.*

परम्परा *continually, from generation to generation.* Used of past time.

सदा *always.*

सदैव *always (intensive of* सदा)

सदा सर्वदा *for ever and ever.*

फिर *once more, again.*

बहुधा *often, generally.*

अक्सर Urdu equivalent, often used in Hindi.

बार बार or बारंबार *repeatedly, again and again.*

327. C. Adverbs of Manner.

अचानक or अचानचक अकस्मात एकाएक or एकाएकी एकबारगी	*suddenly.*
बेग बेग बेग (intensive) शीघ्र तुरन्त or तुरत झट झटपट सहसा जल्द or जल्दी (*Urdu*)	*quickly.*

धीरे *slowly.*

धीरे धीरे (*intensive of above*).

सच or सत्य *truly.*

सचमुच *truly.* An intensive form of the above.

सही *truly.*

अलबत्ता *Urdu equivalent.*

अवश्य *necessarily.*

ठीक *exactly, truly.*

ठीक ठीक or ठीक ठाक } Intensive forms of the above.

सेंत or सेंतमेंत *gratuitously.*

साक्षात *manifestly, openly.*

सहज *easily.*

अनायास *easily, without effort.*

यथा or जथा *just as.*

तथा *so.* Correlative of the above.

यथार्थ *as is fit, as is necessary.*

निरन्तर *uninterruptedly.*

वृथा *vainly, uselessly.*

हौले *softly.*

धड़ाधड़ *boldly, with a crash.*

मनमाने *according to one's will.*

ऐसे, वैसे, जैसे, कैसे. See Section 194, where

ऐसा, वैसा, जैसा, कैसा are treated of as Pronominal Adjectives. In their inflected form, these become Adverbs, and are much used. It is not uncommon to find the adjectival forms in आ used where the adverbial forms in ए would be more correct.

It may be pointed out that many Adjectives may be used as Adverbs of Manner. उसने अच्छा किया, उसने बुरा किया, *He did well. He did badly.*

328. D. Adverbs of Degree.

बहुत *much.*

कम *little.*

कुछ *somewhat.*

निपट }
अति } *very.*
बड़ा } बड़ा is an Adj. "great," but is frequently used as an Adverb.

अत्यन्त *exceedingly.*

केवल *only, merely.*

निर्केवल Intensive of केवल.

निरा *entirely.*

एक बेर *once.*

दो बेर *twice.*

तीन बेर etc., *thrice*, etc.

As the Pronominal Adjectives of Quality are used in their inflected form as Adverbs of Manner, similarly the Pronominal Adjectives of Quantity, जितना, etc., (see Sect. 193) are used as Adverbs of Degree, but are not generally inflected. Adjectives also may be used in a similar way.

ही, sometimes हीं, is an intensive Adverbial Particle which may be added to many, if not most, words. The ह often disappears, or rather combines with the previous letter, converting it into its corresponding aspirate, *e.g.*, अभी *just now*, from अब + ही. Where the previous letter is already an aspirate, the ह is omitted; thus मुझी from मुझ + ही, वही from वह + ही. This ही may be sometimes translated by "even," "indeed;" at others, it only corresponds to a word which would, in English, be italicized in writing, or emphasized in speaking. मुझी को मारोगे, *Will you strike even me?* वह है ही नहीं, *Indeed, he is not (here).*

The use of ही with the Present Participle in the constructive form, called the Adverbial Participle, has already been noticed. Joined with parts of the Verb which have an auxiliary, it is inserted before the auxiliary: thus जाता ही था, *(while) he was actually going.* With the Future, it is even inserted before the Conjugational termination, *e.g.*, **जायहींगे**, *they will assuredly go.* **देहीगा**, *he will assuredly give.*

329. E. Miscellaneous Adverbs.

The propriety of classing one or two of the following as Adverbs may be questioned, but no more suitable heading for their notice suggests itself.

हाँ *Yes.*

तो *Yes.* Not found in literature, but much used by villagers.

Other words also are used for expressing assent, **अच्छा**, *very well*; **निस्सन्देह**, *without doubt*, etc.

नहीं *No, not.* Used mostly with the Tenses, which would belong to the Indicative Mood, less commonly with Tenses of the Subjunctive; *i.e.*, it is more common with the denial of a fact than the negation of a contingency or possibility. It is *not* used with the Imperative. It may be used absolutely, "*No.*"

न *No, not.* Absolute "*No,*" also with the Verb, more especially for Subjunctive Tenses, and for the polite forms of the Imperative.

Speaking generally, **न** seems to be more abrupt and less formal than **नहीं**, though it is less emphatic, *e.g.*, **मैं कभी नहीं करूँगा**, i. e., *I will never do it.* **न** would not generally replace **नहीं** in this sentence: **न आऊँगा न करूँगा**, *I will neither come nor do it*, might be said; but **नहीं** in both places would be still more emphatic.

मत *Not.* Used only with the Imperative, **मत, जाओ**, *don't go.* It must not be used with the polite forms of the Imperative.

जिन a colloquial equivalent for **मत.**

There are various idiomatic uses of these Adverbs of negation, **नहीं तो**, *if not.* **अभी जाओ, नहीं तो मैं दूसरे को भेजूँगा**, *Go at once, if you don't (if not), I will send some one else.*

न......न...... } *neither—nor—*, **न करता है न**
न तो......न...... } **कराता है**, *He neither does (it), nor gets (it) done.*

क्यों नहीं *Yes*, lit. "*Why not,*" used in much the same way as the English "*of course;*" though, in many cases, it is used where in English the simple "yes" would be used. Thus, if a man be asked if he can do a certain kind of work, he will answer, **क्यों नहीं**. This, of course, means *literally* "*why not?*" but, *idiomatically* it is simply "*yes.*"

कदापि *possibly, perchance.*

शायद *Urdu equivalent.* More common in Hindi than कदापि.

अर्थात *namely, that is to say.*

याने *Urdu equivalent.* Frequently used in Hindi.

उलटा *on the contrary.*

सारांश *in short, briefly.*

प्राय: *probably, usually, for the most part.* (In the form प्राय: करके, it means *often, generally,* and is equivalent to the Urdu अक्सर).

मात्र *merely.* Only used after another word, combining with it into a semi-compound, *e.g.*, वचन मात्र, *merely a word.* (This must not be confused with another use of मात्र । meaning, *all, every, each,* e.g., मनुष्य मात्र, *all men,* or *every man.*

3. ADVERBIAL PHRASES.

330. Adverbial phrases are very numerous, and are formed in various ways; not a few are simply some case of a Noun with its Postposition.

The Instrumental and Ablative Cases, with से, or से added to a word already used as an Adverb, *e.g.*, गुप्त रीति से, *secretly,* सहज से, *easily,* क्रोध से, *angrily,* धीरे से, *slowly,* किस प्रकार से, *how, in what manner?*

नम्रता से, *gently.* So for Adverbs of place, **वहाँ से**, **यहाँ से**, etc.

The Locative Case in **में**. **अन्त में** *finally* **प्रगट में**, *manifestly, apparently*, **वास्तव में**, in very truth.

The Accusative Case, with or without **को**, *e.g.*, **अन्त को**, *finally*, **उस समय**, *at that time*, **एक दिन**, *one day*, i.e., *on a certain day.*

The Conjunctive Participle is very frequently used as an Adverb. **जान बूझ के उसने किया**, *He did it wittingly.* **छिपकर**, *secretly.* **एक एक करके**, *singly.*

Various other ways of forming Adverbial phrases are also met with, *e.g.*, **सर्प्प की भाँति**, *in a snake-like way.* **एक साथ**, *unitedly.* **इसी तरह**, *in this way.* **वैसे ही**, *in the same manner.*

CHAPTER XIII.

POSTPOSITIONS. { सम्बन्धबोधक अव्यय or सम्बन्धसूचक अव्यय.

331. The Case-signs **का, की, के,** etc., partake of the character of Postpositions. These have a special name given to them by Indian Grammarians, *viz.*, **विभक्ति.** It is not apparent what essential difference there is between **पर,** as a Case-sign of the Locative, and **नीचे,** a Postposition. As a matter of fact, the **विभक्ति** or Case-signs are as truly Postpositions as those dealt with in the present Chapter: it is only their identification with the Case system that has led to their separation.

These words correspond with the English Prepositions, but as they are almost invariably used after the word to which they are related, they have been appropriately called Postpositions. The Hindi name, **सम्बन्धबोधक अव्यय,** *the particle indicating relation,* is excellent.

Dr. Kellogg has pointed out that many of these Postpositions were originally Nouns. This accounts for the fact that, with some of them, the related word is used in the masc. Genitive, with others in the fem.; the Postposition having been originally a masc. or fem. Noun. We have उसके नीचे, *Beneath it*, but उसकी सन्ती, *In its place.*

Occasionally, a Postposition becomes a Preposition, *i.e.*, it may be used *before* the related word. This is optional with some Postpositions. बिना is the outstanding example of freedom in this matter: it may be used before or after the related word, with के or without.

In the following lists, the endeavour has been made to arrange the words according to meaning, so that synonymous words or those similar in meaning may be noted and differences of idiom pointed out. Many Urdu equivalents have been included, as they are so frequently found in Hindi books.

Postpositions marked—

*are preceded by के.	घर के पीछे, *Behind the house.*
† ....की	बालक की सन्ती, *In the place of the child.*
‡ are used without के or की.	सेना सहित, सेना रहित, *With (his) army. Without (his) army.*
* ‡ may be used with or without.	घर के पास, *Near the house.*
	उस पास, *By him.*

It has been mentioned in Chapter XII that several words are both Adverbs and Postpositions.

*साम्हने, now more commonly written सामने, *in front of*. In addition to its literal use, this word has two idiomatic uses also. 1. Equal to "*in his estimation.*" परमेश्वर के साम्हने हम पापी हैं, *We are sinners in God's sight.* 2. To indicate comparison. शेर के साम्हने कुत्ता क्या है, *What is a dog in comparison with a tiger?*

Notice the difference between साम्हने and आगे. साम्हने means, *in the presence of*; आगे *ahead. He stands before the king*, is वह राजा के साम्हने खड़ा है, but, *He walks before the king*, i.e., *ahead of the king*, वह राजा के आगे चलता है.

*आगे *before*. Used both of time and place. Notice in previous Chapter about the possible reference to either the past or the future. For time, से as well as के may be used.

*पहिले *before*. Used chiefly of time. Though constructed with its governed word as a Postposition, it is adverbial in force. Thus, इसके पहिले, *before this*, or *previously*. (This can also be used with से, *e.g.*, उस से पहिले, *before that, previously*).

*पूर्व *before.* Of time only.

*पीछे *behind, after.* Of place and time.

*बाद Urdu equivalent of पीछे. Used of time.

*अनन्तर *after.* Used of time occasionally, of logical succession.

*उपरान्त *after.* Of time. Occasionally in the sense of "*in addition to,*" "*moreover.*"

*ऊपर *over, above.*

Notice the distinction between पर and ऊपर; the former is *on, upon*; the second, *over.* An ornament is *on*, or, *upon* the mantelpiece, a picture is *over* it. In the first sentence, the word is पर, in the second ऊपर. A man is *on* (पर) the roof of his house, a kite flies *above* (ऊपर) it. This distinction is sometimes lost sight of, and quite recently it has become a fad to use ऊपर in many cases where पर is more appropriate, *e.g.*, उसके ऊपर दया करते हैं, *He shews mercy on him,* instead of using the word पर as was practically always done in such phrases in past days.

*नीचे *beneath, under.* Of place and also of status.

*‡ तले *beneath, under.*

*‡ बीच *between.* Used of place and time, in the

latter case, it may often be translated "*meanwhile.*" Commonly followed by one or more of the Particle Postpositions, *e.g.*, **उनके बीच में,** *among.* **घर के बीच में,** *in the centre of the house.* **उनके बीच में से,** *from among.* **बीच में,** *meanwhile.*

* **दर्मियान,** Urdu equivalent of above.

* **बाहर,** *outside.* Sometimes written **बाहिर. द्वार के बाहर,** *outside the door.* An idiomatic use of this word, with the governed word in the ablative, may be noted *e.g.*, **गिनने से बाहर हैं** (*They*) *are outside of counting,* i.e., *cannot be counted.* **जो आप की इच्छा से बाहर है,** *which is not according to your wish.*

* **भीतर** *inside, within.* Used both of place and time, *e.g.*, **परदे के भीतर,** *inside the curtain.* **एक महीने के भीतर,** *within a month.*

* **अन्दर,** *Urdu equivalent.*

*‡ **पास** *by, near to.* Used both of *position* and *motion to, e.g.*, **उसके पास वह बैठा है,** *He is sitting by him.* **उसके पास वह गया,** *He went to him.* It is also used

idiomatically of *possession*. **मेरे पास कुछ नहीं**, *I possess nothing.*

* **निकट** *near.*

* **समीप** *near.*

* **नज़दीक**, Urdu equivalent.

* **नगीच**, *Corruption of the above.*

* **परे** *beyond.* (Used also with **से**)

* **लगभग** *near, round about.*

* **आस पास** *near, round about.* Used in such a phrase as *the villages near the city.* This can also be expressed by......**के चारों ओर**, or ...**की** (or **के**) **चारों तरफ़**, *in the four directions, on the four sides.*

* **गिर्द**, Urdu equivalent.

† * **ओर** *In the direction of, side.*

A peculiarity of the word should be specially noted. In the sing. it is fem., in the pl. masc., *e.g.*, **मेरी ओर देखकर**, *Having looked in my direction.* **गंगा के दोनों ओर**, *On both sides of the Ganges.* **घर के चारों ओर**, *On the four sides of the house.* Probably this arises from the word having two meanings. As fem., it means *direction*, as masc. *side.* (Compare the same peculiarity with reference to the word खोज noticed in Sec. 77). This suggestion receives some confirmation from the fact that with the meaning, *side*, this word is found in the masc. even in the sing, *e.g.*, उसके एक ओर मङ्गला की झोंपड़ी थी, *On one side of that was Mangala's little shed.*

† तरफ़, Urdu equivalent.

‡ लों
‡ लग
‡ पर्यन्त
‡ तक

Up to, as far as. Used of time, place and degree.

A special use of तक may be noticed, *e.g.*, in the sentence, प्रवेश तक न करेगा, *He will not so much as enter.*

* संग *with*
* साथ *with*

Very occasionally used without के.

‡ समेत *with.* Used without के, *e.g.*, स्त्री पुत्र धन समेत, *With wife, son and wealth.*

‡ * सहित *with.* Used in the same way as the above. It is also often used with adverbial force, *e.g.*, चिन्ता सहित, *with thought,* i.e., *thoughtfully.* Occasionally found with के (*e.g.*, ऋषियों के सहित, *with the saints*), but better without.

‡ रहित *without.* The exact reverse of सहित, constructed generally in the same way, but occasionally with its Noun in the Ablative Case, *e.g.*, सब पापों से रहित होकर, *Having become devoid of all sins.*

Both सहित and रहित are not properly Postpositions, but their usage justifies their inclusion in this list.

‡ पूर्वक *with.* Used in much the same way as सहित and समेत. क्षपनक निरादर पूर्वक नगर से निकाला जाता है, *Kshapanak is being expelled from the city with dishonour.*

‡ * बिना or बिन *without.* When the governed Noun is not used with के, this Postposition may be used before or after its Noun. It is also used with some parts of Verbs.

पूरे विश्वास बिना, *Apart from perfect* (lit., *full*) *faith.* बिना भेस बदले, *Without changing his dress* (or *appearance*). जो अपने बल बिना और अनेक दुखों के भोगे बिना राज्य मिलता है, *That kingdom which is acquired without one's own exertion, and without the endurance of many troubles.* दूसरे पहिये के बिना, *Without a second wheel.* बिना

किसी परिश्रम या प्रयत्न के, *Without any labour or effort.*

The form बिन is mostly confined to poetry and proverbial sayings.

* बग़ैर, Urdu equivalent of बिना.

* लिये *for the sake of, in order that.*
* कारण *on account of.*

Although the distinction is not always strictly observed, there is a very real and exceedingly useful difference in meaning between these two words. लिये rather looks to the future, *in order that,* कारण to the past, *because of,* e.g., वह देखने के लिये आया था, *He came in order that he might see...* निर्बल हाने के कारण वह नहीं आया था, *On account of his weakness he did not come.* This point is worth careful consideration.

With the phrase, इस लिये, equivalent to *therefore,* के is not used. In इस कारण, *i.e.,* for इस कारण से *on account of this,* कारण is a Noun, not a Postposition.

‡ * लगि *for the sake of.* Mostly used in poetry.

* ‡ निमित्त *for the sake of.*

† ख़ातिर, Urdu equivalent.

* **हेतु** *for (this) reason,* or with persons, *on behalf of.* (More generally used as a Noun, *e.g.*, **इस हेतु से,** *for this reason.*)

* **मारे** *on account of, by reason of.*

‡ **वास्ते,** Urdu equiv. Generally used with Demonstrative Pronouns, etc., in the Oblique Case, as **इस वास्ते,** *for this reason,* **किस वास्ते,** *for what reason?*

* **विषय** or **बिषय** *in the matter of, with reference to.* Generally followed by **में,** *e.g.*, **इसके विषय में,** *with reference to this (matter).* Where **के** is omitted, *e.g.*, **इस विषय में,** *in this matter,* **विषय** is a Noun. It is a Noun in all cases, but has come to be numbered with the Postpositions, and is as much a Postposition as many others included in the list.

† **बाबत**
† **निस्बत** } Urdu equivalents, "*with reference to.*"

* **द्वारा** *by means of.* Occasionally a pleonastic **से** is added, **उस के द्वारा से,** *by means of him.*

*‡ **योग्य** *suitable for.* **यह देखने के योग्य है,** *This is worth seeing.* Not infrequently, the **के** is omitted. **देखने योग्य है.**

* समान
* तुल्य } *like, equal to.*
* सदृश्य

† नाईं *in the manner of*, e.g., पिता की नाईं उसने बालक की सुध ली, *He took care of the child as a father would.* This word generally possesses an adverbial force.

* बराबर, Urdu equivalent.

* अनुसार *according to, in conformity with.*

* अनुकूल *according to.*

* प्रतिकूल, Adversative of the above.

* मुआफिक, Urdu equivalent.

* प्रति. From its first meaning of *Substitution*, the *meaning of the* Postposition branches out into two uses: 1. *with*; सबके प्रति, *i.e.*, सबके साथ. 2. *for*; रोगी के प्रति, *For a sick person*, such and such things are necessary.

† सन्ती *in the place of.*

* बदले } Urdu equivalents. बदले is often followed
* इवज़ } by में, *e.g.*, इसके बदले में, *in the place of this.*

* विरुद्ध or बिरुद्ध }
* विपरीत or बिपरीत } *opposed to, on the contrary.* विरुद्ध is very occasionally found with an Ablative. आपकी इच्छा से विरुद्ध कोई व्यवहार नहीं होने पावेगा, *No custom shall be observed which is opposed to your wish.*

* ख़िलाफ़, *Urdu equivalent.*

There are two inseparable prefixes, स *with*, and बे *without*, which have a prepositional force. सपरिवार, *with (his) household.* बेफल, *without fruit.* These might be equally well expressed by परिवार सहित and फल बिना.

CHAPTER XIV.

CONJUNCTIONS.

Conjunction संयोजक अव्यय.

Disjunction विभाजक अव्यय.

332. The English name, Conjunction, is exceedingly unsatisfactory, as it by no means covers the scope of the words included under the name. Indian Grammarians extend the scope by using two names, Conjuncton and Disjunction. Even this, however, does not fully meet the case.

In the following paragraphs, the endeavour will be made to group the words commonly included in this class and to offer a few words in the way of explanation as to their meaning and use.

333. 1. Cumulative Conjunctions.

ओर, *and.* This is the simple copula for connecting words or sentences. With pairs of words it is often omitted, *e. g.*, ऊँचनीच, *high and low*; राजाप्रजा, *king and subjects.* Also with strings of words, *e.g.*, माता पिता भाई बहिन सब के सब मर गये, *Mother father, brothers and sisters, all are dead.* Or, for the sake of emphasis, it may be used between all the words, माता ओर पिता ओर भाई ओर बहिन सबके सब मर गये हैं.

ओर is often found written **औ**, occasionally **अरु**, and sometimes **व** is used.

It should be remembered that there is another use of **और**, *i.e.*, as a Pronominal Adjective. In the sentence, **लल्लू आ गया है और कौन आवेगा,** *Lallu has come, who else will come?* **और** is a Pronominal adjective; in the following, **वह आ गया है और रहेगा भी,** *He has come and will also remain*, it is a Conjunction. Care is sometimes necessary lest ambiguity should occur, one being understood for the other.

भी *also, moreover.* **वे भी आवेंगे,** *they also will come.* **उन्होंने आने को कहा वे आवेंगे भी,** *they promised to come, they will come also.* Sometimes, it approximates in force to the intensive Adverb **ही**, and may then have to be translated by "even," or some such word: **एक भी नहीं,** *there (is) not even one.* Somewhat similarly, it may occur in a sentence with another Conjunction, **यदि आवै भी,** *should he even come.*

एवं, Occasionally the Sanskrit **एवं** takes the place of **भी**. Its meaning seems to hover between **भी** and **फिर**.

फिर *again.* Used as the English "again," and in making an additional statement or beginning a new point in an argument. Occasionally, this word assumes the form **फेर.**

पुनर, the Sanskrit equivalent of the above. It is sometimes found in Hindi.

बरन. See the next section.

334. 2. Adversative.

पर
परन्तु
बरन or
बरञ्च or
बं,
किन्तु
} *but.*

Of these, **पर** is frequently used with the force of an exceptive rather than with an adversative force. **दो आये पर केवल एक रहा,** *Two came, but only one remained.* **परन्तु** is more strongly adversative, *e.g.*, after relating how Ravan had tempted and threatened Sita, a writer states, **परन्तु सीता...बिचलित न हुई,** *but Sita......wavered not.* Again, a writer, after relating certain adverse circumstances, says, **परन्तु यदि विचार कर देखा जाए,** *but if the matter be looked at thoughtfully.* **बरन** has often more of a cumulative than adversative force, *not only so, but also.* **न केवल दो दिन बरन दो बरस तक रहूँगा,** *Not merely for two days, I will remain for two years.* Sometimes, however, it has an adversative force. **किन्तु,** is often equal to **परन्तु.** Occasionally, it approximates in meaning to **बरन.**

लेकिन, बल्कि (corrupted to बल्कन in the colloquial), मगर, Urdu equivalents. लेकिन especially is very common in Hindi.

तौभी *nevertheless.*

335. 3. **Alternative.**

वा या अथवा	*or.*	These are used between alternative words or sentences. मेरी बातें अच्छी लगती हैं वा नहीं, *Are my words acceptable or not?* but in the case of

या, we may also have it in both sentences, या तो...या तो, or, या तो...या, *e.g.*, उसका यत्न या तो उल्टा हो या निष्फल होगा, *His effort will either produce an unexpected result* (lit., *will become turned*) *or become fruitless.* (Cf. the old-English use of nor, "*I whom nor avarice nor pleasures move.*")

कि *or.* लोग चाहते हैं कि नहीं, *Do the people desire* (*it*) *or not?* See also the use of कि under No 6 Explanative.

नहीं तो *if not*; followed by तो *then* (cf. § 329.)

न...न......*neither, nor.* न सुनता है न बोलता है, *he neither hears nor speaks.* Sometimes only one न is given for both sentences, especially in poetry. इन्हें हम जानते हैं न बूझते हैं. *I neither know nor recognize this gentleman.* Compare Eng. "*Eye, nor ear, nor mind ever tired by these sandy dunes.*"

चाहे......चाहे...*whether......or* (cf. § 304).

क्या...क्या...*either......or.*

336. 4. **Hypothetical.**

जो *if.* Generally followed by तो *then.*

यदि *if.*

अगर Urdu equivalent.

337. 5. **Concessive.**

यद्यपि *although.* Followed generally by तौभी or यथापि, *nevertheless*, and occasionally by किन्तु. यद्यपि वह नाटासा है तौभी वह बलवन्त भी है, *Although he is dwarfish, yet he is very strong.* शकटार यद्यपि बन्दीखाने से छूटा किन्तु अपनी अप्रतिष्ठा का शोक उसके चित्त में बना रहा, *Although Shakatâr was released from prison, yet the grief on account of the disgrace remained fixed in his mind.*

जो......भी *even if, if also*, followed commonly by

तौभी, *nevertheless.* **जो आवे भी**, *even if he come.*

चाहे *should, though, even if*, followed commonly by **तौभी**.

338. 6. **Explanative.**

कि *that*, in such sentences as, "*he said that......*" "*he saw that......*" "*it came to pass that......*"

कि is also used of purpose, "*he went that he might see.*"

क्योंकि or **क्यौंकि** *because, for*, e.g., **क्योंकि पूरे विश्वास बिना**...*For apart from perfect faith.*

339. 7. Dependent, indicating Result.

तो *then.* Introducing what will result, if certain conditions be fulfilled. **यदि मेरे प्राण की रक्षा होगी तो मैं आपको छुड़ाऊँगी**, *If my life be saved, then I will effect your deliverance.*

CHAPTER XV.

INTERJECTIONS.

Interjection, विस्मयादिबोधक अव्यय (Lit., *that which indicates astonishment, etc.*)

340. The Hindi name for Interjection is very appropriate, as विस्मय signifies not only surprise, but also wonder and consternation.

The following are the principal Interjections :—

हे The common Vocative Interjection.

हो More used towards inferiors. हो तुम, *Hallo you ?*

अजी is used alone, not as an addition to a Vocative. It is used to call the attention of some one, something like the English, "*I say,*" or to indicate slight surprise, "*Ah!*"

जी or जी हाँ is used rather in the way of assent or approval than as a pure Interjection; but it may be called an Interjection, as it is frequently used when no question has been asked. It somewhat corresponds to the "Yes, yes," with which some hearers encourage a speaker.

अरे (with fem. अरी) generally indicataes (1) surprise, sometimes impatience or anger, but may be used

(2) as an ordinary Vocative Interjection. Though very commonly used, it is not regarded as an *elegant* word.

(1) **अरे ब्राह्मण क्रोध मत कर,** *O, you Brahman, don't get angry.* **अरे जाना,** *Ah! I see.* "**अरे!**" uttered by a man to himself on receiving a letter containing some startling news.

(2) **अरी बहन,** *O sister!* **अरे कुमार आपही आ गए,** *My prince! have you come?* (Here there is some measure of surprise.)

रे is a very different Interjection as regards usage: it is a Vocative Interjection, expressing contempt or disgust, *e.g.,* **रे मूढ़ याद रख कि,** *You fool! remember that......* **वाह रे कौटिल्य वाह,** spoken of a person as though present, *Oh that Kauṭilya!*

अहा or **आहा** expresses admiration or surprise.

ओः expresses mingled surprise and sorrow.

ओःहो „ wonder and surprise.

अबे „ contempt.

अहह (or **अहहहह** *ad lib.*) expresses sorrow (on receiving sad news).

हाहा, हाय or **हाय हाय** } „ „ „ „

हाए or **हाए हाए** } „ „ Eng. "alas!"

हा questioning surprise.

अहो somewhat of surprise.

छिः or **छीछी,** *avaunt! away with the thought!*

> **छिः मूर्ख क्या तू गुरुजी से भी धर्म्मविशेष जानता है,** *Away with you, you fool! what, do you know about religion better than the guru?*

ओफ disgust.

वाह or **वाह वाह** may express nearly any emotion, the emotion being indicated by the *tone* in which the word or words are uttered. They may convey the idea of admiration, astonishment, grief, disgust, etc.

राम राम, in addition to being used as a salutation, is uttered on hearing any statement which the hearer would desire were not true, something like the English, "*Don't say that!*"

341. Other words also are used with the force of Interjections :—

दोहाई *hear me! help me!* or, more fully, **आपकी दोहाई,** *I make my plaint to you.*

त्राहि *mercy! Shield me!*

भला *well! all right!*

बस *enough!*

धिक or **धिक्कार**, expressive of very strong disgust. With the Acc. of the person, almost equivalent to "a curse on him."

धन्य धन्य might almost be defined as a *religious Hurrah!* It indicates exalted admiration and praise.

जय or **जय जय** Victory!

342. Of forms of salutation, the more common are:—

राम राम which may be taken as about equivalent to "*God bless you.*"

जय "*good luck to you.*"

नमस्कार / **पालागी** } reverential salutations, addressed principally to Brahmans. The return salutation is **कल्याण**, *prosperity.*

नमस्कार has become a very common salutation among equals, of recent years.

स्वस्ति, salutation among equals, much adopted at the present time by members of the Árya Samáj.

सलाम *peace!* **बन्दगी** *my obeisance to you*, **तस्लीमात** (connecte with **सलाम**) *greeting!* are Urdu, but are occasionally used by Hindus, especially to Europeans.

CHAPTER XVI.

343. NUMBERS, DIVISIONS OF TIME, WEIGHTS AND MEASURES.

In the present chapter, many mat ers are included which do not strictly belong to Grammar. As, however, the points may be very useful to the student, and as the information may not be available in compact form elsewhere, they have been brought together here.

NUMBERS.

344. The Cardinal Numbers. The Numerals up to a hundred, must be committed to memory. In English, after 20 is reached, only the tens need be learned, as the intervening numbers are added quite regularly: this is not so in Hindi; there is not one of the units which unites regularly with all the tens throughout; **एक,** changed into **इक,** does indeed consistently preserve its form, but **इक + बीस** becomes **इक्कीस** (21) **इक + चालीस** becomes **इकतालीस** (41), etc.

Numerical Symbol.		Name.	Alternate form, and form used in compounds.
1	१	एक	इक
2	२	दो	दु

Numerical Symbol.		Name.	Alternate form, and form used in compounds.
3	३	तीन	ति, त्रि
4	४	चार	चौ
5	५ or ५	पाँच	पंच
6	६	छ †	छः, छि
7	७	सात ‡	सत
8	८ or ८	आठ	अठ
9	९, ९, or ९	नौ	नव
10	१०	दस	
11	११	इग्यारह	ग्यारह
12	१२	बारह	
13	१३	तेरह	
14	१४	चौदह	
15	१५	पंद्रह	
16	१६	सोलह	
17	१७	सत्तरह	सत्रह
18	१८	अट्ठारह	
19	१९	उन्नीस	उनीस
20	२०	बीस	

† Notice the aspirated छ throughout for 6, thus distinguishing it from चार. Cf. चौआलीस (44) छिआलीस (46)

‡ Distinguish carefully between सात (7) and साठ (60).

	Numerical Symbol.	Name.	Alternate form, and form used in compounds.
21	२१	इक्कीस	एकईस
22	२२	बाईस	
23	२३	तेईस	
24	२४	चौबीस	
25	२५	पचीस	पच्चीस
26	२६	छब्बीस	
27	२७	सत्ताईस	सताईस
28	२८	अट्ठाईस	अठाईस
29	२९	उन्तीस	
30	३०	तीस	
31	३१	*इकतीस	एकतीस
32	३२	बत्तीस	बतीस
33	३३	तेंतीस	तैंतीस
34	३४	चौंतीस	
35	३५	पैंतीस	
36	३६	छत्तीस	
37	३७	सैंतीस	
38	३८	अड़तीस	अढ़तीस

Notice the Similarity between **पचीस** (25), **पचास** (50) and **पचासी** (85).

* The real sound given in pronunciation is between the two vowels, **इ** and **ए**.

Numerical Symbol.		Name.	Alternate form, and form used in compounds.	
39	३९	उन्तालीस		
40	४०	चालीस		
41	४१	इकतालीस	एकतालीस*	*Cf. No. 31.
42	४२	बयालीस	बेआलीस	
43	४३	तैंतालीस	तैंतालीस	
44	४४	चौआलीस	चवालीस	
45	४५	पैंतालीस		
46	४६	छियालीस		
47	४७	सैंतालीस		
48	४८	अड़तालीस		
49	४९	उंचास	उनचास	
50	५०	पचास		
51	५१	इक्कावन	एकावन, एक्यावन	
52	५२	बावन		
53	५३	तिरपन		
54	५४	चौवन		
55	५५	पचपन		
56	५६	छप्पन		

Numerical Symbol.		Name.	Alternate form, and form used in compounds.
57	५७	सत्तावन	सन्तावन
58	५८	अट्ठावन	अठावन
59	५९	उन्सठ	उनसठ
60	६०	साठ	
61	६१	इकसठ	एकसठ
62	६२	बासठ	
63	६३	तिरसठ	
64	६४	चौंसठ	
65	६५	पैंसठ	
66	६६	छियासठ	
67	६७	सड़सठ	सरसठ or सतसठ
68	६८	अड़सठ	
69	६९	उनहत्तर	
70	७०	सत्तर	
71	७१	इकहत्तर	एकहत्तर
72	७२	बहत्तर	
73	७३	तिहत्तर	
74	७४	चौहत्तर	

	Numerical Symbol.	Name.	Alternate form, and form used in componnds.
75	७५	पछत्तर	पचहत्तर
76	७६	छिहत्तर	
77	७७	सतहत्तर	
78	७८	अठहत्तर	
79	७९	उन्नासी	उनासी
80	८०	अस्सी	
81	८१	इकासी	एक्यासी
82	८२	बयासी	
83	८३	तिरासी	
84	८४	चौरासी	
85	८५	पच्चासी	पचासी
86	८६	छियासी	
87	८७	सत्तासी	सतासी
88	८८	अट्ठासी	अठासी
89	८९	नवासी	
90	९०	नब्बे	नव्वे
91	९१	इकानवे*	एक्यानवे
92	९२	बानवे	
93	९३	तिरानवे	
94	९४	चौरानवे	
95	९५	पंचानवे	पचानवे

* The व is often changed to ब throughout the 90's.

Numerical Symbol.		Name.	Alternate form, and form used in compounds.
96	९६	छियानवे	छानवे
97	९७	सत्तानवे	सतानवे
98	९८	अट्ठानवे	अठानवे
99	९९	निनानवे	निन्यानवे
100	१००	सौ	सै

345. Beyond 100, the numbers proceed regularly, the units are added to the hundreds as in English, but "*and*" is not inserted. एक सौ एक (101), एक सौ दो (102), एक सौ बीस (120), etc.

But सवा सौ (125), डेढ़ सौ (150), पौने दो सौ (175), सवा दो सौ (225), अढ़ाई सौ (250), पौने तीन सौ (275), सवा तीन सौ, साढ़े तीन सौ, साढ़े चार सौ, and so on. This same idiom is used with the thousands in like manner, डेढ़ सहस्र (1,500), etc. (see § 352).

1,000 सहस्र (contracted sometimes into सहस), हज़ार.

100,000 लाख

100 लाख, करोड़ or कड़ोड़, (i.e., 10,000,000).

100 करोड़, अर्ब or अरब

Numerical Symbol.	Name.	Alternate form, and form used in compounds.
100	अर्ब	खर्ब or खरब
100	खर्ब	नील
100	नील	पद्म or पदम
100	पद्म	संख, i. e., 100,000,000,000,000,000.

The last three are seldom met with. अर्ब, खर्ब, are used mainly to convey the idea of innumerable, much as " millions and millions, " in English. करोड़, especially in the reduplicated plural form, करोड़ों करोड़, is used in a similar way.

346. The Ordinals.

पहिला or पहला	First.	चौथा	Fourth.
दूसरा	Second.	पाँचवाँ	Fifth.
तीसरा	Third.	छठवाँ or छठा	Sixth.

From सातवाँ onwards, the Ordinals are formed quite regularly from the Cardinals, by the addition of आँ.

These Ordinals are Adjectives of two terminations, आ or आँ Masc. (with ए or एँ Const. Sing. and ए Pl.) and ई or ईं Fem.

347. Proportionals.

To express "*two-fold, three-fold,*" or "*twice as much, three times as much,*" etc., गुणा or गुना is added to a

Numeral. As the form of the Numeral is sometimes modified in the process of union, a list of those so affected is given.

दुगुना (*f.* ई), दुगनी or दूना	twice as much.
तिगुना or त्रिगुना, also तिगनी	three times as much.
चैागुना	four times as much.
पंचगुना	five times as much.
छगुना	six times as much.
अठगुना	eight times as much.

The rest are formed quite regularly, सातगुना, नौगुना, etc. डेाढ़ा or डेवढ़ा is, *half as much again.* There is a Verb, डेवढ़ाना, *to once and a half.*

These proportionals are treated as Adjectives of two terminations.

माल के दुगुने चैागुने पर बेच कर, *Having sold the goods for twice or four times (their price).* दूने वा तिगुने दाम के बिकी, *(The thing) sold for two or three times its (usual) price.*

That, of which it is a proportional, is indicated by the Ablative Case. चाशनी बेसन से चैागुनी वा पंचगुनी हेा, *The syrup must be four or five times as much as the meal.*

348. **दोहरा करना, तिहरा करना, चौहरा** or **चौपरत करना, पाँचपरत करना,** etc., are used of doubling or folding up cloth, etc., into so many thicknesses.

For the number of strands in a rope, or number of lengths in which it is folded (" double it, " etc., in Eng.) **दोहरा** or **तिहरा** may be used for *two* and *three*; but the addition of **सर** to the numeral is the more appropriate word, **दोसर, तीनसर, चौरसर** or **चौसर,** etc.

349. Collectives.

A few words are in common use, corresponding to our "dozen," "score," etc.

गण्डा is "*a four,*" e.g., **बीस गण्डा,** *twenty fours,* i.e., 80.

This word is principally used in counting out cowries, also in reckoning the *standard* of a seer (weight): thus there is a **बीस गण्डे का सेर** and a **चौबीस गण्डे का सेर,** etc., *i.e.*, weighing 20 × 4 or 24 + 4, in other words, equivalent in weight to 80 or to 96 tolas.

गब्बा or **चौवा, चौकड़ी** are also found for aggregates of four.

गाही "*a five*" is used very largely in counting out the cakes of dried fuel brought into the towns for sale, also in connection with the buying and selling of mangoes, and in counting out quantities of small articles.

सत्ता "a seven."

Among the villagers, large numbers are practically very little used (nothing above 20); it is always so many "fours," so many "fives." I am assured that many of them not only use these aggregates in speech, but think in them; forty mangoes are not even thought of as "forty," but as **आठ गाही**, *i.e.*, eight fives.

कोड़ी "*a score.*" **बीस** is also occasionally used in this collective way. **कोड़ियों बोलियाँ बोली जाती हैं**, *scores of dialects are spoken.* There is a proverb, **एक तीन बीस एक साठ,** *One three score and one sixty* (Cf. "*Six one and half a dozen the other*").

सैकड़ा *a hundred.* Used as we use *hundred* in such a phrase as "How much a hundred?" **बीस आना सैकड़ा,** means "at the rate of one rupee four annas the hundred.

It is perhaps worth noting that सैकड़ा is a varying quantity in different parts of a district, and for different articles (Cf. Eng. *baker's dozen*). "A hundred mangoes" often means छब्बीस गाही, *i.e.*, 130, and in some places it is अट्ठाईस गाही, and over and above that, 8 thrown in as घेलुआ, thus making 148.

जोड़ा or जोड़ी is always *a pair*, never simply *two* in the loose way that "couple" is sometimes used in English.

दर्जन *dozen*, is gradually getting naturalized in Hindi.

350. All the Numerals may be made to assume the character of Collectives (Dr. Kellogg very appropriately calls them Agglomeratives) by the addition of ओं. Thus दोनों (in this case only, न is inserted before the addition), तीनों, चारों, etc., *the two, the three, the four*. चहुँ is also used for चारों, as चहुँ ओर, *in all four directions*. These are used—

(*a*) Of such persons and objects as have something of a collective unity, or are in some way closely connected. Thus, दोनों हाथ, *the two hands*. तीनों लोक, *the three worlds*. चारों

युग, *the four ages of the world.* पाँचों तत्त्व, *the five elements.* छओं रस, *the six flavours.*

(*b*) To designate persons or objects already referred to, or in some way distinctly marked out from others, as, in English, we say, *the five prisoners*; *the first eleven.* जब इन पाँचों देश के राजाओं ने......*When the kings of these five countries*......बिश्वावसु आदि तीनों भाइयों से कहो, *Say to the three brothers, Bishwáwasu and the others.*

(*c*) They are used also in a somewhat reduplicative sense, सैकड़ों और सहस्रों आने लगे, *They began to come along by hundreds and thousands.*

Occasionally, this form is reduplicated with the addition of the Gen. Postposition के, e.g., दोनों के दोनों, तीनों के तीनों, *both of them, all three of them.*

351. Idiomatic uses of the Numerals.

We say, *ten or twelve, eight or ten*, but for the lower numbers take successive numbers, *two or three, four or five.* In Hindi, the former idiom is commonly adopted throughout. Thus दो चार, पाँच सात, *two or four, five or seven.*

The following also are common combinations to indicate *a few*, etc. **दस पाँच,** *ten or five*; **दस बारह** *ten or twelve*; **पंद्रह बीस,** *fifteen or twenty*; **सौ पचास,** *between fifty and a hundred.*

Notice also such a phrase as **कोई दस एक,** which means *some ten or so.* **एक** is frequently in this way placed after a round number, to signify "*about.*"

उन्नीस बीस is used to indicate a slight difference. If enquiries be made about any one who is ill, the reply may be made, **कुछ उन्नीस बीस,** which means *he is somewhat better*, really *one-twentieth way towards recovery.*

Notice the following idiom : **एक को बीस बीस बनाके सुनाया करती हैं,** *they go on making twenty out of one, and keep on telling it to others* (i.e., *spread abroad exaggerated tales*).

The repetition of a number has a distributive force. **इसकी टोपियाँ दो दो तीन तीन आने को बिकने लगीं,** *The caps she made began to sell at two and three annas apiece.* **एक एक करके वे चले गये,** *They went away one by one.* **सब लोगों को दो दो तीन तीन मिले,** *They got two or three apiece.*

When the number is a compound one, only one part of the number, generally, is repeated, *e.g.*, **अढ़ाई**

अढ़ाई सौ पर मिलेगा *You will get them for two hundred and fifty (rupees) apiece.* पौने दो दो सेर होंगे, *They must weigh about a seer and three quarters each.*

The following idioms are worth noting:—

तीन तेरह करना, *to scatter* (transitive); तीन तेरह होना, *to scatter,* (neuter, *i.e., to be scattered*); सात पाँच करना, *to shilly shally*; नौ दो ग्यारह हुए, *They scuttled off*; धर्म कर्म सबही नौ दो ग्यारह हुए, *all moral and religious restraints went to the winds.*

352. **Fractions.**

$\frac{1}{4}$	चौथा, चौथाई, चौथा हिस्सा, पाओ or पाव
$\frac{1}{4}$ less	पौने or पौन
$\frac{1}{4}$ more	सवा
$\frac{1}{2}$	आधा
$\frac{1}{2}$ more	साढ़े
$1\frac{1}{2}$	डेढ़
$2\frac{1}{2}$	अढ़ाई or ढाई

As पाओ (commonly pronounced पौवा) is generally used for $\frac{1}{4}$ seer, it is safer to use चौथा or चौथाई or चौथा हिस्सा for the quarter of other things.

तीन चौथाई ग्रन्थ हमारी प्रति में नहीं है, *Three quarters of the books are not in the edition which I possess.*

पौने signifies $\frac{1}{4}$ less, and is placed before the number, thus **पौने दो** ($1\frac{3}{4}$); **पौने तीन सौ** (275). When used with **एक**, the **एक** is commonly omitted, and **पौन**, not **पौने**, is often used; thus **पौन गज,** $\frac{3}{4}$ of a yard. **हिंदू प्रति सैकड़ा पौन (·७७) बढ़े,** *The Hindus have increased at the rate of three-quarters in every hundred* (77), *i.e.*, 75 %. It is not used before 100 ; 75 is **पचहत्तर,** not **पौने सौ.**

सवा alone is $1\frac{1}{4}$. Placed before numbers higher than I, it signifies $\frac{1}{4}$ more, thus **सवा सेर** $1\frac{1}{4}$ seer, **सवा दो सेर** $2\frac{1}{4}$ seers, **सवा तीन सौ** 325.

आधा is *half of*. **आधा सेर** $\frac{1}{2}$ *seer*. **आधा राज्य,** *half of the kingdom.* When used with a word which is not a number, it is generally written *after* the word and has the Genitive Case sign, *e.g.*, **इसका आधा उसको दो,** *Give half of this to him.*

साढ़े is a half more, and is placed before the other number. **साढ़े तीन** $3\frac{1}{2}$, **साढ़े पाँच सौ** 550. Notice that **साढ़े** is *never* used with 1 and 2.

डेढ़ and अढ़ाई (or ढाई) are *always* used for $1\frac{1}{2}$ and $2\frac{1}{2}$. डेढ़ गज़ $1\frac{1}{2}$ yds. अढ़ाई हज़ार 2,500.

It is important to acquire facility in using these idioms; दो सौ पचास would sound to a Hindu as uncouth, as "*two hundred and a half of one hundred*" would to an Englishman.

DIVISIONS OF TIME.

353. General Names.

Year, बरस, also साल. For "*about a year,*" बरस दिन, is a common phrase. परसाल is *last year*, or *next year.* परिआर, *the one before* or *after that.*

For Century, the Urdu सदी is commonly used, less commonly शतक, शताब्दी, शत वर्ष

Month, महीना or मास.

Half a Month (which may be 14 or 15, occasionally 13 or 16, days), पक्ष or पाख.

The first half, reckoned from the day after full moon, is called बदि; कृष्णपक्ष or अन्धियारा पाख, *the dark half.*

The second half, from new moon to full moon, is सुदि; शुक्लपक्ष or उजियाला पाख (Colloq. अंजोरा;) *the light half.*

Although, for ordinary purposes, the months are reckoned from full moon to full moon, Pundits, for astronomical purposes, reckon from new-moon to new-moon.

Week, **हफ़ता**, occasionally **अठवारा**, or **सप्ताह**.

Day, **दिन**, is the ordinary term for a day of the week. **दिवस** also is in use, and the Urdu **रोज** or **रोज़. वार** is used in the Compounds. **सोमवार** *Monday*, etc.

For the *date*, the day of the **पक्ष** (1st, 2nd, etc.), **तिथि** must be used. It should be noticed that it is the day of the *fortnight* or **पक्ष** that is always mentioned, not the day of the *month*.

To-day, **आज**. Yesterday or to-morrow **कल**. The day after to-morrow, or, the day before yesterday, **पर्सों** (Colloq. **परों**). The third day from the present (*i.e.*, next Friday, if speaking on Tuesday) is **तरसों** or **चौथे दिन**. The fourth day from the present is **नरसों**, also occasionally **अतरसों**; but these are seldom used. The Hindus always reckon the two boundary, as well as the intervening days. Thus, if a man, speaking on a Thursday, says, **चार दिन हुए मैं आया**, he means, *I came on Monday*.

Night, रात. (also रात्र, रात्रि, रात्री, रैन)

Early morning, भिन्सारे, बिहान, तड़के, प्रातः-काल, प्रभात, सवेरे, etc.

Evening, साँझ, संझावेला, सायंकाल, etc.

पहर is the fourth part of a day or night, averaging therefore 3 hours. दो पहर means *noon.* पहर रात बीते, *about* 9 *p.m.* (lit., *when a pahar of the night shall have passed*). पहर रात रहे, *about* 3 *a.m.* (i.e., *when a pahar of the night remains*). So पहर दिन रहे, of, 3 *p.m.* पहर दिन चढ़े is *about* 9 *a.m.* (lit. *when one pahar of the day has ascended*).

घण्टा was a fourth part of a पहर, *i.e.*, 45 minutes, but is now largely identified with the English hour.

घड़ी was a still shorter period (22½ minutes ?). " आठ पहर चौंसठ घड़ी" The word घड़ी is sometimes used for *hour*, more commonly for *watch* or *clock*.

The idiom for the time of the day is now accommodated to the English method of reckoning, बजा (*struck*) being added to the numeral, दस

बजा, 10 O'Clock. **नौ बज के बीस मिनट हुआ**, 9 *having struck* 20 *minutes have passed*, i.e., 20 *past* 9. **जब ठीक चार बजे**, *Exactly at four.*

Sometimes the sing. is used, **बजा**, sometimes the pl. **बजे**, e.g., **रात को १० बज गया था**, *At night, ten had struck.* **नौ बज गये हैं**, *Nine has struck.*

354. Days of the week.

Sunday	**इतवार** or **रविवार, रविबार**
Monday	**सोमवार**
Tuesday	**मंगल**
Wednesday	**बुध**
Thursday	**बीफै** or **बृहस्पति**
Friday	**सुक** or **सुक्रवार, शुक्र**
Saturday	**सनीचर** or **शनैश्चर, शनिवार**

Other names also are found, but are mainly confined to literature. e.g., **आदित्यवार**, *Sunday*; **इन्दुवार**, *Monday*; **भौमवार**, *Tuesday*; **गुरुबार**, *Thursday.*

355. Months and Seasons.

COMMON NAME.	CORRECT SANSKRIT NAME.	CORRESPONDING TO, ABOUT.	NAME OF RITU.
1. चैत	(चैत्रः)	March.	वसन्त (Spring)
2. बैसाष	(वैशाख)	April.	
3. जेठ	(ज्येष्ठ)	May.	ग्रीष्म (Hot season)
4. असाढ़	(आषाढ़)	June.	
5. सावन	(श्रावण)	July.	वर्षा (Rainy season)
6. भादों, भादवँ	(भाद्र or भाद्रपद	August.	
7. कूआर	(आश्विन)	September.	शरद (Autumn).
8. कातिक	(कार्त्तिक)	October.	
9. अगहन	(मार्गशीर्ष)	November.	हेमन्त (Winter).
10. पूस	(पौष)	December.	
11. माघ	(माघ)	January.	शिशिर (Cold or Dewy Season).
12. फागुन	(फाल्गुन)	February.	

The Year begins with the second half of चैत,

The Months are divided into six seasons, of two months each. The names of these are given above, but they are mostly confined to poetry. For practical purposes, there are three Seasons: जाड़ा or जड़काल

(occasionally, शीतकाल), *The Winter.* गर्मी or धूपकाला, *Summer.* बरसात or बरखाकाल or बसकाला, *The Rainy Season.* These may be roughly reckoned as three periods of four months, beginning from कातिक.

The Hindi Months are Lunar Months; reckoned from the day after full moon to the next full moon. The year therefore is only about 354 days. To correct this inaccuracy, an extra month is added every three years or less. This extra month is known as मलमास, or अधिमास, or अधिकमास (occasionally, लौंद or लौन), and may come in the first seven months, but not in the last five. For religious purposes, this month begins after the first पक्ष of the month in which it occurs, and is followed by the remaining half of that month; but, for ordinary purposes, the month is doubled, and thus there is a 1st Chait and 2nd Chait, or 1st Baisakh and 2nd Baisakh, or whatever the month may be which is doubled.

English reckoning is now very commonly adopted. The English months are written as follows (with variations):—

जनवरी	अप्रैल
फ़रवरी	मई
मार्च	जून

जुलाई	अक्तूबर
अगस्त	नवम्बर
सितम्बर	दिसम्बर

356. Days of the Month.

The days of the पक्ष bear Sanskrit names, and not the ordinary Hindi Ordinals.

1st	परिवा	8th	अष्टमी
2nd	दूज or दूइज	9th	नौमी
3rd	तीज	10th	दसमी
4th	चौथ	11th	एकादसी
5th	पंचमी	12th	द्वादसी or दुआदसी
6th	छट्ठ	13th	तेरस
7th	सप्तमी	14th	चतुर्दसी or चौदस

The day before the new moon is called अमावस, the day of full moon, पूरनमासी (occasionally, पूनों or पूनेा). They may occur on the 14th or 15th, or very occasionally on the 13th or 16th of the पक्ष.

It is perhaps worthy of mention that in the case of such a short or long पक्ष, the day is not cut off or added at the end, but is arranged for, according to astronomical calculations, at its proper place, so that a पक्ष may have no 2nd (or other day), or may have two 2nd's, etc.

357. Eras or Epochs.

There are now three Eras in common use for reckoning in India (exclusive of the Mahommedan or **हिजरी**, 1326 of which commenced in February, 1908). The word **सम्बत** (prop. **संवत**) is applied both to the Era, and to the year in that era.

1. The most common Era in use among Hindus is that of Vikramáditya 56—57 B. C. This is used for most transactions. The year begins at the second-half of **चैत**. The English January 1919 is **माघ** 1975, according to Hindu chronology.

2. Another Era, which is used for transactions connected with the payment of rents for land, is called **फ़सली**. This year commences from the 1st of the month **कुआर**. The **फ़सली** year 1316 commenced on October 5, 1908.

3. The Christian Era also is now used for all legal documents; for this the word, **सम्बत**, is not commonly used. It is written **सन् ईस्वी १९१८** or **सन् ई० १९१८**, *i.e.*, 1918 A. D.

An example or two of the way in which these dates are printed may be useful.

आषाढ़ शुक्ल १२ भौमवार संवत १९४३, *On the 12th day, Tuesday, of the light-half of Asárh*, 1943.

वैशाख शुक्ल अष्टमी का विवाह है, *The marriage is (fixed for) the eighth day of the light-half of Baisákh.*

यह ईसाई सन् के ४७१ वर्ष पहिले हुआ, *This occurred in* 471 *B. C.*

There is still another Era, occasionally used, *viz.*, **शाक,** 78 years later than the Christian era.

"...**का जन्म १७९९ शकाब्द (वि० संवत १९३४),**" *i.e.*, 1877 A. D.

WEIGHTS AND MEASURES.

358 Weights.

5 **तोला** = 1 **छटाँक** — A tola is the exact weight of a rupee.

4 **छटाँक** = 1 **पाओ** or **पाव**

16 **छटाँक** = or 1 **सेर**

4 **पाव**

4 **सेर** = 1 **धरा**

5 **सेर** = 1 **पसेरी**

40 **सेर** = 1 **मन**

Considerable differences exist in different districts, and even in different markets in the same district, about weights. The **तोला, छटाँक, सेर** and **मन,** as given in the above table, are reckoned as *the* standard, and are recognized as such even where they are not used. But, frequently for local purposes, other **सेर** are in use, and there is the same variety in **मन, धरा,**

and पसेरी. The correct सेर is what is called the बीस गण्डा का सेर, *i.e.*, 20 times 4 tolas, the weight of 80 rupees, *i.e.*, 2lbs. and about $\frac{9}{10}$ of an oz., but in one district alone, known to the writer, there are current (in different parts) a 48, 72, 84 and 96 tola सेर.

The तोला and smaller weights are used mainly for precious metals, and the more valuable drugs, etc.

There is no Measure of capacity widely used. Milk, oil, grain, etc., are all sold by weight, though frequently milk and other liquids are actually measured, not weighed.

The word भर idiomatically used with weights, etc., *e.g.*, सेर भर actually means full, but is purely idiomatic, giving no additional or exact force.

359. Measures of Length.

The गज or गज़ is a fraction over 40 inches, but the cloth-sellers take kindly to the English yard, and it is now largely used in the towns.

The गज़ is divided into 16 गिरह, or गिरिह, *i.e.*, about $2\frac{1}{2}$ inches.

The following are not standard measures, but are in common use for things not actually bought and sold :—

अंगुल the breadth of a finger, something under an inch.

तस्सू the breadth of two fingers, about $1\frac{1}{2}$ inch.

बित्ता or बालिश्त a span, about 9 inches.

चौवा or चव्वा is a measure of four fingers.

हाथ from elbow to tip of middle finger, about 20 inches.

The following is found as a "table:"—

जव = a grain of barley.

8 जव =1 अंगुल

24 अंगुल=1 हाथ

For measuring the depth of wells, the word पर्सा is commonly used. It is the height a man can reach, including his height, *i.e.*, about 7 or 8 feet.

The कोस (prop. कोश) is about 2 English miles.

गोली (the distance a bullet will travel) is generally used of any distance somewhere about half a mile, or less, or more.

Both words, however, are very *broadly* used, as a traveller has often to experience. कोस भर may be anything between 2 miles and 5, except when used by the driver of a hired conveyance, when it is *very* much less.

The following is given as a "table" by some:—

4 हाथ =1 दण्ड

2000 दण्ड = 1 कोस
4 कोस = 1 योजन

360. Land Measure.

The बीघा in the U. P. (at least around Benares and Mirzapur), is 3025 sqr. yards, 55 yards, respectively, in length and breadth, *i.e.*, about $\frac{5}{8}$ of an English acre.

20 बिस्वांसी or धूर = 1 बिस्वा
20 बिस्वा = 1 बीघा
A गट्ठा is $2\frac{3}{4}$ yds. in length,
लट्ठा „ $5\frac{1}{2}$ „ „ „
20 गट्ठा or 10 लट्ठा = a जरीब, which is 55 yards *in length*. The Square of this is a बीघा.

361. Coinage.

3 पाई = 1 पैसा	अधेला	is half-a-pice.
4 पैसा = 1 आना	टका	„ two pice.
16 आना = 1 रूपी	दमड़ी	may be $\frac{1}{4}$ or $\frac{1}{8}$ of a pice.

For the exact English equivalent to the rupee, reference must be made to the daily paper. There was a time when it was worth two shillings, it stood for some time at 1s. 4d., recently (1919) it has been between 1s. 5d. and 1s. 6d.

In some parts, two kinds of pice (पैसा) are

current: the ordinary government coin, called गड़ाड़ीदार पैसा, and an uncoined, one not a very shapely bit of metal, called the गोरखपुरी पैसा, The latter is less in value than the former, and has largely gone out of use during the last few years.

The कौड़ी (a small shell, Eng. Cowrie) is used for buying small quantities of condiments, etc. The rate of exchange varies, but बीस गण्डा, *i.e.*, 80 for a pice, may be taken as their average value.

The names for a two-anna, four-anna, and eight-anna piece are, respectively, दुअन्नी (or दुइअन्नी), चौअन्नी (or चवन्नी, also सूका), अठन्नी (sometimes among villagers अधेली).

The following illustrate the method of writing down rupees, annas, and pice:—

For rupees, the number is written with this mark) after it. ५) = 5 Rs. २) = 2 Rs.

For annas, a small horizontal or oblique stroke signifies 1 anna, a perpendicular stroke 4 annas, written in the same way before the mark).

Thus –) or ⁄) is 1 anna, ≡) or ⫽) is 3 annas, |) is 4 annas, |⫽) is 6 annas, |||≡) is 15 annas, etc.

Pice are indicated by similar horizontal strokes written to the right hand of this). Thus)।। is 2 pice.)। is 1 pice. २॥) is Rs. 2-8-0. ४॥ =)।।। is Rs. 4-10-9.

It should be noticed that, in expressing Indian money in English, the number of *pice* is never written, but the number of *pie*. Rs. 5-4-3 means 5 rupees, four annas, 3 pies (*i.e.*, 1 pice), *not* 3 pice.

362. Addition, Subtraction, etc.

The idioms for the four simple rules of Arithmetic will be sufficiently illustrated by the following :—

Addition.	**जोड़ना**	5+8	**पाँच और आठ को जोड़ना.**
Subtraction	**बाकी निकालना**	8—5	**आठ में से पाँच को घटाना.**
Multiplication	**गुणा करना**	8×5	**आठ को पाँच से गुणना.**
Division	**भाग देना**	40÷5	**चालीस में पाँच का भाग देना.**

जोड़, बाकी, गुण, भाजन are also used as shortened forms for Addition, Subtraction, Multiplication, and Division.

The Multiplication Tables present peculiarities of their own. They begin from *once one is one, once two is two*, and differ from the English tables in having tables for one-and-a-half, two-and-a-half, etc. The words also for the cardinal numbers differ from those in general use. One table is given below to illustrate this:—

दो एक्के दो
दो दूना चार
दो तियाँई छः
दो चौक्के आठ
दो पंजे दस

दो छक्के बारह
दो सत्ते चौदह
दो अट्ठे सोलह
दो नवाँ अठारह
दो दहाँई बीस

CHAPTER XVII.

PROSODY.

363.

Poetry	पद्य
Prose	गद्य
Word	शब्द
Word with its Case-ending	पद
Syllable or letter	वर्ण
Instant	मात्रा
Long syllable or letter	गुरु or दीर्घ
Short " " "	लघु or ह्रस्व
Verse	पद or पाद
Line	पंक्ति or दल
Half-line	चरण
Foot	गण
Full pause at end of line or चरण	विश्राम
Pause at end of गण	यति
Poetry measured by number of syllables.	वर्णवृत्त
" by number of instants	मात्रिक छन्द
Rhyme.	तुक or तुकान्त
Rhythm or Cadence	लय
Arrangement of words	योजना
Alliteration, etc.	अनुप्रास

It should be understood that these are only approximate, and not exact equivalents.

364. Hindi literature is written in **गद्य**, Prose, and **पद्य**, verse. Since the beginning of the 19th century, prose has been steadily gaining ground and may now be considered to have taken the place of verse for the general diffusion of knowledge. Up to the end of the 18th century, practically all Hindi literature was written in verse. Not only were the subjects usually relegated to the domain of verse in English so treated in Hindi, but all subjects were thus dealt with. Not merely were there love poems and poems dealing with nature and human passions, but such prosaic subjects, as grammar and arithmetic, were done in verse. During the last century matters were steadily changing, and though verse is up to the present often used for subjects that an English writer would scarcely dream of dealing with in anything but prose, yet the main body of Hindi literature, history, biography, fiction, educational books, is now produced in prose, and verse is more largely reserved for religious subjects, for erotic writings, for descriptions of nature and the reproduction of episodes from the great works in Sanskrit, such as the Mahabharat. Incidents also from the lives of Ram and Krishna are continually being produced in various metres.

Considering the position that verse took in the past of Hindi literature and the place which it still occupies, Hindi Grammar would be very incomplete were Prosody to find no place in it. The subject is so wide that not a chapter but a volume seems called for, and it may be hoped that some really good comprehensive work on the subject may be produced in English. All that can be attempted here is to give a brief introduction to the subject.

Dr. Kellogg has devoted some 39 pages to Prosody in his Hindi Grammar. This is possibly the best we have in English on the subject. In Hindi, Babu Jagannath Prasad of Bilaspur has written two very important works dealing with Hindi Prosody, the larger book, called **काव्यप्रभाकर**, aims at covering the whole ground, the smaller book, **छन्दःप्रभाकर**, treats of metre or **पिंगल.** The latter has proved of great service to the writer of this Grammar, and he desires to acknowledge this, and to express his high appreciation of the work. Babu Jagannâth Prasad is an enthusiast, and writes with great ability and judgment.

There are three main divisions for us to consider:

I. **भाव** and **रस**, The Emotions and Styles (see below.)

II. Metre, **छन्द** or **पिंगल.**

III. Mataphors and Figures of Speech, **अलंकार.**

भाव AND रस.

(THE EMOTIONS AND STYLES).

365. भाव. It is not easy to find English words suitable to translate भाव and रस. *Emotions* and *Styles* are probably about the nearest equivalents.

भाव may be regarded as the emotions which are to be expressed. रस originally means *flavour* or *taste,* the *essence,* or *juice* of anything which produces the flavour, and so, as applied to Prosody, stands for the *Styles* through which the emotions, or भाव, are expressed. The रस is the appropriate medium for reproducing in the mind of the reader something like the emotions which have been stirring the mind of the writer.

There is a natural bent in the Indian mind to elaborate in the way of dividing and sub-dividing a [illegible]t. and Prosody is a fine field for such elaboration. There are not only भाव, but विभाव, which apparently refer to the states of mind which precede the fully-blown भाव or emotions. There are also अनुभाव, which indicate the external expression of the emotions.

भाव are of two kinds, स्थाई and संचारी or व्यभि-चारी. The former, eight in number, by some reckoned as nine, refer to the great fundamental emotions or passions which sway human conduct. The latter, generally numbered at 32 or 34, are connected with the more fugitive or secondary or minor emotions or feelings.

The eight स्थाई भाव are 1. Desire, or amorous passion; 2. Mirth; 3. Sorrow; 4. Heroism; 5. Anger; 6. Fear; 7. Aversion; 8. Astonishment. The संचारी भाव are generally numbered as 32, 33 or 34, but one writer reckons them as 41, including in the number 8 which apparently most writers on the subject regard as अनुभाव. If the 8 be included, then they form a separate class, called तन संचारी भाव, *i.e.*, bodily, such as *crying*, *trembling*, *horripilation* (the standing up on end of the hairs of the body), etc. The remaining states are called मन संचारी भाव, *i.e.*, mental. This group is quite a miscellaneous company, including *doubt*, *flurry*, *pride*, *lassitude*, *delight*, *dejection*, *sickness*, and even *death*.

366. The रस are nine in number, sometimes a tenth is added.

1. शृंगार, the *erotic* style; 2. हास्य, the *comic* or *humorous*; 3. करुणा, the style in which *pathos* prevails; 4. वीर, the *heroic* style; 5. रौद्र, setting forth *wrath*; 6. भयानक, the *terrible*; 7. बीभत्स, arousing *disgust*; 8. अद्भुत, arousing *wonder*; 9. शान्त,

the *quietistic* style; 10. **वात्सल्य,** the style in which there is a *tenderness*, corresponding to that which parents manifest.

METAPHORS AND FIGURES OF SPEECH. अलंकार.

367. With Indian writers, this subject is treated in separate treatises, being considered too large and important to be included with "metre." According to western taste, Hindi poets appear to run riot in various metaphors and devices of versification, but from the Indian standpoint it is regarded as essential that strict rules and canons should be applied to the use of **अलंकार** or ornamentation.

Words are said to be used, 1. *literally*, 2. *idiomatically*, or *with a conventionally accepted meaning not strictly literal*, 3. *figuratively*, i.e., *in a poetic sense.*

In the next place, **अलंकार** are arranged under three heads according to 1. *Sound* **शब्दालंकार,** 2. *Sense*, **अर्थालंकार,** 3. The two combined, **उभयलंकार.**

These are, again, sub-divided. 1. includes various forms of alliteration, the use of words with similar sound but different meanings, of equivocal words, etc. Under the second come well-nigh innumerable rules about different kinds of metaphors, of the common qualities which must be found in the thing compared and the thing with which it is compared, the consideration of suitable styles for praise, blame, irony, etc.

In भूषणग्रन्थावली, edited by two brothers, Pundits Shyámbihāri Mishra and Shukadevabihári Mishra, 129 forms of अलंकार, as illustrated in शिवराजभूषण, are enumerated, and a further list of between 20 and 30 is given which were not illustrated in that work.

For the further study of this subject, students may be referred to the book just mentioned, published by the Nagari Pracharini Sabha, Benares, price 12 annas, and also to a little book, अलंकारप्रबोध, written by Adhyāpak Rāmaratna and printed at the Shresth Printing Press, Agra, price 5 annas.

METRE. छन्द or पिंगल.

368. This subject is one with many ramifications, and cannot be treated with any fulness. All that can be undertaken is an endeavour to set forth some of the main principles and to offer a few details with reference to some of the very common metres and verses.

369. बर्णिक and मात्रिक, These are two main divisions into which metres have been divided. छन्द is applied to both of these methods of reckoning metre in versification, but the word छन्द is more particularly appropriated for those forms of verse counted according to their number of मात्रा. It may be well therefore to write of मात्रिक छन्द and use the word वृत्त for metres worked out according to their वर्ण or syllables, वर्णवृत्त.

The first point to consider is the exact meaning or use of these two words, वर्ण and मात्रा.

370. वर्ण or बर्ण. This word means, literally, *letter*, but in considering Prosody it must be taken to signify a *sounded* letter, not a written one. It may be a vowel alone, or a consonant with its vowel, or a compounded consonant with its accompanying vowel. It is that part of a word which is sounded at one movement of the vocal organs. This movement may commence with a consonant or not, but must conclude with a vowel (with very rare exceptions). Thus इ is one वर्ण, so is कि. स्त्रि also is but one वर्ण. The essential of a वर्ण is one vowel sound, whether that vowel be preceded by a simple or conjunct consonant, or be alone. A vowel there must be in a बर्ण and *only* one. We may call this a *letter* or a *syllable*, but in neither case does it correspond with the English *letter* or *syllable*, e.g., in English, *son*, is one syllable, in Hindi it is two, स + न; *i.e.*, स with its inherent अ is one वर्ण, and न with its

inherent अ is a second वर्ण. On the other hand, in English, *so* is two letters, *sea* is three, *slay* is four, *screw*, five; but the nearest equivalent sounds to these in Hindi, सो, सी, स्ले, स्क्रू, are each but one वर्ण.

The वर्ण are of two kinds, long and short, depending on the length of the vowel, not in any way on the number of the consonants. The long is called दीर्घ or गुरु, the short ह्रस्व or लघु. In indicating these long and short वर्ण, the long is represented by ऽ, the short by । It may be more convenient for us to keep to the English signs — and ⌣ for the long and short वर्ण, respectively. In Hindi, the phrase, कारज धीरे होत है, *work is accomplished slowly*, would be written down ऽ । । ऽ ऽ ऽ । ऽ, *i.e.*, 8 वर्ण, 5 of which are long, 3 short. We may express it thus, — ⌣ ⌣ — — — ⌣ —.

The दीर्घ or गुरु consists of one of the long vowels, आ, ई, ऊ, ए, ऐ, ओ, औ, standing alone, or preceded by a consonant, simple or compound.

The ह्रस्व or लघु of one of the short vowels, अ, इ, उ, ऋ, with or without a consonant or consonants.

The principal exceptions to the above are the following :—

1. A short syllable, followed by a syllable beginning with a Conjunctive Consonant, is reckoned long, *e.g.*, in पण्डित, the syllable प would be, ordinarily, short, but as the following syllable begins with the Conjunctive, ण्ड, this प is reckoned long, and the word would be represented by — ⌣ ⌣ *i.e.*, प = गुरु, ण्डि = लघु, and त = लघु.

2. A short syllable, followed by visarg, or by anusvár, when it represents a *strong* nasalization, is reckoned long (for this nasalization, with its accompanying consonant, is practically a conjunct. consonant). Thus अंतरज्ञानी, if reckoned by vowel sounds, would be ⌣ ⌣ ⌣ — —, but, by the above rules, it becomes — ⌣ ⌣ — —, because अंत equals अन्त and the Conjunct न्त makes the preceding short vowel अ equal to a long syllable. So संग becomes — ⌣, and दुःख — ⌣ .

Anunasik does not affect the length of a syllable or वर्ण.

3. Sometimes the conjunct. does *not* lead to the preceding vowel being reckoned long. This is especially the case when the second member

of the Conjunct. is र or ह, *e.g.*, तुम प्रिय मोहि भरत जिमि भाई, *You are as dear to me, my brother, as (my brother) Bharat.* Here म followed by प्रि is reckoned short, *not* long, and the line scans ⏑ ⏑ ⏑ ⏑ — । ⏑ ⏑ ⏑ ⏑ । ⏑ ⏑ — । — ‖ So in the following: जिन्ह रघुबीर चरण रति मानी, (*who have yielded their hearts' devotion to the feet of Raghubir*). Here, although before the Conjunct. न्ह, the जि is reckoned short; the line scans ⏑ ⏑ ⏑ ⏑ — । ⏑ ⏑ ⏑ ⏑ । ⏑ ⏑ — । — ‖.

4. The long vowels, ए and ओ, are sometimes reckoned short, *e.g.*, in जेहि सायक मारा मैं बाली, (*with which arrow I slew Báli*). ⏑ ⏑ — ⏑ ⏑ । — — । — — । — ‖ Here जे is reckoned short. So is मे reckoned short in the following: निज बुधिबल भरोस मोहि नाहीं, *On the power of my own wisdom I have no confidence*) ⏑ ⏑ ⏑ ⏑ ⏑ ⏑ । ⏑ — ⏑ । ⏑ ⏑ — । — ‖.

5. Other exceptions may be summed up in the words of an Indian writer. और जो कवि लोग गुरु को भी लघु कर पढ़ते हैं उस को

भी लघु जानो, *and if poets read even a long syllable as a short one (then) understand that also to be a short one.* Poets take considerable license in this matter.

371. **मात्रा.** This is a standard of metric measure equalling a short वर्ण, the long वर्ण being reckoned as two मात्रा. Lines are frequently measured not by the number of वर्ण, but by the number of मात्रा. As a matter of practical working, while certain parts of the line may be regulated by long and short syllables, in a definite order there may be other portions of the line where this is not so, but the number of मात्रा must be correct. As an illustration, take the following *doha* :—

क्यों कीजै ऐसौ जतन जा तें काज न होय।
परबत पै खोदै कुआँ कैसे निकसे तोय॥

Why spend your energy in such a way that the work will not be effected. Dig a well on a mountain! how will water issue?

In the 1st and 3rd चरण, there must be 13 मात्रा, 6+4+3=13; in the 2nd and 4th, 6+4+1=11 मात्रा. The last 3 मात्रा of lines 1 and 3 must be ⏑ ⏑ ⏑ or ⏑ —, not — ⏑, but the 1st 6 मात्रा, and the 2nd group of 4 मात्रा, may be arranged in any way the poet chooses.

The 1st — — — =6; the 2nd — — =4; 3rd ⏑ ⏑ ⏑ =3 total 13.
" 3rd ⏑ ⏑ ⏑ ⏑ — =6 .... — — =4 ...... ⏑ — =3 ...... 13.

In the same poem we find the following arrangements for other lines :—

The 1st ⏑ ⏑⏑⏑⏑⏑ =6; the 2nd ⏑ ⏑ — =4; 3rd ⏑ — =3, total 13.
...... ⏑ ⏑ — — =6 ...... ⏑⏑— =4 ⏑ — =3 ...... 13.
...... — ⏑ — ⏑ =6 ......— ⏑ ⏑ =4 ⏑ — =3 ...... 13.
...... — ⏑ — ⏑ =6 ...... ⏑ ⏑ — =4 ⏑ — =3 ...... 13.

372. We are now in a better position to understand the broad distinction between the two great divisions of Hind verse, **वर्णवृत्ति** and **मात्रिक छन्द**. The words, *broad distinction*, are used advisedly, *essential difference* there is not. In **वर्णवृत्ति**, the length of the line is reckoned by the number of syllables or **वर्ण**; in **मात्रिक छन्द** by the number of **मात्रा**; but forasmucn as there are invariably *some* regulations about long and short syllables and their order in some part of the **चरण**, and also about the number of **मात्रा** in each **चरण**, the **वर्णवृत्त** is not quite distinct from the **मात्रिक छन्द**. Again, the **मात्रिक छन्द** are never regulated simply by the number of **मात्रा** there must be some observance of the arrangement of long and short syllables in some part of the line, and thus the **मात्रिक छन्द** are not completely different from the **वर्णवृत्त**. All that can be said is that, in the one class, the stress is on the number of syllables, वर्ण, in the other on the number of instants or मात्रा. When the matter is carefully worked out, it transpires that the differences between the two great classes of Hindi poetry are not so great, nor so absolute, as the statements of some writers might lead us to expect. It must be self-evident to any one that the grouping of a number of lines, either with a certain number of instants or a certain number of syllables, could not be poetry, in the sense of metrical poetry. What is effected by accent in English verse is effected in Hindi, *more or less*, by the arrangement of long and short syllables and the grouping of the words into चरण. Apart from this and rhyme, we should not obtain metrical composition.

373. Cæsura, Rest, or Pause. विश्राम and यति. Verses in Hindi poetry are of various lengths (two, four, six lines, etc., as in English), but these are mostly made up of various combinations of smaller divisions or groupings of syllables. The most common form of verse is one of four चरण. An example before us will be useful for reference.

समाचार तेहि समय सुनि सीय उठी अकुलाइ।
जाइ सासु पगकमल युग बंदि बैठि सिर नाइ॥

At that time, having heard the news
Sita arose, in great distress
Having gone; to her mother-in-law's two lotus feet
Bowing her head in obeisance, she sat down.

Here there is a full pause (॥) at the end of the verse, a half-pause (।) at the end of the half-verse, and pauses (unmarked) at the end of the 1st and 3rd lines or चरण. Before each of *these* pauses, a word is usually completed, *i.e.*, the pause does not occur in the middle of a word. We shall notice that within these चरण there are frequently minor divisions, between which there are unmarked and less distinguishable pauses. These pauses must come at the end of a syllable or वर्ण, but not necessarily at the end of a word. The pauses at the end of these minor divisions are called यति.

374. गण. The word गण (corresponding in a general way to the English word "foot" as applied to poetry) is the name given to the minor divisions noticed at the end of the last paragraph. A गण is a group of syllables or instants.

a. As applied to वर्णवृत्त, the गण, of course, may stand for various numbers of syllables, but it is employed especially for the aggregate of 3 syllables; eight varieties of this गण are possible, according to the order and number of long or short syllables. For these eight varieties, special symbols are used.

Thus :—

Symbol.	Name.	Value.	English equivalent.*
म	मगण	— — —	Molossus.
य	यगण	⏑ — —	Bacchic.
र	रगण	— ⏑ —	Cretic.
स	सगण	⏑ ⏑ —	Anapest.
त	तगण	— — ⏑	Antibacchic.
ज	जगण	⏑ — ⏑	Amphibrach.
भ	भगण	— ⏑ ⏑	Dactyl.
न	नगण	⏑ ⏑ ⏑	Tribrach.

For less than three syllables, ग (short for गुरु) and ल (short for लघु) are used. Thus गल = — ⏑; लल = ⏑ ⏑ etc.

b. As applied to मात्रावृत्त, the गण stand for numbers of *instants*, not *syllables*. Symbols also exist for these :—

ण = 2 instants.

ठ = 3 „

ड = 4 „

---

*It is not, of course, intended that these English names *exactly* represent the Hindi गण or feet, but the long and short syllables of the latter do correspond, in no small measure, with the accented and unaccented syllables of English poetry.

Considering the position that verse, took in the past of Hindi literature and the place which it still occupies, Hindi Grammar would be very incomplete were Prosody to find no place in it. The subject is so wide that not a chapter but a volume seems called for, and it may be hoped that some really good comprehensive work on the subject may be produced in English. All that can be attempted here is to give a brief introduction to the subject.

Dr. Kellogg has devoted some 39 pages to Prosody in his Hindi Grammar. This is possibly the best we have in English on the subject. In Hindi, Babu Jagannath Prasad of Bilaspur has written two very important works dealing with Hindi Prosody, the larger book, called काव्यप्रभाकर, aims at covering the whole ground, the smaller book, छन्दःप्रभाकर, treats of metre or पिंगल. The latter has proved of great service to the writer of this Grammar, and he desires to acknowledge this, and to express his high appreciation of the work. Babu Jagannath Prasad is an enthusiast, and writes with great ability and judgment.

There are three main divisions for us to consider:

I. भाव and रस, The Emotions and Styles (see below.)

II. Metre, छन्द or पिंगल.

III. Mataphors and Figures of Speech, अलंकार.

भाव AND रस.

(THE EMOTIONS AND STYLES).

365. **भाव.** It is not easy to find English words suitable to translate **भाव** and **रस.** *Emotions* and *Styles* are probably about the nearest equivalents.

भाव may be regarded as the emotions which are to be expressed. **रस** originally means *flavour* or *taste*, the *essence*, or *juice* of anything which produces the flavour, and so, as applied to Prosody, stands for the *Styles* through which the emotions, or **भाव**, are expressed. The **रस** is the appropriate medium for reproducing in the mind of the reader something like the emotions which have been stirring the mind of the writer.

There is a natural bent in the Indian mind to elaborate in the way of dividing and sub-dividing a subject, and Prosody is a fine field for such elaboration. There are not only **भाव**, but **विभाव**, which apparently refer to the states of mind which precede the fully-blown **भाव** or emotions. There are also **अनुभाव**, which indicate the external expression of the emotions.

भाव are of two kinds, **स्थाई** and **संचारी** or **व्यभिचारी.** The former, eight in number, by some reckoned as nine, refer to the great fundamental emotions or passions which sway human conduct.

with either झ, ह, र, भ or ष might spell disaster. Should, however, the poet, for some reason or other, feel greatly moved to begin his poem with a word commencing with one of the banned letters, he can mitigate the danger involved, if not absolutey nullify it, by using with it a long vowel or placing near the word the name of a deity or some other word of equal efficacy.

377. Dialects used in Poetry. Even in English, the language of poetry is not quite identical with that of prose. Such words as *morn, eve, erst, ope, chanticleer, the flight of time,* and a thousand other words and phrases, are felt at once to belong to the realm of verse rather than to that of prose. In Hindi, however, until comparatively recently, the language of poetry was far more widely marked off from that obtaining in prose than it is in English. It is not perhaps so much in the vocabulary as in the forms of the words that the differences are most marked, especially in the forms of the Tenses of the Verbs. In prose, there has been the steady endeavour to eliminate dialectical differences, to "standardise" the forms; in poetry, these dialectical forms are deliberately, if not always consistently, retained. Braj bhāshā, Avadhi, Eastern Hindi or some other dialect may be selected, or forms from more than one dialect may be used in the same poem. Braj is the favourite dialect, but the large use of Avadhí by Tulsi Das has led very many to follow him in this respect as in many others.

During recent years, a school of "Kharí bolí" has grown up, whose aim is to adopt in poetry the forms commonly current in prose writing. Quite a large quantity of verse has been produced on these lines. Naturally, a foreigner might be expected to have a prejudice in favour of the course advocated by the members of this new school, making, as it does, for simplicity, and lessening the difficulties of understanding the language of the poem; but it must be confessed that there is a sweetness and a swing in the dialectical verses that one does not catch in the "Kharí bolí" lines. One of the great advantages of the dialectical forms is their pliability in the hands of a master; they may be stretched or compressed or twisted or modified to meet the needs of the moment, remaining recognizable and wearing no appearance of grotesqueness or uncouthness. For instance, in the Ramayan of Tulsi Das are found no less than eleven different forms for the word ऐसा; it may be one syllable अस, or two ऐसे, or three ऐसेउ, according to the corner to be occupied.

At present, a somewhat heated controversy is being

waged by the champions of the old and the new styles. Both styles are being used ; both have their merits. The new may grow, the old will not easily die. Probably both will live on side by side and flourish, each admired and adopted by many, both by some.

378. Divisions of lines, etc. Not a little uncertainty exists with regard to some of the technical terms used in Prosody. छन्द may be used for a *verse*, but the word has other meanings and uses. पद or पाद is perhaps the best equivalent for *line*, but is not an unequivocal word, as it is used in other ways. चरण is the half line. The sub-sections within the चरण may be गण, or they may not be so. If a certrin arrangement of long and short syllables within that sub-section be required, then the sub-section is a गण, if not, but only the number of मात्रा be laid down, then the name गण is not appropriate.

The Cæsura or Pause occurring at the end of a पद or चरण or sub-section is called a यति.

Generally, a word is completed at the pause occurring in the middle of the line, *i.e.*, at the end of the 1st चरण; but this is not necessary at the pauses within the चरण, *i.e.*, at the ends of the sub-sections, *but* a वर्ण must be complete at these minor pauses, *i.e.*, if the चरण be made up of 13 instants or मात्रा, arranged as follows, 6+4+3

=13, the last instant of each sub-section must be either a short syllable or the second half of a long one, it must not be the first half of a long one. For illustrating this point, take the second sub-section, *i.e.*, the one containing four **मात्रा.** These four must conform to one of five arrangements, 1. ⏑ ⏑ ⏑ ⏑, 2. — —, 3. ⏑ — ⏑ 4. ⏑ ⏑ —, or 5. — ⏑ ⏑. It must not be ⏑ ⏑ ⏑ — for that would involve the second half of the last long syllable passing over into the following sub-section; and this is not permissible.

The sign । is used for the pause at the half line, or first line of a dohā, ॥ for the end of the line or dohā.

379. Metres. Very elaborate and exceedingly ingenious methods have been worked out for ascertaining how many different arrangements of long and short syllables are possible in a line containing a certain number of **मात्रा** or **वर्ण.** The scheme for working this out is called **संख्या.** There is another scheme, called **प्रस्तार,** for working out the order in which these various arrangements will arise. By **सूची** it can be ascertained how many varieties will end with a long vowel, how many with a short one. By means of **उद्दिष्ट** may be discovered what number in the series, worked out according to **प्रस्तार,** any particular grouping of long and short syllables will be. Other schemes for working out other details are given, eight or nine in all.

Of the ingenuity of these methods and their adequacy to secure accurate results, it is impossible to speak too highly, but whether the ascertainment that in a line containing 32 instants 3,524, 578 different arrangements of long and short syllables are possible is of great value for those who desire to cultivate poetry, may be doubted by some.

वर्णवृत्त.

380. Common to both Varnavritt and Matrik Chhand are the three sub-divisions: (1) सम, in which are included all verses in which the four चरण or lines have an equal number of वर्ण or मात्रा; 2) अर्द्धसम, in which the alternate lines or चरण agree: (3) विषम, under which are grouped all other varieties.

Within these sub-divisions are almost infinite possible and actual varieties, according to the number of syllables, in varying order of long and short. Every group of 4 वर्ण is capable of 16 varieties, with 16 वर्ण 4,096 varieties are possible. In the case of lines with 30 and more वर्ण, the possible arrangements of long and short syllables must run into millions.

As so many of the popular metres are composed according to the मात्रिक छन्द method perhaps one form of the वर्णवृत्त, may suffice. The कवित्त is selected, as it is probably the best known; though, in making this selection, it should be pointed out that probably there is no other form of verse in this division which is so free from trammels as regards the observance of the order of long and short syllables as is the कवित्त. In this way, it is not quite typical of this division of poetry.

The poet who most excelled in this metre was Padmākar; Tulsi Das has also used it very effectively in his Kabitt Ramayan.

The कवित्त contains 31 वर्ण in each line, arranged as follows:—8+8+8+7=31. If possible, a word should close at each of the four pauses, but this is not absolutely essential. A word must close, however, at the 16th and 31st वर्ण. This condition and the further one that the last वर्ण of the line must be long, are the only restrictions placed on the full freedom of the poet; yet probably there is no more melodious measure in Hindi poetry than the Kabitt.

Two specimen lines are given—

1. रैनदिन आठों जाम राम राम राम राम सीताराम सीताराम सीताराम कहिये.

2. (As written)—

कहैं पदमाकर पवित्रपन पालिबे को चेारचक्रपाणि के चरित्रन केा चाहिये ।

(As read) **कहैं पदमाकर पवित्रपन पालिबे को चेारचक्रपाणिके चरित्रनकेा चहिये ।**

To illustrate the freedom of this form of verse, the metric arrangement of the lines 1 and 2 is placed one over the other, by which it will be seen how greatly they vary.

— ⏑ ⏑ ⏑ — — — ⏑	— ⏑ — ⏑ — ⏑ — ⏑	— — — ⏑ — — — ⏑	— — — ⏑ ⏑ ⏑ —
⏑ — ⏑ ⏑ — ⏑ ⏑ ⏑	— ⏑ ⏑ ⏑ — ⏑ — —	— ⏑ — ⏑ — ⏑ — ⏑	⏑ ⏑ ⏑ — ⏑ ⏑ —

In the first example, the words conclude at each of the four pauses, according to the strict rule; in the 2nd it is not so, the **प**, though belonging to the second group as regards meaning, is read with the first group, so as to make up the 8 **वर्ण**. So with the **च**, in the word **चरित्रन**; but, as stated above, this liberty is allowed to the poet.

मात्रिक छन्द.

381. Most of the Hindi poems which enjoy the widest reputation, are written in the styles which conform to the Matrik method of scanning.

Generally, a poet adopts the use of several different metres in the same poem, something after the manner of

Tennyson in his "Maud." Writers vary greatly in this matter. Occasionally, a poet exclusively, or almost exclusively, adopts one special metre, *e.g.*, Girdhar Kabiraya made himself master of the Kundaliya, and uses no other form of verse; Bihari Lal's favourite was the Dohā; Padmākar excelled in the Kabitt; Nābhā Daș used the Chhappaya largely. Tulsi Das seemed greatly at home with all forms of verse; but possibly the Chaupai was that in which he wrote with the greatest freedom. In his Ramayan, the general method is 4 chaupais (8 lines), followed by a Dohā, with here and there a Soraṭhā, and, scattered up and down the book, some Chhands of various metres. Some of these latter are very fine.

It has been already noticed that in the Matrik Chhand the lines are regulated by the number of instants or मात्रा, not by syllables, वर्ण.

Three points should be noted.

1. Sometimes only the number of the instants in the line or Charan is fixed.

2. Sometimes certain sub-divisions within these Charan are fixed, with the number of instants in each sub-division.

3. Sometimes the गण in these sub-divisions are also fixed, *i.e.*, the order of long and short syllables is definitely laid down. Frequently this only applies to

certain parts of the line: it may be arranged that a long syllable must stand at the end of the Charan, or that certain गण must occur in this or that sub-division of the line.

With reference to 2, it may very naturally be asked, if the line be only measured by instants, what difference can it make whether it be said that the Charan must contain, say, 13 instants, or that it must have one foot of 6 instants, another one of 4, and a third of 3, making a total of 13? The answer is that in the second way of stating it, a slight restriction is put upon the arrangement of long and short syllables; a foot must always conclude with a completed syllable, and, therefore, under the second method, there must not be a long syllable for the 6th and 7th instants in the line, for then the first half of the syllable would belong to the 1st foot, and the second to the 2nd, which is not permissible, *e.g.*—

काल करे जो आज कर, *he who does to-morrow (the work) of to-day,* is correct – ⏑⏑ –।– –। ⏑ ⏑ ⏑ ॥, *i.e.*, 6+4+3, total 13; but were the Charan written, आज कर जो काल करे, the meaning would be the same, and the total number of instants the same, but they would not fall correctly as regards the feet;

जो would belong partly to the 1st foot and partly to the 2nd, which is not allowed, or the Charan would have to be scanned —⏑ ⏑⏑ — | —⏑ | ⏑ —‖ 7+3+3, or —⏑ ⏑ ⏑ | — —⏑ | ⏑ —‖ 5+5+3, neither of which is correct.

382. Of the numerous species and varieties of Matrik Chhand, only a few will be explained and illustrated.

1. Dohā (**दोहा**). The Dohā consists of 4 Charans. The 1st and 3rd Charans contain 3 feet of 6, 4, and 3 instants, respectively, total 13; and the 2nd and 4th Charans, 3 feet of 6, 4, and 1 instants, total 11. The last foot of the 1st Charan must be either ⏑ ⏑ ⏑ or ⏑ —, but not — ⏑. The last syllable of the 2nd and 4th Charans must be short.

राम अनंत अनंत गुण अमित कथा बिस्तार ।
सुनि आचरज न मानिहहिं जिनके बिमल बिचार ॥

— ⏑ ⏑ ⏑ — | ⏑ ⏑ ⏑ — | ⏑ ⏑ ⏑ ‖ 6+4+3
⏑ ⏑ — ⏑ — — | — — | ⏑ ‖ 6+4+1
⏑ ⏑ — ⏑ ⏑ | ⏑ ⏑ — | ⏑ ⏑ ⏑ ‖ 6+4+3
⏑ ⏑ — ⏑ ⏑ | ⏑ ⏑ — | ⏑ ‖ 6+4+1

Ram is eternal, his attributes endless, lengthy stories (of him) innumerable; having heard (them) they will not regard them as astounding, whose understanding is clear.

This is the most common Dohā; other varieties are also found, *e.g.*—

मन मोती अरु दूध को इनको यही स्वभाव ।
फाटे पीछे ना मिलैं कोटिन किये उपाव ॥

The heart, a pearl, milk, of these the nature is, that, when broken, they cannot afterwards be reunited, though myriads of devices be adopted.

Here it will be noticed that, though there are 11 instants in the 2nd and 4th Charans, the arrangement of feet is different, being apparently 4+6+1 or 4+4+3; it cannot be 6+4+1, as there is a long syllable at 6, 7.

383. 2. Soraṭhá (सोरठा). The Soraṭhá is a transposed Dohá, the 1st and 3rd Charans of the latter becoming the 2nd and 4th of the Soraṭhá, and the 2nd and 4th the 1st and 3rd. Thus, instead of 6+4+3 =13, 6+4+1 =11, we get 11 instants in the 1st Charan and 13 in the 2nd, and the rhyme also comes in the middle of the half-verse instead of the end.

अब विचार मति धीर तजि कुतर्क संशय सकल ।
भजहु राम रघुबीर करुणा कर सुंदर सुखद ॥

⏑ ⏑ ⏑ — ⏑ | ⏑ ⏑ — | ⏑ ॥ 6+4+1

⏑ ⏑ ⏑ — ⏑ | — ⏑ ⏑ | ⏑ ⏑ ⏑ ॥ 6+4+3

⏑ ⏑ ⏑ — ⏑ | ⏑ ⏑ — | ⏑ ॥ 6+4+1

⏑ ⏑ — ⏑ ⏑ | — ⏑ ⏑ | ⏑ ⏑ ⏑ ॥ 6+4+3

Thus having thought, O steadfast in wisdom, putting away every evil counsel and doubt, worship Râm, the hero of Raghu's line, the home of mercy, the excellent, the giver of peace.

384. 3. Chaupāi. चौपाई, i.e., *four-footed.* A Chaupāi is made up of 4 Charans, each Charan containing 16 instants. The 2nd Charan rhymes with the 1st, and the 4th with the 3rd. The last two instants must be — or ⌣ ⌣, that is to say, a long syllable must not precede a final ⌣. As regards the earlier 14 instants of each Charan, various arrangements are possible and permissible.

For the whole Charan perhaps, the most general arrangement is 6+4+4+2 =16. Other arrangements are also given. The following are quoted from Babu Jagannath Prasad's book already referred to.

(1) 2+2+2+2+2+2+2+2=16, *e.g.* झूठा लेना झूठा देना ॥

(2) 2+2+3+3+2+2+2 =16, „ बंदौं राम नाम रघुबर को ॥

(3) 2+2+2+2+3+3+2 =16, „ जग मंगल गुण ग्राम राम के ॥

(4) 3+3+2+2+2+2+2 =16, „ विश्वनाथ पहुँचे कैलाशा ॥

(5) 3+3+2+3+3+2 =16; *e.g.* कहहु राम की कथा सुहाई ॥

(6) 3+3+3+3+2+2 =16, ,, हृदय बिचारि शंभु प्रभुताई ॥

Take the following as an illustration of an average Chaupāi.

तातें मैं संतन सिर नाई ।
गावों हरियश जन सुखदाई ।
जो वृज में हरि कियो बिलासा ।
सेा कछु कहिहैं। सहित हुलासा ॥

Wherefore I, having bowed my head before the saints, will sing the glory of Hari, the giver of peace to his people, the sportive life he lived in Brij, of this will I tell something with joy.

It will be noticed that the 3rd Charan of the above does not scan correctly; it is 6+5+3+2, instead of 6+4+4+2; but there is no difficulty in reading it, because कियो, though correcly ⏑ —,reads more like— ⏑, the य seems to lengthen the previous कि nearly into की, and the ओ after य does not get its full length, and becomes practically short. This example well illustrates how a poet is not a slave to rules, but trusts his ear.

385. 4. Kunḍaliyá (कुण्डलिया). This is not an uncommon verse, and is a good illustration of the peculiarities which some writers delight in.

Its peculiarity consists in this, that the first Charan of the third line must be the same as the second Charan of the second line, and the whole verse must close with the same words as it commences with.

The Kunḍaliyá consists of 6 lines. The first two are a dohā, the last four a **रोला**. This **रोला** has four lines, with 24 **मात्रा** in each, the 1st Charan containing 11 **मात्रा**, the 2nd 13. The 11th **मात्रा** must be a short syllable.

बिना बिचारे जो करै सो पाछे पछताय ।
काम बिगारै आपनो जग में होत हँसाय ॥
जग में होत हँसाय चित्त में चैन न पावै ।
खान पान सनमान राग रंग मनहि न भावै ॥
कह गिरिधर कबिराय दुःख कछु टरत न टारे ।
खटकत है जिय माँहि कियो जो बिना बिचारे ॥

He who acts without thought, will afterwards repent;
He will ruin his work and become a laughing-stock in the world;
He will become a laughing-stock in the world, and will obtain no peace of mind,
Eating and drinking, the courtesies of life and festivities will yield no pleasure to his mind;
Girdhar kabiraya tells you that trouble cannot be kept back, try how you will.

It comes hammering away at the life of the man who has acted without thought.

In some Kuṇḍaliyās, the 5th and 6th lines scan 13+11, instead of 11+13.

Paltu Das, or, as his disciples prefer to call him, Paltu Sahib, wrote many verses, and among others 200 (actually 198) Kuṇḍaliyās have been collected and published. He appears to have invented a Kuṇḍaliyā of his own. Each verse contains nine lines, the first and last are identical, and the last half of the 1st line is repeated as the first half of the 2nd.

Ṭhis is but a brief introduction to a very large subject. Not only are there a very great number of different verses, but frequently numerous varieties of one form of verse, *e.g.*, one writer speaks of 23 *principal* forms of the Dohā.

CHAPTER XVIII.

BRAJ BHASHA.

386. For the study of the Braj Bhasha, few prose works are available. About the best is the राजनीति of Lallu Ji. In modern editions of this, however, the tendency is to substitute modern Hindi forms for the more distinctly Braj forms. Probably the best edition obtainable is that published by the (Government) Board of Examiners, Council House Street, Calcutta. Rs. 3. It has useful notes.

Sometimes, even by Indian readers, the Prem Sagar (also by Lallú Jí) is spoken of as written in the Braj Bhasha; but this is not the case. It was put into the Hindi prose that was then being developed by Lallú Jí from a Braj original. The Braj forms are largely confined to the scraps of verse with which the prose is interspersed. Commentators on the Ramayan and other Hindi books not uncommonly affect a style which approximates, in a larger or less degree, to the Braj dialect, but the true domain of Braj Bhasha is poetry. Hindi writers may adhere to modern Hindi in their prose; but, as soon as they use verse, Braj is the dialect most frequently brought into requisition. It is therefore necessary for the student at an early stage of his reading to acquire some familiarity with the more common forms of the Braj declensions and conjugations.

As Braj forms predominate largely in most Hindi works written in verse, it is needless to refer to many by name. The **ब्रजबिलास**, by Brajbásí Dás, would, I believe, be accepted as a good specimen. An exceedingly useful book is the "Sabhá Bilás." Of this a good edition was published at the Medical Hall Press, Benares, in 1900; it has an English translation and full notes. A most helpful book for a student. (The price is about Rs. 6, I believe).

In the following lists, no pretence is made to completeness, and not every form given is to be taken as necessarily pure Braj. The charge of slavish purism cannot be fairly brought against the majority of Hindi writers. Tulsi Das wrote in Purabi Hindi, but was quite ready to use forms from other dialects, and, in case of need, to make up new forms of his own. The glamour of Tulsi Das' style has so influenced poetry since his time, that few writers adhere strictly and exclusively to Braj forms, but introduce Purabi and other dialectic forms; probably few could decide which are Braj forms and which belong to some other dialect.

In these circumstances, it has been thought better to give some of the more common forms met with in poetry, whether these forms be Braj or not. As the writer has, in a separate pamphlet, dealt with the more distinctive Ramayan forms, they have not been specially included in the following lists.

PARTICLE-POSTPOSITIONS USED IN THE DECLENSION OF NOUNS AND PRONOUNS.

387.

	High Hindi.	Braj, etc.
Accusative. Dative.	को	कौं, हि
Agentive.	ने	very seldom used.
Ablative.	से	तें, सों
Genitive.	का	कौ, कर. With some of the Pronouns, सु is used for the Genitive, *e.g.*, जासु, *i.e.*, जिसका.
	के	के
	की	की
Locative.	में	में, मां, महं
	पर	पै, पर
	तक	लौं, लग

PLURALS OF NOUNS.

388. As regards the Nominative Plural, there is nothing very special to note, except that, *when* used, एँ is preferred to एं for feminines— बातैं, not बातें. In the Construct., Plural न or नि commonly takes the place of ओं, *e.g.* लोगन कौ (लोगों का), पुत्रनि कौ (पुत्रों का), स्त्रिन कौ, स्त्रिन कर (स्त्रियों का).

PRONOUNS.

389. 1st Personal Pronoun.

		High Hindi.	Braj, etc.
Sing.	Nominative.	मैं	मैं, हौं
	Construct. Base.	मुझ	मो, *e.g.*, मोपर (मुझपर)
	Accusative.	मुझको	मोहि, मुहि, मोकौं
	Genitive.	मेरा	मेरौ, मोर, मम
Plu.	Nominative.	हम	हम
	Construct. Base.	हम	हमन
	Accusative.	हमको	हम कौं, हमहि
	Genitive.	हमारा	हमार, हमारौ

2nd Personal Pronoun.

Sing.	Nominative.	तू	तैं
	Construct. Base.	तुझ	तो
	Accusative.	तुझको	तोहि, तोकौं
	Genitive.	तेरा	तेरौ, तोर
Plu.	Nominative.	तुम	तुम
	Construct. Base.	तुम	तुम
	Accusative.	तुमको	तुमकौं, तुमहि

	High Hindi.	Braj, Etc.
Genitive.	तुम्हारा	तुम्हार, तुम्हरौ, (तिहार)

3RD PERSONAL PRONOUN, AND PROXIMATE AND REMOTE DEMONSTRATIVE.

Sing.	Nominative.	यह	यह, ई
	Construct. Base.	इस	या, ई, *e.g.*, यापर (इस पर)
Plu.	Nominative.	ये	ये, ए
	Construct. Base.	इन	इन
Sing.	Nominative.	वह	वह, ओ
	Construct. Base.	उस	वा
Plu.	Nominative.	वे	वे
	Construct. Base.	उन	उन, विन

REFLEXIVE PRONOUN.

अपना	आपन

RELATIVE PRONOUN.

Sing.	Nominative.	जो	जौ, जौन
	Construct. Base.	जिस	जा
	Accusative.	जिसको	जाकौं, जेहि
	Genitive.	जिसका	जाकौ, जासु
Plu.	Nominative.	जे	जौ, जौन
	Construct. Base.	जिन	जिन

Correlative Pronoun.

		High Hindi.	Braj, etc.
Sing.	Nominative.	सो	सो, तौन
	Construct. Base.	तिस, उस	ता, वा
Plu.	Nominative.	ते, वे	ते, वे
	Construct. Base.	तिन, उन	तिन, उन, बिन

Interrogative Pronoun.

		High Hindi.	Braj, etc.
Sing.	Nominative.	कौन	को, कौन, कवन
	Construct. Base.	किस	का
Plu.	Nominative.	कौन	कै, कौन
	Construct. Base.	किन	किन

Indefinite Pronoun.

		High Hindi.	Braj, etc.
Sing.	Nominative.	कोई	कोऊ, कोय
	Construct. Base.	किसी	काहू
		क्या	का, कहा
		कुछ	कछु

390. The verb "To be."

	High Hindi.	Braj, etc.
Infinitive.	होना	होनौं
Imperfect Participle.	होता	होतु
Perfect Participle.	हुआ	भयौ
Conjunctive Participle.	होके, etc.	होयकै, ह्वैके
Noun of Agency.	होनेहारा	होनहार, होनिहार

* PRESENT TENSE.

Singular.		*Plural.*	
1.	हौं	1. 3.	हैं
2. 3.	है	2.	हौ

PAST TENSE.

1. 2. 3.	हतो	1. 2. 3.	हते

or more commonly—

1. रह्यौं } from रहना
2. 3. रह्यो }

CONTINGENT FUTURE.

Generally the same as High Hindi, but औ sometimes is substituted for ओ, *e.g.*, हौऊँ for होऊँ, etc.	1. and 3. हौंय

ABSOLUTE FUTURE.

1.	होइहौं, ह्वैहौं, होऊँगो,	1. 3.	होइहैं, ह्वैहैं
2. 3.	होइहै, ह्वैहै	2.	होइहौ, ह्वैहौ.

IMPERATIVE.

2.	हो	2.	हो

INDEFINITE IMPERFECT.

1. 2. 3.	होतु, होत.	1. 2. 3.	होतु, होत

* From this point, the High Hindi forms will not be given.

INDEFINITE PERFECT.

1. 2. 3. भयौ	1. 2. 3. भये

PRESENT IMPERFECT.

1. होतु हौं	1. 3. होतु हैं, होत हैं.
2. 3. होतु है.	2. होतु हौ, होत हौ.

PRESENT PERFECT.

1. भयौ हौं	1. 3. भये हैं
2. 3. भयौ है	2. भये हौ

It is unnecessary to go through the remaining Tenses of the Verb; they are seldom met with, and, from the forms given above, will be readily recognized.

391. A VERB WITH CLOSE ROOT.

Two courses were possible in illustrating the forms of the general Verb: (1) to give forms of *different* Verbs, as actually met with, in the various Tenses, etc., or (2) to apply these forms to one simple Verb. The latter course has been adopted, as being less confusing to the student.

INFINITIVE.	चलनौं
IMPERFECT PARTICIPLE.	चलतु, चलत
PERFECT PARTICIPLE.	चल्यौ
CONJUNCTIVE PARTICIPLE	चलकै
NOUN OF AGENCY.	चलनहार

CONTINGENT FUTURE.

1. चलौं	1. 3. चलैं
2. 3. चलै	2. चलौ

ABSOLUTE FUTURE.

1. चलिहौं, चलौंगो	1. 3. चलिहैं, चलैंगे.
2. 3. चलिहै, चलैगो	2. चलिहौ, चलौगे.

IMPERATIVE.

2. चल, चले	2. चलौ

INDEFINITE IMPERFECT.

1. 2. 3. चलतु, चलत	1. 2. 3. चलत

INDEFINITE PERFECT.

1. 2. 3. चल्यौ.	1. 2. 3. चले, चलैं

PRESENT IMPERFECT.

1. चलत हौं	1. 3. चलत हैं
2. 3. चलत है	2. चलत हौ

PRESENT PERFECT.

1. चल्यौ हौं	1. 3. चले हैं
2. 3. चल्यौ है	2 चले हौ

PAST IMPERFECT AND PAST PERFECT.

In these Tenses, instead of the ordinary auxiliary था parts of the Verb रहना are commonly used, रह्यो or रह्यौ for 1. 2. and 3. Sing., रहे for 1 and 3 Pl. and रहौ for 2 Pl. Thus चलत रह्यो, चलत रहे, चल्यौ रह्यो, चले रहे, etc.

392. With the above forms before him, the student will not experience much difficulty in recognizing the various parts of other Verbs. In Verbs with an open root, य is often inserted, *e.g.*, आयौ (आया), ल्याऊँ (लाऊँ). With the Verbs करना, लेना, देना a न is often inserted, sometimes न्ह, *e.g.*, कीनौ, (किया), दीनौ (दिया), लीन्हा (लिया).

APPENDIX.

HINDI GRAMMATICAL TERMS.

Grammar ...	व्याकरण
Etymology ...	व्युत्पत्ति
Orthography { concerning letters	वर्णविचार, or वर्ण-विभाग
Orthography { ,, words	शब्दविचार, or शब्द-विभाग
Syntax ...	वाक्यविचार or वाक्यविभाग
The Letters, etc.— ...	
Letter ...	अक्षर or वर्ण
Alphabet ...	वर्णमाला
*Group of kindred Letters...	वर्ग
Gutturals ...	कंठ्य
Palatals ...	तालव्य
Cerebrals ...	मूर्धन्य
Dentals ...	दन्त्य
Labials ...	ओष्ठ्य
Sibilants (श, ष, स and ह) ...	ऊष्म
Nasals (ङ, ञ, ण, न, and म) ...	अनुनासिक or सानुनासिक

* See classification on page 24.

Liquids or Semi-Vowels (य, र, ल and व) ...	अन्तस्थ
Hard Letters ...	विवृत प्रयत्न or अघोष प्रयत्न
Soft ,, ...	घोष प्रयत्न
Unaspirated ,, ...	अल्पप्राण
Aspirated ,, ...	महाप्राण
Gutturo-palatals (ए and ऐ)	कंठतालव्य
Gutturo-labials (ओ and औ)	कंठोष्ठ्य
Dento-labial (व) ...	दन्तोष्ठ्य
ड़ and ढ़ ...	द्विस्पृष्ठ
Form of letter (written or printed) ...	आकार
Pronunciation ...	उच्चारण
Place of utterance ...	स्थान
Organ ,, ,, ...	अवयव
Vowel ...	स्वर
Consonant ...	व्यंजन
Short Vowel ...	ह्रस्व or एकमात्रिक
Long ,, ...	दीर्घ or द्विमात्रिक
Extra long vowel ...	प्लुत
Nasal mark ...	अनुस्वार and अनुनासिक
do. semi-nasal ...	अर्धचन्द्र or चन्द्रबिन्दु
Final aspiration ...	विसर्ग

Closed letter ...	हल
Stroke for indicating closed letter ...	विराम
Moment or Syllable ...	मात्रा
Compound Consonant ...	संयुक्त अक्षर
Coalescence of sounds (Sandhi)	संधि
„ of Vowels ...	स्वरसंधि
„ of Consonants	व्यंजनसंधि
„ of Visarga and other letters	विसर्गसंधि
Prefix ...	उपसर्ग
Affix ...	प्रत्यय
Word ...	शब्द
Word, in a sentence, especially when subject to inflection ...	पद
Change, in the form of a word by inflection, &c. ...	विकार
A Sound inexpressible by letters	ध्वन्यात्मक
„ composed of letters ...	वर्णात्मक
„ without meaning ...	निरर्थक
„ having a meaning ...	सार्थक
An original word from one root	रूढ़ि
A word in which two roots are combined.	यौगिक
do. (with arbitrary meaning)	योगरूढ़ि
A word imported from Sanskrit	तत्सम

A word derived through Prakrit... तद्भव

A language or dialect ... भाषा

Parts of speech are, according to Indian grammarians, 3, *viz.* :—

1. Including Nouns, Adjectives & Pronouns. } संज्ञा
2. Verb ... क्रिया
3. Undeclined words ; (including Adverbs, Affixes, Postpositions, Conjunctions, Disjunctions, and Interjections). } अव्यय

Some, Indian Grammarians would make 5 main divisions instead of 3, *i.e.* 1. संज्ञा Noun. 2. सर्वनाम Pronoun. 3. विशेषण Adjective. 4. क्रिया Verb. 5. अव्यय Adverbs, etc.

Noun (see above) ... संज्ञा

Adjective ... विशेषण or गुणवाचक

Pronoun ... सर्वनाम

Verb ... क्रिया

Adverb ... क्रियाविशेषण

Postposition ... संबन्धबोधक अव्यय

Conjunction ... संयोजक अव्यय

Disjunction ... विभाजक अव्यय

Interjection ... विस्मयादिक अव्यय

Common to Nouns, Adjectives, and Pronouns.

Case ...	कारक
Case-Sign ...	विभक्ति or कारकार्थक अव्यय
*Nominative Case ...	कर्त्ता
Accusative „ ...	कर्म
First Accusative ...	मुख्य कर्म or प्रधान कर्म
Second Accusative ...	गौण कर्म or अप्रधान कर्म
Instrumental Case ...	करण
Dative „ ...	सम्प्रदान
Ablative „ ...	अपादान
Genitive „ ...	सम्बन्ध
Locative Case ...	अधिकरण
Vocative „ ...	सम्बोधन
Signs of Vocative (हे हो, etc.)	सम्बोधन कारक के चिन्ह
Gender ...	लिंग
Masculine gender ...	पुँल्लिंग
Feminine „ ...	स्त्रीलिंग
Neuter (not used in Hindi)	नपुंसक लिंग

* Though कर्त्ता means "doer," it is equivalent to "subject."

Number ... वचन

Singular number ... एकवचन

Plural „ ... बहुवचन

Dual „ (Not used in Hindi) द्विवचन

Noun (but generally including, in Hindi, Adjectives and Pronouns) संज्ञा

Common Noun .... जातिवाचक

Proper Noun ... व्यक्तिवाचक

Qualitative Noun (also used for Adjective). गुणवाचक

Abstract Noun ... भाववाचक

Adjective ... विशेषण

Qualified Noun *or* Pronoun विशेष्य

Pronominal Adjective (Quantitative) परिमाणवाचक

Pronominal Adjective (Qualitative). सादृश्यवाचक

Pronoun ... सर्वनाम

Personal Pronoun ... पुरुषवाचक सर्वनाम

1st Person ... उत्तमपुरुष

2nd Person ... मध्यमपुरुष

3rd Person ... प्रथमपुरुष or अन्यपुरुष

Demonstrative or Definite Pronoun (used only of the Proximate Demon. Pronoun यह	निश्चयवाचक सर्वनाम or संकेतवाचक सर्वनाम
Remote (included under 3rd Pers. Pronoun).	
Indefinite Pronoun (*i.e.*, कोई)	अनिश्चयवाचक सर्वनाम
Relative Pronoun (*i.e.*, जो).	सम्बन्धवाचक सर्वनाम
Interrogative Pronoun (*i.e.*, कौन)	प्रश्नवाचक सर्वनाम
Reflexive Pronoun (*i.e.*, आप)	निजवाचक सर्वनाम
Honorific Pronoun (*i.e.*, आप)	आदरप्रदर्शक सर्वनाम
Verb ...	क्रिया
Root ...	धातु or मूल
Transitive Verb ...	सकर्मक क्रिया
Intransitive ,, ...	अकर्मक क्रिया
Transitive Verb taking one Accusative	एककर्मक
do. two Accusatives	द्विकर्मक
Active Verb ...	कर्तृप्रधान or कर्तृवाच्य क्रिया
Passive Verb ...	कर्मप्रधान or कर्मवाच्य क्रिया
Impersonal Verb ...	भावप्रधान or भाववाच्य क्रिया

Causal Verb	...	प्रेरणार्थक क्रिया
Compound Verb	...	संयुक्त क्रिया
Mood	...	No Hindi equivalent.
Tense	...	काल (but in speaking of a certain tense, the word क्रिया is often added to the name of the Tense, instead of काल)
Infinitive (Mood)	...	No Hindi equivalent. धातु (root) is sometimes used, but incorrectly. क्रियार्थक संज्ञा and भाववाचक संज्ञा are also sometimes used.
* Imperfect Participle	...	क्रियाद्योतक संज्ञा
* Perfect "	..	कर्मवाचक संज्ञा
Conjunctive Participle	...	पूर्वकालिक क्रिया
Noun of Agency	...	कर्तृवाचक संज्ञा
Present (Tense)	..	वर्तमान
Past	...	भूत
Future	...	भविष्यत्

* These names are unsatisfactory, as they may be used of Nouns as well as of Participles.

	Contingent Future ...	सम्भाव्य भविष्यत् or सम्भावनार्थ क्रिया
	Absolute Future ...	सामान्य भविष्यत्
	Imperative ...	विधि
	Indefinite Imperfect ...	हेतुहेतुमद्भूत
	Present Imperfect ..	सामान्य वर्तमान
	Past Imperfect ...	अपूर्णभूत
	Contingent Imperfect ...	सम्भाव्य वर्तमान
	Presumptive Imperfect ...	संदिग्धवर्तमान
	Past Contingent Imperfect	अपूर्ण हेतुहेतुमद्भूत
	Indefinite Perfect ...	सामान्य भूत
	Present Perfect ...	आसन्न भूत
	Past Perfect ...	पूर्ण भूत
	Contingent Perfect ...	सम्भाव्य भूत
	Presumptive Perfect ...	संदिग्ध भूत
	Past Contingent Perfect ...	पूर्ण हेतुहेतुमद्भूत
Adverb ...		क्रियाविशेषण
	Adverb of time ...	कालवाचक क्रियाविशेषण
	,, ,, place ...	स्थानवाचक ,,
	,, ,, manner ...	भाववाचक ,,
	,, ,, quantity, or degree	परिमाणवाचक ,,
Postposition ...		सम्बन्धबोधक अव्यय or सम्बन्धसूचक अव्यय

Conjunction	...	संयोजक अव्यय
Disjunction	...	विभाजक अव्यय
Interjection	...	विस्मयादिक अव्यय
Syntax	...	वाक्यविचार or वाक्य-रचना
Sentence	...	वाक्य
The qualifying word or sentence	}	विशेषण
That which is qualified	...	विशेष्य
Subject	...	उद्देश्य
Predicate	...	विधेय
Analysis	...	वाक्य विभाग
Parsing	...	पदान्वय
Written Composition	...	काव्य
Prosody	...	
Prose	...	गद्य
Poetry	...	पद्य or कविता
A poem	...	कवित or कविता

There is a very large vocabulary for different kinds of poems and various kinds of verses.

Style, as regards the subject-matter, रस

There are ten varieties, as वीररस (heroic), करुणारस (pathetic), etc.

Rhyme	...	तुक

Alliteration ...	अनुप्रास
Metre according to number of letters	वर्णिक
do. instants (or syllables)	मात्रावृत्त
Instant ...	मात्रा
Long instant ...	गुरु or दीर्घ
Short „ ...	लघु or ह्रस्व
Line or half-line ...	चरण
Foot (or group of instants)	गण
Syllable (*i.e.*, each Consonant, single or conjunct., with its vowel; or a vowel alone)	वर्ण
Pause ...	विश्राम
„ (mirror) ...	यति

INDEX I. (ENGLISH).

Hindi Grammatical Terms are given at the heads of the Chapters and in the Appendix. They are not included in the Index.

The numbers refer to the Paragraph, not to the page.

Where more than one reference is given the earlier number generally refers to the more important section.

ENGLISH INDEX.

INDEX II (Hindi).

In indexing, ब, both as initial and medial, has been included with व (with exceptions).